Kissing the Mango Tree
Puerto Rican Women Rewriting
American Literature

Kissing the Mango Tree
Puerto Rican Women Rewriting American Literature

by

Carmen S. Rivera

Arte Público Press
Houston, Texas

This volume is made possible through grants from the City of Houston through The Cultural Arts Council of Houston, Harris County.

Recovering the past, creating the future

Arte Público Press
University of Houston
452 Cullen Performance Hall
Houston, Texas 77204-2004

Cover design by James F. Brisson

Rivera, Carmen, S.
    Kissing the mango tree: Puerto Rican women rewriting
American literature / by Carmen S. Rivera
    p.   cm.
    ISBN 1-55885-377-4 (alk. paper)
    1. American literature—Puerto Rican authors—History and
criticism.   2. Puerto Rican literature—Women authors—History
and criticism.   3. Feminism and literature—United States—
History—20th century.   4. Women and literature—United
States—History—20th century.   5. American literature—Women
authors—History and criticism.   6. Puerto Rican women—United
States—Intellectual life.   7. Puerto Ricans in literature.   I. Title.
PS153.P83 R48 2002
810.9'9287'097295—dc21   2002066675
                                                           CIP

♾ The paper used in this publication meets the requirements of the American National Standard for Information Sciences—Permanence of Paper for Printed Library Materials, ANSI Z39.48-1984.

2 3 4 5 6 7 8 9 0 1   10 9 8 7 6 5 4 3 2 1

Para Mami, who gave me the passion for reading.
Para Papi, who gave me the gift of writing
and for Phil, who gave me faith . . .
I kiss you all.

Contents

Preface

This book focuses on the work of Puerto Rican women writers in the United States, that is, *Latinas*. Whether they were born on the island or on the continent, they have spent most of their adult lives in the United States. The majority started writing around the seventies, and are still publishing today. Thematically and stylistically they stand apart from the many Nuyorican male writers, such as Tato Laviera, Miguel Algarín, Pedro Pietri, and Victor Hernández Cruz, who have left their own imprint on the literary world.

Each chapter is dedicated to the work of one writer in particular, although there are overlaps, and references are made, when necessary, to the works of others. The chapters are written as independent essays. The translations of quotes are all mine, unless otherwise stated.

I am greatly indebted to Wingate University for the Spivey Instructorship and its extension to allow me reduced course work and the precious gift of time. I also want to thank The Ethel K. Smith Library and its staff, especially Susan Sganga of Inter-Library Loans, for their resilience and perseverance in locating even the most obscure journals. Mrs. Iris Rodríguez Parrilla from the University of Puerto Rico, Río Piedras, eased my access to the Biblioteca General and most importantly, to the Colección Puertorriqueña. The Centro de Estudios Puertorriqueños at Hunter College, N.Y., also provided valuable resources. Dr. Gregory S. Crider gave me innumerable historical references. Dr. Philip B. Rollinson's diligent proofreading of the manuscript was indispensable in disguising my Puerto Rican accent on its pages. I also appreciate the encouragement of the many colleagues within the profession who have kept me going *pa'lante*. My deepest gratitude goes to the editors of Arte Público for their faith in and support of this project.

Ultimately, I want to thank the Rivera-Delgado family, both here and there, who were my best resources and researchers, always on the lookout for books and articles that might be relevant. My friends, Andy, Liz, Lizzy, Mayra, and Pam, like my family, stood patiently in the margins of a nonexistent social life, while I wrote and wrote. My children, Antonio and Adriana Rodríguez, continued with their adolescent pains, becoming beautiful young adults, and at the same time gave me the necessary space for my professional growth. To Phil, Antonio, and Adriana, I can only say, *mil gracias de todo corazón.*

Introduction
Female Invisibility and Literary Representations of Puerto Ricans in the United States

The dark-skinned woman has been silenced, gagged, caged, bound into servitude with marriage, bludgeoned for 300 years . . . For 300 years she was invisible . . .

Gloria Anzaldúa, *Borderlands*

"I, as a Puerto Rican child, never existed in North American letters," declares Nicholasa Mohr ("Puerto Rican Writers" 113). She finds herself equally invisible in Puerto Rican literature. Her experiences are not unique. Roberto Santiago relates instances when primary schoolteachers told him and others that Puerto Rico had no history, no culture, nothing worth studying (*Boricuas* xiv). In spite of those efforts to erase the contributions, the impact, the mere existence of Puerto Ricans on the continent, there have been throughout the years fictional and nonfictional records of the journey and the lives of thousands of Puerto Rican immigrants in the United States. A quick historical overview of literary works about Puerto Rican migration and the subsequent process of acculturation will show that the female experience has been essentially overlooked. Gradually, *Puertorriqueñas* have begun to write themselves literally into his/story.

❦ ❦ ❦

This migration of Puerto Ricans to the United States dates back to the late nineteenth century when they sought refuge from the Spanish colonial government. Eugenio María de Hostos, Ramón Emeterio Betances, and Lola Rodríguez de Tió were among the revolutionary leaders who spent time in exile in New York City. Their writings express the political ideologies of people struggling for independence. Although there are beautiful renditions of their patriotic love, not much is devoted to the everyday life of the Puerto Rican immigrant.

In 1898, Puerto Rico was invaded and declared a territory of the United States. At first, the island was ruled by a military government and later by a civilian one appointed by the U.S. Congress. In 1952, Puerto Rico became a Commonwealth of the United States, with its own gubernatorial and legislative powers. Although the Jones Act had granted American citizenship to Puerto Ricans in 1917, those living on the island still are not allowed to vote for U.S. presidents or members of Congress.

The change in colonial powers only facilitated emigration, which was usually sanctioned by both the island and federal governments. The agricultural economy of the island was transformed into an industrial one, leaving thousands of farmers without means of support. "Operation Bootstrap"[1] in the fifties helped consolidate the industrialization of the economy. An estimated 500,000 Puerto Ricans emigrated to the United States between 1947 and 1961 (Morales Carrión 288). Francisco Scarano points to the dramatic increase in the numbers from an annual average of 1,800 emigres in the thirties to 31,000 during the late forties, and 45,000 during the fifties (754). Such dramatic increases had a disastrous impact on the lives of the immigrants in the States.

Bernardo Vega, who arrived in New York in 1916, gives us one of the most detailed accounts of the life and trials of a Puerto Rican immigrant during the first half of the twentieth century. Edited and published a decade after his death in 1965 (Andrew Iglesias), Vega's memoirs chronicle the political and economic struggles faced by thousands like him. He also devotes two sections to "historical antecedents" based on the experiences of his uncle, who had been in the States since the late 1800s. The unusual historical breadth of the book provides a unique look at the changing circumstances of Puerto Ricans in the United States, from the prosperity of the cigar factories at the turn of the century to the desolation of unemployment and underemployment that robbed them of human dignity, all the way to serving in the armed forces during World War II. His detailed descriptions of organizations that emerged, both social and political, are invaluable. His photographic memory and accounts of public events, political debates, and negative campaigns are amazing. What is missing in his memoirs is the private space where his wife, his family, and other women moved. References are made to women being present at some meetings, serving coffee and snacks. A few women, such as Lola Rodríguez de Tió, were at times in positions of leadership, but they were quite often absent from the narratives that have come down to us.

Like Vega, Jesús Colón arrived in New York in 1918 and went on to write his collection of sketches, *A Puerto Rican in New York*, during the fifties. Colón's vignettes depict the abject poverty and struggles for survival of Puerto Ricans. He had been a *tabaquero* (a cigar worker), the same as Vega. While both give a detailed look into the working environment of the cigar factories, with their readers and learned debates, Colón's work differs from Vega's in two important respects. As an active member of the Communist Party, Colón's writings are impregnated with a strong militant tone. As a black man, some of his sketches deal with double discrimination: for being Puerto Rican and for the color of his skin. Once again, this collection focuses on the public arena of politics, the job market, and social issues. Not much is said about the private lives of the protagonists. Aside from his wife's name, not much information is given about his family. The only episode dealing with a female describes the conversion of his mother-in-law, recently arrived from Puerto Rico, from Roman Catholicism to Socialism. The account does not reveal much about women's lives and/or roles in society.

While Vega and Colón were writing their biographical texts, a whole generation of Puerto Rican writers in the island were also recording in fiction the experiences of the emigrés. René Marqués, José Luis González, Pedro Juan Soto, and Emilio Díaz Valcárcel are among the members of what is known as the "Generation of the '40s." Except for Soto, who lived in New York for ten years, the others spent only a year or two studying under the sponsorship of a grant or scholarship. As opposed to Colón, who made a deliberate choice to write in English during the 1950s (he had earlier written and published substantial work in Spanish), these writers' literary language is Spanish. Their short stories about the emigrés are considered classics of Puerto Rican literature, regularly included in anthologies and literary studies. Unfortunately, as outsiders, the works of these writers only register "the alienation, exclusion and traumatic desperation, an anguished culture-shock leading inevitably to existential nostalgia for the Island" (Flores, *Divided* "Foreword" xv).

In 1953, René Marqués produced his play, *La Carreta* (*The Oxcart*), about a poor family's migration from the countryside to the metropolis. It is divided into three acts, each of which depicts the misery of the family, first in the rural countryside, then in the slums on the outskirts of San Juan, and finally in New York. As they move, "modern life" seems to gnaw and bite chunks out of the family. The aging grandfather stays behind to die in a cave, knowing that he will never adapt to an urban setting. The youngest boy gets involved in drugs and goes to jail in San Juan. The daughter turns to prostitution in New York, and the oldest son is literally devoured by a machine at work. At the center is the mother, self-sacrificing and helpless to protect her family. At the end, she decides to take her dead son and her fallen daughter back to their home on the island.

González's and Soto's fiction share in the desolation and pessimism of Marqués' characters. In the short novel *Paísa* (1950) and the short story "El pasaje" ("The Airplane Ticket" *Veinte cuentos*), González depicts two Puerto Rican men who die while committing a robbery. Andrés, in the first work, sits in a dark room with his partner-in-crime. As he waits, he reminisces about his childhood on a farm in Puerto Rico and the starvation that forced his father to uproot them to the city in search of a better life. In the short story, Jesús confides to a friend at a bar that he has not been able to find a job and has decided to return to the island. The problem is he cannot afford the "airplane ticket." A week later, his friend goes into the bar, where the bartender shows him the newspaper with a picture of a man shot to death in front of a deli he tried to rob, armed with a small knife. With complete mastery of a succinct, laconic style, González gives insight into the psyche of these men, who are not criminals, but are driven to commit criminal acts out of desperation and misery.

Soto published his collected short stories in 1956 under the title *Spiks*, co-opting the insulting term used to refer to Puerto Ricans in the Northeast, in order to emphasize the collective experience of his people: "seres abrumados por la tecnología, el aislamiento y la correspondiente inseguridad de los exploradores en cualquier selva" ("human beings crushed by technology, by isolation, and by the corresponding insecurity of explorers in any jungle" 9–10). "Garabatos" ("Doodles"), one of the most famous stories in the collection, echoes many of these sentiments, except this time it examines the impact on the soul of an artist. The protagonist, a painter, is not only struggling with poverty and unemployment but also with his frustrated creativity, especially as Christmas approaches and there are no gifts for his wife and five children. But he has a surprise; he will make a painting for her using the bathroom wall as a canvas. Painstakenly he traces the silhouettes of a naked couple embracing, making sure that the features are exactly those of his wife when he first met her. When he comes back from an errand, he finds that she has erased his "dirty drawings."

For the most part, the few women depicted in González's and Soto's stories are alcoholics and/or prostitutes. These women constitute one more affront that the Puerto Rican man has to suffer in this city-jungle that has robbed him of his dignity. Even "our women" are being corroded and destroyed. As they expose the atrocious circumstances of the immigrants' lives in the metropolis, their main focus is on the impact on the generic character, "the Puerto Rican male." Female characters are introduced as satellites, and their moral and economic ruin only adds to the ignominy of the male protagonists. "Garabatos" is a good example of this, as the wife's insensitivity and constant nagging for money and food only hasten the sealing of "la lápida ancha y clara de sus sueños" ("the clearly wide gravestone over his dreams" Soto 38).

A dissonant voice from the forties was that of Julia de Burgos, who lived the last twelve years of her life in New York, where she also wrote many of her poems. In contrast to the writings of the Generation of the '40s, Burgos' poems exist in the emotive world of love, death, abandonment, and isolation. There are a few poems lamenting the cold and inhuman atmosphere of the big city, but there is very little in terms of concrete experiences from daily life. On the other hand, her death on a street in New York has transformed her into an emblem of the tragic fate of many Puerto Rican immigrants.

❧ ❧ ❧

During the sixties, more and more Puerto Ricans living in New York begin to record *their own* experiences. Most of them represent the first generation born in the States, who still suffer discrimination because of their parents' ethnic background. In 1967, Piri Thomas published his autobiography, *Down These Mean Streets*, a detailed account of a Puerto Rican boy in a ghetto plagued with drugs, gangs, and violence. The book provides an illuminating look at the issue of race for Puerto Ricans within the context of the United States. The son of a dark-skinned father and a white mother, Piri is the only one in his family who inherited the paternal African features, both in skin color and hair texture. Influenced by his friend Brew, an African-American from the South, Piri proclaims his blackness only to come into conflict with his father, who wants to be white, and his white siblings, who pretend to be blind to his dark skin. Piri chronicles his journey with Brew to the South and his encounter with Jim Crow laws and the ambiguity and irrationality of segregation: if he calls himself a Puerto Rican, they will let him in at commercial establishments; if he declares himself a black man, then he is denied entrance.

The female characters in Thomas' autobiography fall into two categories. One is that of the devoted mother who, from his perspective, accepts him as he is. While in jail and fighting drug addiction, the mother's unconditional love is his sole beam of hope. The other women are girlfriends, his and his friends. They are to be beaten into submission to ensure their faithfulness and compliance, while the men fool around with other women. Marta E. Sánchez explains that this violence against women is to some extent a means to cope with his own oppression:

Piri compensates for his tenuous Puerto Rican cultural identity by identifying as a predatory Puerto Rican male. By implication, he affiliates himself with the imperial conqueror, the racially and sexually "superior" male who penetrates and colonizes the racially and sexually "inferior" female. (122)

This bleak portrait of life in *El Barrio* became an instant best-seller and, together with *West Side Story* (1959), it reinforced some stereotypes of Puerto Ricans in New York which are still prevalent today. A few years later, during an exhibition of her work, Nicholasa Mohr was approached to write her own memoirs, accompanied with her own illustrations. When she submitted the manuscript that later would become *Nilda* (1973), the publishers rejected it because it was not what they had expected: a female version of Thomas' turbulent life.

❦ ❦ ❦

The *Nuyorican*[2] poets that began to organize impromptu readings and poetry recitals in the sixties, found publishing outlets in the seventies. Pedro Pietri, Miguel Algarín, Miguel Piñero, Tato Laviera, Lucky Cienfuegos, Sandra María Esteves, and Victor Hernández Cruz are among the many writers whose work began to leave the imprint of a new aesthetic, to be reckoned with whenever discussing Puerto Rican literature in the States. Algarín's article "Nuyorican Aesthetics" summarizes their *ars poetica*. In his introduction to the groundbreaking *Nuyorican Poetry: An Anthology of Puerto Rican Words and Feelings*, Algarín describes the search for a new language because "raw life needs raw verbs and raw nouns to express the action and to name the quality of the experience" (19). Theirs is the language "of short pulsating rhythms that manifest the unrelenting strain" that the Nuyorican endures day after day (16). They appropriate the street language combined with the beat of their *Salsa* music to put the "raw" feelings of the Puerto Rican working class into words.

The verses of Pedro Pietri's "Puerto Rican Obituary" (1973) are the "raw nerves" of an eulogy to all of those who have worked and died in the streets of Spanish Harlem and now lie anonymously in "long island cemetery" (Santiago, *Boricuas* 117–126). Pietri's magnum opus soon became the national anthem of the Nuyorican, the epic poem of a collective consciousness fighting for cultural identity. Six years later, Tato Laviera reaffirms the presence and permanence of Puerto Ricans in the States with his visionary collection of poems, *La Carreta Made a U-turn*. While René Marqués' cart returned to the island with its defeated passengers, Laviera introduces a cart whose passengers turned around and planted themselves on continental ground, determined to fight against everyday hardship.

The work of these writers delves mainly into the public sphere of everyday life. There are highly emotive renditions of the daily sounds and smells of the streets in *El Barrio*. The struggles against poverty, unemployment, drugs, AIDS, racism, and other social problems are depicted with "raw" honesty. But the female perspective is either absent or unrecognized. For example, in his introduction to *Nuyorican Poetry*, Algarín insists on using the generic "he" in references to the Nuyorican poet in spite of the fact that women are among the "poets" included in the anthology. By the late seventies and early eighties, however, Latina *Puertorriqueña* writers begin to trace with indelible ink their own experiences.

This book looks at the contributions of six of them and their rituals of survival, the quest for creative expression, and the fight to assert their right to become artists. They are representative of Puerto Rican women writing in the United States but do not comprise the totality of them. The writers included here would be the first to acknowledge their indebtedness to other "sistas" such as Carmen Valle and Lorraine Sutton.

The women selected for this volume are of Puerto Rican descent who were either born or have lived most of their adult lives in the United States. Although many of them did live in New York, at some point or another, they do not necessarily consider themselves *Nuyoricans*. They write mainly in English, except for Umpierre-Herrera's first two collections. They are contemporary writers very active in the literary world. They have chosen to portray "the humdrum insignificance . . . the forgettable, unheroic little dramas that make up the lives of regular working people" (Flores, "Back" 53). In so doing, they also challenge traditional literary discourses, from both Puerto Rico and the United States, to author/ize their own voices at the margins and at the center of the printed page. The first chapter examines Esmeralda Santiago's autobiographical novels and how they echo the *bildung* or process of formation of the Puerto Rican community in New York. Chapter Two looks at the intrinsic tension of the mother-daughter relationship in Nicholasa Mohr's fiction, as it parallels a woman's struggle for a space of her own. Mother and daughter, Rosario Morales and Aurora Levins Morales, are the subject of the next chapter that discusses the mechanics of liquids as a metaphor for their fluid identity. Chapter Four shows how Sandra María Esteves co-opts the rhythmic sounds of *Salsa* and the incantations of *Santería* to articulate a political discourse of liberation. The following chapter studies Luz María Umpierre-Herrera's systematic attacks on social and intellectual institutions with their patterns of racial and sexual discrimination. Finally, Chapter Six studies Judith Ortiz Cofer's notion of storytelling as a sacred ritual that brings about the transformation of experiences and reality.

The chapters can be read independently but there is a common thematic thread: the primal need of these Latina *Puertorriqueña* writers to give voice to their own experiences, to their creative spirits, to their souls. As the experiences of Puerto Ricans in the States have evolved, so has their cultural and artistic expression, and Nicholasa Mohr insists that it should be recognized as such:

> We are no longer an island people. This reality has become increasingly incomprehensible to the Puerto Rican from the island. This new world, which we are still creating, is the source of our strength and the cradle of our future. ("Puerto Ricans in New York" 160)

In 1981, Ana Lydia Vega published in Puerto Rico her short story "Pollito Chicken," a satire that uses "spanglish" to depict the sexual liberation of a Nuyorican woman. Mohr, among many others, took great offense to the story both for its language and the stereotypes depicted that had nothing to do with the reality of thousands of Puerto Ricans in New York. No longer will Latina writers allow others, especially those in the island, to record the experiences of those who live at the crossroads of the "here and there," of what Luis Rafael

Sánchez calls "*la guagua aérea*" ("the aerial bus"). When discussing her skills as storyteller, Nicholasa Mohr likes to say that "she must have 'kissed the mango tree,'" (Flores, "Back" 52). The Latina *Puertorriqueñas* studied in this book have done just that: they kissed and ate the forbidden fruit and in so doing, they have been anointed with the power of words that enables them to re/create "new worlds." Their works are indeed the "cradle of our future" in that they place their "words" in front of our eyes as an offering of strength for our souls.

Notes

1. "Operation Bootstrap" was an economic plan to attract industrial corporations to open plants in Puerto Rico. The local government offered them cheap labor, physical plants, and other infrastructure at low costs, and above all, tax exemptions for up to 25 years (Scarano 743).
2. Term used to designate people of Puerto Rican descent living in the United States, mainly in New York.

Chapter 1
Esmeralda Santiago and the
Bildungsroman of El Barrio

*You are an amazing hybrid—a tree that
gives forth both mangoes and magnolias.
And Carmita, you don't have to stop
eating the fruit to smell the flower.*
—Carmen Agra Deedy

Scholars of German literature may immediately object to the title
of this chapter because once again the term *Bildungsroman* is being
used loosely. In the introduction to *Reflection and Action: Essays on
the Bildungsroman*, James Hardin laments "the imprecise use of the
word to categorize virtually any work that describes . . . a protagonist's
formative years" (x). Jeffrey Sammons similarly objects that the definitions of the literary genre usually cite English and/or American novels as its best examples.[1] Years before, Sammons set out in search of
the "invisible *bildungsroman*" of German literature and called it the
"phantom genre."[2] Marc Redfield borrowed the term for his 1996
book, *Phantom Formations: Aesthetic Ideology and the Bildungsroman*, where he discusses the challenges to genre theory as emblema-
tized by this German form.

Frederick Amrine had already observed in 1987 the lack of a con-
sensus regarding a canon of the *bildungsroman* and the problematic
issues of defining the literary genre. At the end of his article, Amrine
recommends the study of three "neglected" characteristics of this
genre. First, it should be considered a "hybrid genre" as opposed to a
"pure" one. Second, critics ought to recognize the novel's modality

1

with its predominantly "satiric/ironic features." And finally, they need to reconsider the "revolutionary poetics" of the genre as originally suggested by Friedrich Schlegel and other Romantics (134–135).

John H. Smith discusses the problem of sexual difference and concludes that "the strict gender codification at the basis of *Bildung*, taken in its historical context, makes female *Bildung* a contradiction in terms" (220). Borrowing Lacan's theory of desire, Smith argues that the *bildungsroman* attempts "to represent the self's developmental trajectory within the bourgeois patriarchal order and thereby to expose the structuration of (male) desire" (215). Thus, women, as the Other being desired, as the object of male desire, are inherently excluded from the process of *bildung*.

At best, these critics seem to acknowledge the problematic complexity and ambiguity of defining the *bildungsroman*. At worst, they betray a regionalist, elitist, sexist mentality that can only conceive a literary form in eighteenth-century Germany depicting a German male hero in a process of acculturation and integration into a bourgeois society.[3] In discussing the historical development of the meaning of the word *bildung,* James Hardin points to two important considerations: "first, *Bildung* as a developmental process and, second, as a collective name for the cultural and spiritual values of a specific people or social stratum in a given historical epoch" (xi–xii). Notice that no specification of gender or historical period is given. To exclude female voices from *bildungsroman* is to insist on excluding women from a life experience that is not limited to Germans and/or to men.

In their introduction to *The Voyage In: Fictions of Female Development,* Abel, Hirsch, and Langland observe that throughout the revision of theories of development and the gradual expansion of variables within this literary genre, "gender . . . has not been assimilated as a pertinent category" (5). Critics, such as John H. Smith do admit that gender should be taken into account, but ultimately insist that stories of female self-development be called something else, such as "novels of awakening" (221).

One might argue, on the other hand, that it is precisely because of Hardin's emphasis on "process" and "collectiveness" and because of Amrine's underlining characteristics of "hybridity" and "revolution," that the literary form of the *bildungsroman* has become the ideal locus for the discourse of socially, politically, economically, racially, ethnically, and sexually disenfranchised groups. In fact, Blacks, Chicanos, Jewish-Americans, homosexuals, and others have co-opted this genre to depict their growing-up experiences as "a series of disillusionments or clashes with an inimical milieu" (Abel et al. 6). While Fritz Martini insists that the end result should be one of harmonious integration into society (Hardin 17), Margot Kelley believes that "the *Bildungsroman* is an ideal genre for writers interested in making literary texts that *disorganize* the form and content of a predominant genre for *revolutionary* purposes" (65, emphasis mine). Unfortunately for women who have been traditionally denied the "social options available only to men" (Abel et al. 7), their awakenings have often ended in death, whether physical and actual or symbolic. In recent years, though, the *bildungsromans* of minority groups have begun to explore alternative notions of self and cultural identity as they construct a discourse of resistance toward any "harmonious" assimilation into the dominant culture. They seem to relish "hybridity," "*métissage*,"[4] "fragmentation," "ambiguity," and "fluidity."

Piri Thomas' 1967 autobiography, *Down These Mean Streets,* became synonymous with the *bildungsroman* of a Puerto Rican boy in the ghetto. It is almost a continuation of Oscar Lewis' 1965 anthropological study *La Vida: A Puerto Rican Family in the Culture of Poverty—San Juan and New York.*[5] Thomas' realistic and bleak portrait of life in *El Barrio* was an instant best-seller. However, as Nicholasa Mohr has observed, his highly popular "adventures" with gangs, violence, drugs, and imprisonment are not altogether typical of Puerto Ricans in *El Barrio*, and only depict a limited and sordid aspect of inner-city life. In fact, Esmeralda Santiago in *Almost a Woman* observes with poignant irony that she only knew *one* Puerto Rican on drugs, her friend and neighbor Neftali. True, there were family members abusing alcohol, but none of them ever, including four brothers, got into trouble with the law. On the other hand, drugs seemed to her to be the recreational activity of choice for many of her white American classmates.

Bothered by the stereotypes promoted in Thomas' book and the invisibility of her own experiences, Mohr wrote her first novel, a semi-autobiographical account about the everyday life of a Nuyorican girl, about "the humdrum insignificance of it all, the forgettable, unheroic little dramas that make up the lives of regular working people" (Flores, "Back Down" 53). Since *Nilda*'s publication in 1973, Mohr has written many other award-winning stories of children and their everyday lives in Spanish Harlem and the South Bronx. Judith Ortiz Cofer has also chronicled her experiences of growing up between the island and New Jersey in her collection of essays and poems *Silent Dancing: A Partial Remembrance of a Puerto Rican Childhood* (1990). *An Island Like You* (1995) is a collection of stories about teenagers in *El Barrio,* recording their experiences from their own point of view, combining male and female perspectives.

The ambivalence and ambiguity of Esmeralda Santiago's two-part autobiography, *When I Was Puerto Rican* (1993) and *Almost a Woman* (1998), epitomizes the *bildung* of *El Barrio.* In the first book (*WPR*), Santiago adopts the innocent voice of a girl as she rubs her eyes and focuses them on the world around her. Negi,[6] Esmeralda's nickname when she was little, narrates her childhood in a poor rural town and in the slums of the metropolitan area of San Juan until her family moves to New York and her admission to the Performing Arts High School. The second book (*AW*) begins with the arrival of the family in New York and goes on to describe Esmeralda's adolescence until, at almost twenty-one, she is on the brink of leaving home. These two autobiographical texts provide the reader with a kaleidoscopic view of the "humdrum" everyday life of ordinary people with their "unheroic little dramas" as they live in poverty in the island's countryside, as they try to stay afloat in the stinking waters of El Mangle, as they struggle between employment and welfare in New York, and as they fight against the maladies of cancer, pregnancies, racism, and discrimination. While Esmeralda's father, Pablo, struggles between jobs in construction, her mother, Monín, does sewing and laundry for other people and cleans houses. As a teenager attending high school, Esmeralda and, later on, her siblings get odd jobs at theaters and pizza stores to help the family. After high school, her college studies are interrupted by periods of full-time work so that she can enroll for another semester. Like Nicholasa Mohr's books, *Nilda* (1974), *El Bronx Remembered*

(1975), and *In Nueva York* (1988), Santiago's work is populated with families struggling not only to provide a protective and safe environment for their children but also opportunities so that they can rise above "the culture of poverty."

Unfortunately, such financial and social progress is not always smooth. Santiago is painfully aware of this as the controversial title of her first book and the imprecise adjective "almost" of her second one indicate. Instead of the natural progression from ignorance and innocence into wisdom and maturity, Negi/Esmeralda depicts the anguishing disintegration of her Puerto Rican being and the painful descent into the chaos and confusion of her cultural identity.

Santiago's process of *bildung* (formation) actually becomes a process of de/formation, of unraveling, of coming apart as opposed to coming into being, of fragmentation as opposed to achieving a monolithic identity. This process echoes in many ways the development of the Nuyorican community in *El Barrio*. Although it is obvious that the text is written by an adult, Santiago deliberately chose the "eyes" of a naive child and bewildered adolescent to be the prism through which we encounter her experiences. Negi's painful childlike point of view resonates with the collective experiences of the displaced Puerto Ricans in New York. The clashes and disillusionment with the "American dream" and the "land of the free" leads to the fragmentation of what is perceived to be the Puerto Rican identity, until, that is, the voices begin to emerge from the spaces of ambiguity and ambivalence to proclaim an identity from the margins of the ghetto.

In the award-winning essay "'Qué assimilated, brother, *yo soy asimilao*': The Structuring of Puerto Rican Identity," Juan Flores outlines the four stages in the development of the Puerto Rican identity in the United States. First, he talks about the total disillusionment with the reality of life in New York City—the poverty, welfare, discrimination, unemployment, and/or slave-like working conditions. At this point, a sense of total despair prevails. The second stage is when Puerto Ricans begin to look at a mythical notion of their island in hopes of a paradisiacal refuge/escape from New York. The third is the moment of reentry into the community, reaffirming their presence on the continent with a strong sense of cultural context and belonging. And finally, in the fourth stage Puerto Ricans identify with other ethnic groups and recognize in them their own painful experiences. This last stage does not mean an integration and/or assimilation with other groups. As Puerto Ricans say, *"juntos pero no revueltos"* ("together but not mixed"), they have learned to embrace other colonized and/or ghettoized communities without giving up their own sense of cultural identity.

Santiago records these stages as they occur both on the island and in New York. She depicts the slow disillusionment of Negi not only with American society but with the patriarchal inconsistencies of her own native land. In the figure of her mother who has eleven children, the adolescent girl begins to suspect the suffocating and limiting roles that society wants to impose on her and her body, and she finally surpasses her idyllic view of *"ser jíbara"* (to be a country girl) to reaffirm her presence in North America.

It is very appropriate for Esmeralda Santiago to use the autobiographical form to trace the process of her *bildung*. Sidonie Smith and Julie Watson explain how this mode "becomes the site on which cultural ideologies intersect and dissect one another, in contradiction, consonance, and adjacency" (*De/Colonizing the Subject* xix). The two critics believe that in adopting "traditional patterns" of writing, a woman reveals "their gaps and incongruencies, wrenches their meanings [. . .] for 'illegitimate' speakers have a way of exposing the instability of forms" (xx). Santiago appropriates the apparently straightforward discourse of autobiographical narrative to underline the contradictions of the social expectations of women, the friction between their ethnic pride and the cultural stereotypes of Puerto Ricans, the dichotomy of an "I" constructed by others and by self.

Underneath the seamless linear progression of the narrative are the constant moves of the family to different places in Puerto Rico or to various apartments in New York City. In fact, both texts start with references to a move. *When I Was Puerto Rican* begins with the move to a house in Macún without electricity or running water. The book describes the zigzagging journey from Macún to Santurce and back, to El Mangle, and finally to New York. The first chapter in *Almost a Woman* is about moving so much during the first twenty years of her life that even as an adult she can pack all her belongings in a couple of suitcases. As they leave behind possessions, neighbors, and friends, Esmeralda begins to store away "sights and sounds [. . .] as if their meaning would someday be revealed in a flash of insight to transform her life forever" (AW 3). Thus begins a series of epiphanic moments where the protagonist realizes slowly and painfully that things are not what they seem to be. Even her trips to New England with a Children's Theater company force her to confront ethnic and racial issues.

Santiago deliberately subverts the metaphor of journey and the motif of the quest for the cup of self-knowledge as she maps the zigzag movements on the island and the circular searches in the Big City to underline the constant disruptions in the development of a young girl. As she moves in and out of places and steps in and out of costumes, the protagonist/narrator, an illegitimate child herself, destabilizes the process of becoming a woman, a Puerto Rican, an artist.

Between "puta" and "pendeja"

Most of Monín's talks with her daughter Negi are warnings against the evils lurking in the streets. One would assume that naturally her mother would advise her children to beware of robbers, rapists, drug dealers, murderers, etc. Yet, the threat that preoccupies her the most is the one posed by men and their "*pocavergüenzas*, shameless acts that included drinking, gambling, and squandering money on women not their wives" (AW 14). Women that participate in these shameless acts are considered *putas* (whores), and those that have fallen victims to men's lies are *pendejas* (fools). Esmeralda is supposed to grow up not being one or the other, but something else not quite defined.

In *Subjectivity, Identity, and the Body*, Sidonie Smith explains how the body becomes the locus where a woman "negotiates the autobiographical 'I,'" (22) and wages war with the dominant culture's notions of gender (139–144). As the naive observations of the child Negi grow into Esmeralda's adolescent questioning of her mother's expectations and her own experiences with men, the clash between the traditional patriarchal definition of women's roles and Esmeralda's own search for sexual identity intensifies and erupts at different moments with devastating results for her.

In *When I Was Puerto Rican*, Negi inquisitively observes the conflicting gender roles imposed by society with growing confusion and an incipient nagging feeling that something is amiss. In *Almost a Woman*, the teenager Esmeralda grows impatient and downright rebellious as she confronts the contradictions between her mother's and men's expectations of her and their own behavior.

Obviously, Negi's first notions of gender roles come from her parents. Throughout her childhood, Pablo is the hero who constantly rescues the family from misery—both when living in El Mangle where she is overwhelmed by the stench of the putrid waters and later on in Santurce where she is being verbally abused by her teacher. In each case, her father shows up unexpectedly to take his family back to their hometown. Even years after her mother has moved them to New York, Negi/Esmeralda dreams of the day when her father will come to claim his family and to take them all back to Macún. Pablo is the source of infinite wisdom, according to Negi. Only he can answer all of her questions about being *jíbara*, American imperialism, the nature of sin, and what is a soul. From him, she learns about poetry and patriotism. Typical of a girl's paternal devotion, her idealized view of her father will not be shattered in an instant. On the contrary, the mask of the hero begins to peel off slowly as Negi observes with bewilderment the world around her and overhears baffling conversations.

Maribel Ortiz-Márquez points out that Santiago's "experiences related to the configuration of gender have to do with viewing and recognizing differences between her and other's bodies, and how those differences come to signify what it is to be a 'woman'" (232). Thus, from an innocent game of "show and tell" with the neighboring male child, Tato, to her realization that her piano teacher is *staring* at her breasts, to *watching* a man masturbate while looking at her, to her own uncle's proposal of a dollar for *a look* at her chest, Negi learns some conflicting and painful lessons about sexuality. In fact, the child's penetrating eyes notice the contradictions of social gender roles and taboos. When her family is forced to seek shelter at a neighbor's house during a hurricane, Negi observes the women cooking and taking care of children, while the men play dominoes. During her father Pablo's occasional absences, she watches her mother struggle to feed the children.

Negi also learns from overheard conversations, radio soap operas, and popular *boleros* (ballads) about love. As the child innocently reports conversations, discussions, and arguments between her parents, the reader soon realizes that Pablo is a womanizer who goes to visit his lover for days at a time, leaving Monín and the children in total misery. Her mother is forced to seek a solution to their economic problem on her own by starting to work at an American textile factory. Each day, she has to get up early, prepare breakfast, cook dinner, do laundry, iron clothes, and get the children ready for school before leaving for work.

In *Política Sexual en Puerto Rico*, Ostalaza Bey discusses the impact that American colonization had on the economy of the island. As part of the industrialization project of Puerto Rico, the United States introduced light industries, such as textiles, and employed women because they could pay them lower wages than men (58). The drastic change from an agricultural economy to an industrial one forced farming men to migrate to the United States. Although this historical fact is not described in Santiago's memoirs, the author nonetheless subtly shows the extent that American political influence had, not only on the family unit, but on gender roles in society as a whole. Even though Negi does feel abandoned by her mother who is at work all day, she cannot understand the neighbors's resentful and indignant gossip about Monín "breaking a taboo" (*WPR* 122) by working outside the home. To her surprise, her father joins his voice to that of the neighbors in criticizing Monín for subverting her role as housewife and mother. Ostalaza Bey points out that "el independentismo tradicional ha respondido con la pretensión de que el estado mantenga los tradicionales controles sobre la mujer" ("traditional independence ideology has responded with the presumption that the state will maintain the traditional control over women" 88). In spite of her ambivalent feelings about her mother's job, Negi resents both systems as equally oppressive: the American colonial economic system that has taken her mother away to work and the Puerto Rican patriarchal society that criticizes women for doing so.

In fact, Negi, not quite sure of the definition of the word, begins to suspect that politics is something that empowers men over women. She explains to her classmates that politics is something that men talk about at the bus stop: "I'd heard Papi tell Mami when he was late that he'd missed the bus because he'd been discussing politics" (*WPR* 71). For the girl, politics is something trivial that men do in their leisure time, while the reader recognizes that men use "politics" as an excuse to cover up their sexual escapades and perpetuate their behavior. Her naive suspicions are confirmed when the new government of Puerto Rico implements new nutritional and hygienic programs in the schools. Puerto Rican women are invited to meetings where American men with bellies bursting out of their sweaty shirts teach the mothers proper nutrition and health care for their children.

Thus, as Sidonie Smith explains, Negi begins "to grapple self-consciously with her identity as a woman in patriarchal culture and with her problematic relationship to engendered figures of selfhood" (*Poetics* 56). As the female autobiographer starts questioning her sexual identity, she "destabilizes notions of male and female difference, rendering gender ideology an elusive thing by conjoining dichotomies" (*Poetics* 59). Negi's awareness of her father's deceitful behavior increases to the point that she realizes he uses her, his own daughter, as an excuse to cover his escapades, and thus her confusion about what is expected of women. The unmarried are called "*jamonas*" (hams, spinsters), a derogatory term to describe women too ugly or too mean to get married. A man that does not get married is called "lucky" according to the bus driver as he laughs at Negi's questions (*WPR* 89). Listening to her grandmother complain about men and marriage while her mother cries, the girl has an epiphanic revelation: being "*jamona*" cannot hurt as much as being married (*WPR* 104). Daughter, mother, grandmother then sit in conspiratorial silence as they all have the same thought (*WPR* 104).

As the title indicates, one of the major concerns in Santiago's *Almost a Woman* is the transformation from girl into womanhood. All of the subtle hints that were given by society and her mother about gender roles in *When I Was Puerto Rican* become clear instructions in the second autobiographical installment.

Esmeralda comes with her mother to New York where they hope that doctors can treat her youngest brother's leg. The remaining siblings arrive months later. By this time, Pablo and Monín have broken up, and he does not move to the big city with the family. The reason Esmeralda was chosen to go on the first trip was not so that she could help with the youngest children, as one would assume, but because at thirteen and already a *"señorita"* (pubescent), she has to be kept under the watchful eye of her mother (*AW* 14). The world, especially the metropolis, is full of dangers and evil threats lurking in dark alleys.

The vague notions the girl has about men in the first text become a physical reality in the second. She sees men standing outside the check-cashing office ready to snap the welfare money out of the women's hands. Many of them will not be back to their families until the next check is due. Esmeralda begins to resent men as she sees them hanging around the corners, at bars, on the stoops, drinking beer and leering at young girls like herself as their families are struggling inside roach-infested rooms for everyday survival.[7]

The protagonist's adolescent body, already confused by the onset of puberty and growing pains, soon becomes the battlefield where dominant male culture will attempt to ravage her innocence. Her uncle will stare at her body and pinch her breasts while throwing a dollar at her to buy her silence. In the subway, men will expose themselves to her or rub against her helpless body trapped in the overcrowded trains. At night she worries that either she is a *puta*, because she might have encouraged such behavior, or that she is a *pendeja*, because she did not do anything to defend herself.

As she begins to map the sexuality of her body, Esmeralda discovers that she is merely an exotic distant country where men want to go for brief exciting adventures but not for enduring commitment. The young adolescent soon finds out that she is the embodiment of what Susana Chávez-Silverman calls "racialized and gendered representations of Latina subjectivity—variously encoded as tropical, exotic, hyper-eroticized sexuality" (101). Halfway through her first date ever, Sidney bursts into laughter as he comments that his Jewish mother would die of a heart attack were she to find out he is out with a "shiksa" (a non-Jewish girl) (*AW* 176). For him, she is just an act of rebellion, a brief incursion into the forbidden land. On the other hand, Avery, a Texas millionaire, would like a more permanent relationship—with her as his mistress, of course, because the sons of nice

American families do not marry Spanish girls. Trying to appease an offended and hurt Esmeralda, he explains his political ambitions and how this is the way it is done: marry a "good ole Texas gal from a prominent family" while keeping a mistress on the side. After all, that's the way Lyndon B. Johnson did it, and for twenty years his father had a *"Mexican one!"* In spite of Esmeralda's questions and objections, Avery never realizes that he is objectifying both Latina and American women by reducing them to some kind of appliance that will enhance both his public and domestic life. Sidney and Avery have obviously been influenced by the media images of the "Latin spitfire . . . volatile and verbal, exhibiting overt sexuality, a hot temper, and mood shifts, spewing broken English full of malapropisms and cosmic misunderstanding" (Kanellos, *Thirty* 133). The biased attitudes of these young men reflect the labels usually applied to Latin women: "Spic, Hot Tempered" and "Explosive / Handle with care," denounced by Luz María Umpierre in her poem "La receta."[8]

That her mother's warnings about men prove to be true does not help an already baffled and mystified young woman. Her mother's advice and her mother's behavior speak of two different and conflicting realities. According to Monín, her daughters are to be married by the church in a big cathedral and have children, even though she never married and no one in the family ever goes to church. As she translates for her mother at the welfare office, the teenager finds out that she, like all of her siblings, is illegitimate.

It is as if Esmeralda is sinking into the "cultural schizophrenia" of becoming a woman in two different worlds, worlds depicted by Judith Ortiz Cofer in her memoir, *Silent Dancing* (124). Here, the author describes the continuing difficulty she has discussing with her mother the definition and the translation of the term "woman" (*Silent* 152). The meaning, connotation, and denotation of the word change according to the language and the culture within which it is defined. The mother only recognizes its reality and significance within Puerto Rican culture. Like Ortiz Cofer, Santiago struggles to make sense of the conflicting instructions for becoming a woman. On one hand, Esmeralda is told that intelligence and education are her best weapons but is harassed in school for applying to the Performing Arts High School and for trying to escape the destiny of all girls like her: welfare and pregnancy! She is told to become an independent woman, but when she plans to move to her own apartment with her cousin, both mothers give a thunderous "NO," reminding their rebellious daughters that the only way out of their homes is in the arms of their husbands. To break away from the gender roles prescribed by the island's culture is an unforgivable sin, as Esmeralda soon finds out. When she rejects the marriage proposal of Neftali, a neighbor's son, family members criticize her for her arrogance and her presumptuousness. The fact that Neftali kills himself a few months later while in jail for drugs and that his alleged enlistment with the Army turns out to be a total lie does not excuse her defiant rejection.

Attendance at the Performing Arts School gives Esmeralda the freedom to travel beyond the streets of El Barrio and to explore the world of Manhattan. As she traverses the different neighborhoods, she begins to construct different identities for herself. Dissatisfied with her life in a crowded apartment and rejecting the alternative solution of marriage as not only unappealing but totally unacceptable, Esmeralda imagines other roles for herself.

First, there is the fantasy world of the comic books in which she imagines herself a teenager without worries, like Archie and his friends. Then come the different performances of Cleopatra and her exotic roles as Hindu princess or mermaid in the Children's Theater. As she steps in and out of exotic costumes, she acts out other "I"s to resist the gender roles that both the patriarchal culture of the island and the American colonizing society have dictated for her. Yet, acting is not only a means of resistance but a means of disguising the disintegration of self that is taking place inside her (AW 74). Accused of not being a good actress on stage, Esmeralda realizes that she cannot act while she is already acting in real life: "Because the minute I left the dark, crowded apartment where I lived, I was in performance, pretending to be someone I wasn't. I resisted the Method's [of dramatic performance] insistence on truth, as I used to create a simulated reality" (AW 74).

Ironically, she ultimately escapes in the arms of a man, and instead of creating her own identity, she relinquishes it all to her lover who invents her all over again. Esmeralda falls in love and elopes with Ulvi, an older Turkish movie director who is as absorbing, demanding, and controlling as her mother. He calls her "chiquita," wants her to imitate his moves when they go out in public, and does not want to know anything about her life. As a director, he is going to instruct her on how to act and what to be. The mature narrator knows that she has thrown herself into an absorbing, not a liberating, relationship. Interestingly enough, the young Esmeralda does acknowledge having taken psychology in college and being able to recognize her Oedipus complex and her need to fill the figure of an absent father in her life. She also makes acute comparisons between Ulvi and her mother, prophetically recognizing that he will turn out to be as suffocating as her mother and the apartment that she is leaving behind.

The ending of *Almost a Woman*, like that of Santiago's first autobiography, leaves the reader with unresolved questions about notions of self, gender, and ethnic identity. Perhaps Santiago needs to "block out the noise, the confusion, the drama of my family's life" that pull her apart between *"puta"* and *"pendeja,"* between *"jíbara"* and "Americanized," before she can stand erect as the "I" that subsequently authored the two texts.

Between "jíbara" and "americana"

In an article appearing in the *New York Times Magazine* in 1994, Santiago describes a painful reunion with her family now residing back on the island. As she admires the choreographed movements of her mother and sisters in the kitchen, one of them asks her: "How can you be Puerto Rican without your rice and beans?" Before she has time to answer, her mother points out that she has become *"americana."* As she fights the tears in her eyes, the words spill out in an emotional meditation of her resentment for being pulled out of the rural town of Macún, where all she wanted to be was a *"jíbara,"* and taken to New York, where she was constantly pushed to set the example for her ten brothers and sisters on how to be successful in America. If becoming a woman was a baffling and painful journey through a maze of contradicting ideologies of gender roles and expectations, defining an ethnic self becomes a process of disillusionment and ultimate disintegration, colored not by the tropical tones of the island but by the dark presence of racial discrimination.

As Juan Flores indicates, one of the stages for exiled Puerto Ricans is the idealization of the island. For Santiago, the process began long before she left the country, when her family moved from one place to the other in an attempt to develop a sense of roots and belonging. In her first autobiography, the child Negi explains how badly she wanted to be a *"jíbara,"* a "country girl," as she listened enthralled to the radio programs with music and poems about rural life. The idealization of this figure goes back to Manuel Alonso y Pacheco's *El Jíbaro*, where a *white* male farmer is the embodiment of the Puerto Rican soul. But soon, Negi realizes the contradiction between the nostalgic admiration for this figure as depicted in the arts and the pejorative connotation that the noun has in everyday speech: "Even at the tender age when I didn't know yet my real name, I was puzzled by the hypocrisy of celebrating a people everyone looked down on" (*WPR* 13). Her precocious suspicion is confirmed when her family moves to Santurce, the metropolitan area, and all her classmates mock her for being exactly what she most wanted to be, a *"jíbara."*

Negi's romantic notion of the *"jíbara"* extends to the island of Puerto Rico. Like many poets, the girl imagines the island as a woman whose feet are caressed by the ocean waves (*WPR* 77). In fact, her favorite part of the national anthem is when Christopher Columbus arrives and admires its beauty as a lover admires a woman.

In spite of her childish tendencies toward romanticism and idealization, there is a gnawing preoccupation with her cultural identity. She describes her bewilderment and questions herself about "multiple personalities" when her mother explains that everyone has two names: the nickname given to us by the loved ones around us and the name used by the government for official business. To discover that her nickname "Negi" originates from her skin color, *"negrita"*[9] (black), only adds to her state of confusion as she begins to study and compare with a great deal of curiosity the color of her skin and the texture of her hair with those of her parents and siblings, who exhibit different "racial" characteristics.

Unfortunately, school does not appease her preoccupations but intensifies them. In the chapter "The American Invasion of Macún," Santiago provides a lighthearted but candid and incisive description of the U.S. government's failed attempts to Americanize the island by forcing "English only" in the schools and new nutritional diets based on American vegetables and fruits not available in Puerto Rico. Negi's young mind is pushed into total chaos when she begins to attend school where classes are conducted totally in English with Miss Jimenez insisting that the children memorize songs phonetically without understanding what the words mean. The child wonders if she will become an *"Americana"* if she eats the "powdered milk and eggs" now served for breakfast. Her father's answer, "only if you like it better than Puerto Rican food," does not assuage her concerns. This sense of confusion and ambiguity resonates with the current polemic about what is cultural identity and the insistence of many on defining it by such tangibles as food, music, and language.

The experiment of "English only" and American food in the schools did not last long in Puerto Rico and was soon cancelled.[10] The experience is enough for Negi to underline the American presence on the island, the disruptive and intrusive impact that colonization has even in a rural town where electricity had not yet arrived.

Negi and the other children in school do not understand the political changes brought with the colonization, and repeat epithets such as *"imperialista"* and *"gringo"* without knowing their meaning or their pejorative connotations. As usual, she asks her father for clarification. After a brief lesson in history, Pablo finally explains that Americans are indeed imperialists because "They expect us to do things their way, even in our country" (*WPR* 73). A few days later, Negi, armed with her new understanding of language, pronounces these insults and throws up the food. Although she gets sick for a few days, she is proud of her small fight for independence.

It is in her slow process of disillusionment with her father that Negi's conflicting awareness of cultural and political ideology is underlined. Throughout this first autobiography, Santiago depicts her father as the great freedom fighter who will rescue her and the whole family from poverty and the misery of their lives. It is in Brooklyn, while she still awaits for father/hero, that she finds out that he already has another family and that all those words of endearment and patriotism were merely empty rhetoric, like the unintelligible words of the Americans at the community center, or the senseless songs of Miss Jimenez, or the political conversations of men hanging around at the corner.

If the first days of school in Macún brought confusion about her island's political identity, Negi's first day in Brooklyn's public school system is a crash course on ethnic diversity and racial tension. As she struggles with the language, she also tries to recognize and distinguish the different groups composed of Blacks, Italians, newly arrived Puerto Ricans, and those born in New York, and how to avoid confrontations with them. Shopping with her mother becomes a lesson on racial and ethnic geography—it is important to know which stores and which restaurants will allow Puerto Ricans to enter!

As the title indicates, *When I Was Puerto Rican* examines the ambiguity of a child trying to become something, a *"jíbara,"* that no longer is appreciated in her culture. Halfway in that conflicting process, Negi is yanked to the United States where the snobism toward a "country girl" turns into discrimination against her whole cultural background. The past tense of the verb "to be" signals the disintegration of a subject: "For me, the person I was becoming when we left was erased, and another one was created. The Puerto Rican *jíbara* who longed for green quiet of a tropical afternoon was to become a hybrid who would never forgive the uprooting" (*WPR* 209).

Almost a Woman then becomes a case study of the phenomenon of grafting and hybridity in an urban setting, where nothing seems to grow except for her fears and confusion as to her cultural identity. Historian Eric Hobsbawm observes that it is usually in exile from their countries that people begin to confront ontological questions about their nationalities because they "can no longer take themselves for granted as people who did not require any definition" (153). Many other Puerto Rican writers in the United States have found themselves forced to answer questions about their national "labels" and to explain their choice of writing in English and/or Spanish.[11]

Two days after her arrival in Brooklyn, a little girl asks Esmeralda: *"¿Tú eres hispana?"* (4). Not knowing what the term means and how to respond, Esmeralda asks her mother, who explains that yes, they are, since they speak Spanish. The whole episode leaves the poor child terrified: "Two days in New York, and I'd already become someone else. It wasn't hard to imagine that greater dangers lay ahead" (*AW* 5). Thus begins the slow fragmentation of her cultural identity as the tension of being pulled between different worlds mounts. Her mother wants her to become an American, to be successful, independent, to strive for the American Dream and to fulfill and live it. On the other hand, every time the teenager talks back, or challenges her authority, or wants to follow modern trends that go against traditional customs, Monín accuses her of changing and becoming "Americanized." In fact, her mother's running criticism of her cousins every time they visit is that Titi Ana is not a good mother because she has allowed her daughters to become "Americanized," afraid that even pronouncing the word will conjure another evil lurking in Brooklyn.

Adding to Esmeralda's confusion are the public notions and stereotypes about Puerto Ricans that she confronts every day. Her sense of humiliation slowly and understandably increases as she is called a "dirty spic" in the subway, as she hears government officials refer to her neighborhood as a ghetto, and as she reads stories in the newspapers always depicting Puerto Ricans as criminals. How could she explain to her mother the disparity of her expectations for her children while the rest of New York "viewed us as dirty spicks, potential muggers, drug dealers, and prostitutes" (*AW* 88). *West Side Story* did not help matters either. At school, everyone expects Esmeralda to lift her skirts and break out into song. She resents that the only virgin in the movie is played by an American while the "sexy spitfire" is played by one of the few Puerto Rican members of the cast, Rita Moreno. Frances Aparicio and Susana Chávez-Silverman discuss the process of "Latinization" or "the appropriation and reformulation of cultural icons such as food and clothing, language, popular music . . . films and religious iconography" (*Tropicalizations* 3) as a way for U.S. culture to deal with the increasing presence of Latinos and their cultural practices. Instead of rendering us "invisible" they make us "visible *only* as stereotypes," such as the erotic and exotic Latin woman (Chávez-Silverman 101).

In the workforce, Esmeralda always feels under the shadow of these stereotypes and assumptions. More than once, colleagues remark that she does not "sound" Puerto Rican. She would try to explain that Puerto Ricans *can* indeed speak good English, dress well, be well-educated and competent in their jobs but to no avail. In fact, she does not get a role as a Puerto Rican student in a movie because "she was too pretty to be Puerto Rican" (*AW* 151). Esmeralda finds herself exhausted from these confrontations and her everyday life performances to avoid the pain and confusion as her Puerto Rican being is torn apart (*AW* 74).

Her skin also becomes the battlefield of racial identity. Although she notices her color every time she takes off her clothes, Esmeralda gradually becomes aware of its social implications. Back on the island, light skin was preferred to dark, "good" hair was better than kinky, and "blue or green eyes proclaimed whiteness, even when surrounded by dark skin" (*AW* 57). But it was also understood that due to the "mestizaje" of the Spanish colonization, no one could claim racial purity. Esmeralda is baffled by official forms in the United States that constantly ask her to check a box as to race: "White, Black, Other" (*AW* 56). With a white mother and a dark father, she always marks "Other," not knowing anymore what she is. Like Esmeralda, dark-skinned Puerto Rican students in the United States feel "grey" as they are forced to confront their obviously racially mixed heritage that only brings them pain, suspicious looks, and outright discrimination. Contrary to Thomas' painful struggle with racial identity fought in the battlefield of his dark skin, Santiago seems to be more concerned with the economic and social ramifications of race. When she applies to the Performing Arts High School and is subsequently admitted, family and classmates accuse her of wanting and pretending to be "blanquita" (a white girl).

Esmeralda realizes that unless she learns "to straddle all of them [the different worlds she inhabits], a rider on three horses, each headed in a different direction" (*AW* 153), she will be quartered and torn to pieces in a process of fragmentation and dissolution of her sexual and cultural being. According to Juan Flores, the third stage in the development of Puerto Rican identity is that of reentry into the barrio with a renewed sense of social and cultural consciousness. Esmeralda honestly recognizes that her sense of "social conscience was pathetically underdeveloped" (*AW* 286). Although she admires Jaime, a fellow Puerto Rican actor, members of the Young Lords, her cousin Corazón, and her siblings Hector and Delsa because of their involvement with different organizations and commitment to the preservation of the Puerto Rican culture and the improvement of living conditions in their neighborhoods, the teenager feels that her first obligation is to "her people" in very concrete terms, that is, all of her own family members whether in New York or on the island. Only when she begins to tour New England with the Children's Theater company and draws attention to herself for being the "darkest person" in every place, does Esmeralda begin to develop a sense of responsibility to educate and inform people about Puerto Rico and its inhabitants.[12] These weak efforts soon die as she returns to New York and once again is overwhelmed by her duty to her family and by the maelstrom of ethnic neighborhoods she traverses daily.

Santiago's two autobiographies echo the ambiguity of the constant challenge to define the self in binary formulas. Toward the end of *Almost a Woman*, Jaime criticizes Esmeralda for pursuing Hindu dancing and for not cultivating the music of her island. She is back to where she was at the beginning of *When I Was Puerto Rican*: "Why should I be less Puerto Rican if I danced Bharata Natyam?" (*AW* 286). She is tired of being snubbed for being a "*jíbara*" and being accused of betraying her people because she has become too "*Americana*," of worrying about whether eating and liking American breakfast or studying Indian classical dance makes her less Puerto Rican. Unfortunately, the nearest and easiest solution for the young woman is to allow others, in her case, Ulvi, to create a label for her—whether it is "*Hispanic*," "*Latina*," "*puertorriqueña*," or "*chiquita*"—just let him "direct" her life, her being. Confusion and conflict resonate in Esmeralda's question to Jaime:

> "What do you think happens to us here?" I contended. "Do you think we're as Puerto Rican in the U.S. as on the island?" "More," he argued. "We have to work at it here." (*AW* 286)

Between the "eyes"/"I"'s of a writer

A variation of the *Bildungsroman* is the *Künstelrroman,* "a tale of the orientation of an artist."[13] In her analysis of *The Awakening,* Marianne Hirsch believes that Kate Chopin might be trying to suggest "the transformation of inner development into an artistic career" as an alternative to the literal and/or figurative death of the heroine in traditional novels of female development (*Voyage* 45). Margot Kelley and Maria Karafilis similarly see Sandra Cisneros' *The House on Mango Street* as a chronicle of Esperanza's "coming of age as a teller of stories" (Kelley, 73). The protagonist of Mohr's *Nilda* is told by her dying mother to hold on to her creative self because it will be the child's only means of survival. Nilda does not understand this advice until, sitting in silence with a new family, she realizes that the secret garden of her childhood summer camp actually exists now in the images and spaces that spill out of her box of crayons and drawings. Like Esperanza and Nilda, Negi/Esmeralda needs to develop an "I" that will speak, draw, and label her own gender and cultural identity. As Jaime tells her, she needs to "work" hard at that. Karafilis insists that the significance of the development of self or *bildung* is its "potential for personal and political agency" (75). Throughout both autobiographies, Santiago struggles to adjudicate meaning to the process of de/composing a self that is no longer familiar to her and to find a new voice that will defiantly challenge the labels superimposed by others.

In both *When I Was Puerto Rican* and *Almost a Woman,* the narrative "I" is forced to surrender to the dominant culture whether it is on the island, in El Barrio, or in Manhattan, which constantly teaches the narrator about gender, love, politics, racism, discrimination, sexuality, etc. The deliberate focalization of both narratives through the eyes of the innocent child Negi and a naive adolescent Esmeralda underlines the contradictions and conflicting notions that are constantly being pounded into her tender mind. In Judith Ortiz Cofer's *Silent Dancing,* the narrator steps in and out of the high heels of the adult mature woman who frequently interrupts and challenges the recollections of the girl Judith. Santiago avoids this analytical and reflective choreography by staying within the gaze of the child/adolescent. Negi learns about her father's womanizing behavior, about "*putas,*" about love and marriage from overheard conversations and popular *boleros*. Her notions of politics and patriotism are derived from her father's words and radio programs that read poetry about Puerto Rico. As she grows up, Esmeralda's mother and grandmother constantly give her lessons about being a *"señorita"* and about what is expected of her. She learns about cultural stigmatization and discrimination from the newspapers and people's pejorative comments in the subway. She becomes aware of sexual stereotypes and their painful repercussions from her boyfriends' "sweet talk." Even when she works in telemarketing, instead of selling, Esmeralda ends up listening to the endless "regrets and resentments": "Each life was a message I had to decode, clues for what lay ahead" (*AW* 196). The reader can almost visualize the wide-eyed child trying to absorb all these disparate lessons coming at her.

At times, Esmeralda allows others to define her identity. Bewildered, she intently studies pictures of herself made by Shanti, a photography student who insists that he can see her soul even if she cannot (*AW* 233). Afraid that others might be able to read in her face what she cannot, she examines the "eight-by-ten glossies . . . as if they are a puzzle, each feature, shadow, line a piece of a larger, undefined whole" (*AW* 234). Later, she lets Avery buy all the clothes she wears on their dates, choose the restaurant, the wines, as if she were a character being written into a fairy tale in which Prince Charming Avery turns out to be a frog. Frustrated with the puzzle, she subsequently gives Ulvi the absolute power to "direct" her in the role of her life.

One could argue that Santiago's insistence on this passive narrator/observer echoes her feelings of being victimized by her uprooting. Again and again, the author insists that her presence in the United States, her hybrid identity, is the result of her mother "yanking" her roots from Puerto Rican soil and throwing her into an unfamiliar flowerpot. Whenever she starts to bloom, it is time to move on and be replanted again. As one reads the anger that permeates both her articles and her narratives, one expects the word "kidnapping" to appear at some point in the text.

This notion of passivity is further reinforced by the use of epigraphs and chapter titles. Every chapter in *When I Was Puerto Rican* includes an epigraph derived from proverbs, sayings, and songs from the island's popular culture. In *Almost a Woman*, the chapter titles are quotes, phrases that someone else has expressed either about her or about life in general. These serve to summarize the truths about life, the lessons to be learned in the process of *bildung*.

Against these words of others, Santiago plants a straight "I" that speaks in the present reality of both texts. In direct contradiction of the past tense "I was" of the title, the prologue of *When I Was Puerto Rican* opens in the present: "Today, I stand before a stack of dark guavas" (4). As she reminisces about the tropical fruit last eaten on the day she left the island, she pushes her cart in the supermarket toward the "apples and pears of my adulthood," confident this time that eating and/or liking the food does not make her any more or any less "*jíbara*" or "*Americana*."

It is noteworthy that the acknowledgments in *Almost a Woman* are placed at the end. They read like an epilogue, as if the reader is invited to turn one more page because there is still something else to say. Like the prologue of her first autobiography, the "I" of the acknowledgments is deeply embedded in the present tense: "This is what I remember, as I remember it" (*AW* 312). However, this "I" is not only a positional counterbalance to the past tense of the previous chapters, but also a defiant challenge to the words said by others. Immediately after describing her ultimate yet incongruous act of rebellion against her domineering mother by eloping with Ulvi, to whom she relinquishes everything, Santiago includes an "I" that takes back her own life, her own voice, her own song for herself.

In the essay, "The Latino Imaginary: Dimensions of Community and Identity," Juan Flores insists that within the debate surrounding the terms "Hispanic" and "Latino," one has to distinguish between "the exterior perspectives" and "the role of the social imagination and the imaginary in the self-conception of nationally, ethnically, and 'racially' kindred groups" (185). Latinos do not shy away from the debate or stand by while they are being labeled. On the contrary, they are responding with what Flores calls the "Latino imaginary," using the term to signify a "'community' represented 'for itself,' a unity fashioned creatively on the basis of shared memory and desire, congruent histories and meshing utopias" ("Latino Imaginary" 188). As Flores and many others have observed, this social-cultural awareness matured during the sixties when Mexicans and Puerto Ricans, among others, organized politically to claim not only their own cultural past, but their presence in the United States, and their rights to a future of equality. Blanca Vásquez believes that "it was only through social movements that sought to *rescatar* (recover and reclaim) our history, honor our culture and ancestors, and to organize collectively to change the historical matrix of societal constraints imposed on us, that we found pleasure and joy and gloried in being Puerto Ricans." Like the Chicanos' claim to Aztlán,[14] Puerto Ricans proudly proclaimed themselves *Boricuas,* tracing their lineage back, not to the Spaniards that colonized most of Latin America, but to the *Taínos*, the original inhabitants, and *Borinquen,* their name for the island of Puerto Rico.

The pride and joy in cultural identity began to seep through "wall murals, bilingual poetry and street theater, and hybrid music and dance styles like salsa and Latin soul" (Flores, "Latino Imaginary" 191). In California, Luis Valdez founded El Teatro Campesino, which provided a venue for Chicanos to explore issues and concerns of their community. In New York, Puerto Rican artists began to create their own venues to read their writings, organizing the Nuyorican Poets' Cafe and the Teatro del Barrio. Such poets as Miguel Algarín, Pedro Pietri, Sandra María Esteves and Nicholasa Mohr acknowledge their debt of gratitude to the important role these organizations, clubs, and societies had in their writing and ultimately in the publication of their work. In fact, Esteves has gone back to her oral roots by directing The Afro Caribbean Poetry Theater.

When I Was Puerto Rican and *Almost a Woman* depict, in many ways, a microcosm of the artistic search for Puerto Rican identity. Like the Latino community, like El Barrio, Esmeralda Santiago has to stop observing through the passive eyes of her childhood in order to "imagine" and "fashion" and create her own self with an authorial/authoritative "I." As Flores concludes, this is not "an act of classification" but "a process of social imagination" ("Latino Imaginary" 191). So Negi/Esmeralda explores, with varying success, her self-identity through different media of creativity. Moving from one crammed apartment to another, Negi finds herself telling stories to entertain her family gathered around the stove to keep warm. During the days, Esmeralda might accompany her mother to the welfare office to translate for her. At night, she translates the ordinary lives of her colleagues in the workplace into dramatic sagas and soap operas for the entertainment of her family. Although she misses her father very much, she is glad that he is in Puerto Rico because she then controls her version of the events of everyday life in her letters to him. She explores the world of theater and dance to create different and exotic notions of self. Toward the end of *Almost a Woman*, the frustrated and bewildered adolescent tells us how desperately she needs to find her own voice: "I longed to cup my hand to my mouth, the way singers did, and listen to myself. To hear one voice, my own, even if it was filled with fear and uncertainty" (210).

Only when Santiago writes, even if it is in ambivalent and ambiguous autobiographies and her novel *America's Dream*, can she proclaim to the world her hybrid identity. *When I Was Puerto Rican* and *Almost a Woman* are not the *bildung* of the *"pendeja"* that is used and seduced by men nor of the "hot tomato" (*AW* 247). Santiago never accomplishes the formation of a *"jíbara"* who idealizes her rural hometown on the island nor of the *"Americana"* harmoniously integrated into the dominant culture. On the contrary, these two texts depict the slow and painful process of de/formation of a discordant "I" that speaks from both the center and the margins, from the "cracked spaces" of the tile floor back in Macún and from the crowded rooms of El Barrio, to sing with a hoarse voice her own hybridity:

> I've learned to insist on my peculiar brand of Puerto Rican identity. One not bound by geographical, linguistic or behavioral boundaries, but rather, by a deep identification with a place, a people and a culture which, in spite of appearances, define my behavior and determine the rhythms of my days. (Santiago, "A Puerto Rican Stew" 36)

Notes

1. "The Bildungsroman for Nonspecialists," Hardin 26–45.
2. "The Mystery of the Missing Bildungsroman, or: What happened to Wil-

helm Meister's Legacy?," 229–246.
3. In "The Bildungsroman," Sammons insists that *bildung* takes place within "the early bourgeois, humanistic concept of the shaping of the individual self" (41).
4. In "Crossing the Borders of Genre," Maria Karafilis argues that Cisneros' *The House on Mango Street* and Kincaid's *Annie John* are *bildungsromans* where the protagonists achieve *métissage* (65), which Edouard Glissant defines as "a pattern of fragmented diversity . . . which is neither chaos nor sterility, [that] means the human spirit's striving for a cross-cultural relationship, without universalist transcendence." "Sameness," he observes, "requires being fixed. Diversity establishes becoming" (97–98).
5. It should be noted that, like Thomas, Lewis focuses on the sordid aspects of the lives of Puerto Ricans living in poverty. Although many of his observations are accurate, his generalizations about the "culture of poverty" of Puerto Rican families are distorted. For example, he emphasizes the obsession of poor people with sex and the tensions caused by prostitution as a currency both within the family and in the community. However, his conclusions are based on his study of the Rios family that had a long tradition of prostitution. It is true that prostitution, drugs, and domestic violence are no strangers to the slums, but to assume that they typify all families living in poverty is biased and inaccurate.
6. In *When I Was Puerto Rican*, most characters refer to Esmeralda by the nickname Negi. In *Almost a Woman*, the teenage narrator becomes Esmeralda. Thus I refer to Negi when discussing the narrator/protagonist of *WPR* and to Esmeralda, the adolescent narrator of *AW*.
7. Tey D. Rebolledo and Eliana S. Rivera believe that one of the contemporary trends of Chicana literature is "the redemption of the male relationships . . . particularly the father-daughter relationships" (*Infinite Divisions* 27). Initially, "their main focus was in rescuing the female maternal figures from oblivion and from silence." Santiago, like many other *Puertorriqueña* writers, seems to be intent on this earlier facet since she feels that up until the seventies Puerto Rican literature has been dominated by male voices depicting the experiences of migration from their own male perspectives.
8. In *El País de las Maravillas* 3. The poem uses the image of cans of food and their labels describing the content and with warnings about their impact as a metaphor of American society's constant attempts to classify people and put them into neat compartments.
9. *Negra* and its diminutive *Negrita* are commonly used in Puerto Rico as a term of endearment, regardless of skin color. In this case, given her racial background, the protagonist makes a direct association with her skin color.

10. After the Foraker Act in 1990 establishing an American colonial tutelage, concerted efforts to "Americanize" the island of Puerto Rico began. The succession of commissioners appointed by the U.S. president to govern the colony issued a series of letters prescribing educational policies in Puerto Rico. In 1903, Commissioner Dr. Roland P. Falkner declared English the official language of the schoolroom (Osuna 345). Commissioner Edwin G. Dexter's language policies from 1907 until 1912 were considered to be "the epitome of absurdity" (Negrón de Montilla 260). In 1934, Commissioner José Padín declared "Spanish officially the language of instruction in all grades" (Osuna 366). It took another ten years to implement Padín's mandate. Other aspects of the "Americanization" process dealt with the imposition and celebration of American holidays, nursery rhymes, food and nutritional standards, etc. (For a more detailed discussion of these events, see Negrón de Montilla and Osuna.)

11. Judith Ortiz Cofer, for example, addresses some of the questions constantly posed to her in "And are you a Latina Writer?" 155–161.

12. The journalist Roberto Santiago explains that many Puerto Rican children including himself were told in school that they had no culture, no literature, no history (xiv). Whatever they learned about these topics was purely accidental: "In New York City's Spanish Harlem in the 1960s and 1970s, guessing was the only way Puerto Ricans like me figured out our culture and history," "Introduction," *Boricuas: Influential Puerto Rican Writings—An Anthology* (New York: One World, 1995), xiii.

13. Jerome Hamilton Buckley, *Season of Youth*, 13.

14. A mythical Aztec area believed to be located somewhere in the Southwest. By claiming Aztlán, Chicanos restored their Indian heritage, tracing their presence on the continent long before "Mexicans" and "Americans" ever existed as cultural and political groups.

Chapter 2
Nicholasa Mohr and Negation/Negotiation of the Mother-Daughter Relationship

And the one doesn't stir without the other.
—Luce Irigaray[1]

In her autobiography, *In My Own Words: Growing Up Inside the Sanctuary of My Imagination*, Nicholasa Mohr describes the mystery that surrounded her father's identity, a man who died early in her life. Her stepfather died two years later, and Mohr became an orphan at thirteen with the death of her mother from uterine cancer. These traumatic events during her adolescent years may explain recurring themes and characters in her fiction. Many of her books are for children and feature a prepubescent girl as the main character. *Nilda*, *Felita*, and *Going Home* depict girls during their formative years, with all the conflicting emotions regarding growing up, becoming women, and relating to their mothers. On the other hand, many of the adult female characters in *Rituals of Survival: A Woman's Portfolio* and *A Matter of Pride and Other Stories* are orphans, and hence alone trying to figure out how to survive as women without repeating their mothers' mistakes. In her own life, Mohr tries to reconcile her mother's words of reproach for not behaving like a *lady* and words of encouragement to become an artist and her own person.

Mohr's preoccupation with the maternal-filial relationship may stem from the simple and obvious truth that "All human life on the planet is born of woman." Thus begins Adrienne Rich's exhaustive study, *Of Woman Born: Motherhood as Experience and Institution*. Rich does not speak "of mother" but "of woman," a woman that is not defined by biology or by her reproductive capabilities. There are no given maternal instincts, no predestination to guarantee that the moment a woman holds a child, she will no longer be able to contain her maternal love and her instincts to care for and to fiercely protect that child. Rich discusses in detail the pre-"conceived" notions, learned paradigms of what it means to be a mother, of what her role and responsibilities should be. Various cultures throughout history have had different expectations of what "motherhood" should and should not be. For example, as guardians of cultural traditions, mothers were expected to bind their daughters' feet in China. In Africa, they were expected to perform clitoridectomies on girls. In the United States, Americans are still very uncomfortable with the notion of a woman being professionally successful, sexy, and a mother at the same time (225). In Latin America, *marianismo* (a prescribed code of behavior emulating the Virgin Mary) dictates self-sacrifice, abnegation, and suffering as essential qualities of any good woman.

Yet, the intricacies and complexities of both motherhood and daughterhood remain absent in most of literature and other systems of cultural representations to the point that critics today speak of "the lost traditions."[2] Even when they have been depicted, what generally is represented is the traditional idyllic image of "Madonna and child." Because we continue to ignore the woman, "the cathexis between mother and daughter" is, according to Rich, "the great unwritten story" (225). If we acknowledge the "woman" in the institution of motherhood, questions begin to emerge. How does the "woman" feel about becoming a mother? How does her new role affect other roles and relationships in her life? How is the child to relate to this "woman" who happens to be his mother? And, in the case of a female child, how does a daughter become a woman and what kind of relationship is she to maintain with the mother—the other significant "woman" in her life?

To this date, theories that analyze and to some extent determine our relationship to our parents are not "of woman born," but originated by men. Oedipus killing his father, marrying his mother, searching for truth, and ultimately mutilating himself have had a tremendous impact on our interpretation and understanding of human behavior up to this day. Freudian concepts of the "Oedipus complex" and "penis envy" are still at the core of psychoanalysis, with theorists, doctors, and scholars situated at both ends: either trying to elaborate and eluci- date Freud's ideas or opposing them while suggesting other alterna- tives which still remain reactions rather than new paradigms of behav- ioral science. Marianne Hirsch begins her book, *The Mother/Daughter Plot*, with an analysis of Oedipus Rex, to showcase the obliteration of the mother's point of view throughout literature. She observes how, in this classic tragedy, Oedipus' feelings are carefully choreographed; however, Jocasta

> is represented by silence, negation, damnation, suicide. The story of her desire, the account of her guilt, the rationale of her complicity with a brutal husband, the materiality of the body which gave birth to a child she could not keep and which then conceived with that child other children—*this* story cannot be filled in because we have no framework within which to do it *from her perspective.* (4)

Hirsch goes on to discuss the Greek stories of Demeter and Perse- phone, Clytemnestra and Electra, and the suppression of the mother's point of view and especially her anger.

Feminist writers have generated extensive research on the sup- pression of women's perspectives.[3] Adrienne Rich's *Of Woman Born* (1976), Nancy Chodorow's *The Reproduction of Mothering* (1978), Judith Arcana's *Our Mother's Daughters* (1979), and Nancy Friday's *My Mother, My Self* (1981) were among the first book-length studies to explore the mother-daughter relationship. Some of them are flawed either by their personal bitterness or by adopting middle-class white women's experiences as the norm.

French feminists, such as Julia Kristeva, Hélène Cixous, and Luce Irigaray, have also tried to redefine the mother-daughter relationship and disarm the pernicious notions of Freudian psychoanalysis still prevalent today.[4] Kristeva is more interested in maternity than in moth- erhood, explaining the former in the realm of the semiotic as important for understanding the socio-symbolic world of our culture. While Kris- teva discusses maternity as a pre-oedipal stage and denies agency to women, Cixous has a more positive view, promoting an image of the "good mother" as a kind protector and generous provider of food, love, and emotional security. Yet, she still recognizes the "voice" of the daughter as a "fragmentation" and "separation" from that of the mother. Irigaray, on the other hand, denounces the fact that motherhood can both "strangle" the life of the mother and suffocate the daughter.

As more feminist critics study the sociocultural representations of motherhood and daughterhood, they discover the discomfort and ambiguity of many female writers toward their own mothers. In fact, many of these studies begin with personal and intimate discussions of their interest in the subject. The books seem to emerge from a personal place in time where the women/authors confronted issues pertaining to pregnancy, childbearing and rearing, and parent caretaking. The introduction to Hirsch's book, for example, details the origins of her project during her maternity leave and participation in discussion groups where the topic was the tension between motherhood, feminism, scholarship, and academe. The one surprising fact that emerged from these meetings was how eager everyone was to speak "as mothers," but "as daughters we could not fully listen to our mother's stories" (Hirsch 26).

Rich goes on to explain this tension. According to her, mothers and the institution of motherhood bear the ultimate responsibility, blame, and guilt for the failures of their children. Often, a daughter will resent her mother for not being stronger, for allowing herself and hence her children to be victimized, whether by the husband, the lover, the boss, or society in general. "Matrophobia," Rich explains, "is the fear not of one's mother or of motherhood but of *becoming one's mother*" (235). It is the fear of making the same mistakes that the daughter attributes to the mother. Why didn't she fight? Why didn't she stand up for her rights, for those of her children? Why did she allow herself to be abused and victimized? The daughter seeks the strength of the mother, and failing to find it, she then searches someplace else. Mothers, on the other hand, seem to identify more readily with their daughters' weaknesses than with their strengths. The mother can anticipate and feel for the daughter's pain in relationships, abuse, and toils of family life. From this pessimistic standpoint, the mother perceives the daughter's resistance to and rebellion against traditional roles as the future source of unnecessary disappointment and grief.

Hirsch recognizes this "matrophobia" in modernist and postmodernist plots where, repeatedly, the heroines reject traditional patriarchal conventions of marriage and family as a means of self-realization. Ironically, in these works, as the protagonist explores her mother's life as part of her feminist awareness, it is the daughter "who occupies the center of the global reconstruction of subjectivity" (136). The mother, like her Greek counterparts, remains marginalized if not altogether silenced. Hirsch suggests four reasons for the "avoidance and discomfort with the maternal" prevalent even now in feminist discourse: first, that motherhood is still perceived as part of a patriarchal system; second, that feminists are uncomfortable with the "vulnerability and lack of control" associated with maternity; third, that they are also uncomfortable with the "pregnant body"; and fourth, that any association of motherhood with anger is still problematic (165–166). Ultimately, Hirsch calls for a pluralistic discourse that will allow the expression of "maternal anger" and "maternal subjectivity," as mother and daughter begin to speak with two voices emerging from one body (196–199).

Rebecca Wells's novel, *Divine Secrets of the Ya-Ya Sisterhood*, seems to be a fictional version of Rich's and Hirsch's discussions of the mother-daughter relationship. In order for Siddalee Walker to go on with her wedding plans and the staging of a new play, she needs to engage first in a journey of discovery of her mother's "secrets" of childhood pain, broken heart, and nervous breakdown. Through the letters and clippings in a scrapbook and the stories told by her mother's "Ya-Ya sisters," Sidda begins to listen to her mother and understand how interconnected and yet separated their bodies and their lives are. "Sidda wondered about the subliminal knowledge that passes between a mother and a daughter. The preverbal knowledge, the stories told without words flowing like blood, like rich oxygen, into the placenta of the baby girl as she grows in dark containment" (202). Only when she accepts that neither her mother nor her lover and their love have to be perfect, can she recognize that she is "good enough" to embrace the happiness of marriage, of family, of life.

Amy Tan's novels similarly explore the disjunction between mother and daughter. Typically in Chinese families, the grown-up woman feels suffocated by the mother, who is constantly giving warnings and expressing her dissatisfaction with the way the daughter leads her life. Tragedy, illness, or ultimately death brings to the surface the conflict between the two. Only then will the daughter listen as the mother begins to speak of her grief, her experiences, and family secrets. At the same time, the mother learns to listen to her daughter's fears, confusion, and anxiety about the choices ahead, and they both engage in "the development of a sense of voice, mind and self."[5] In *The Joy Luck Club*, the mother's death forces the protagonist to listen to others tell her about her mother's life in China and the search for her twins lost during the war. It is now the daughter who must bring that search to a conclusion by traveling to China, meeting her sisters and her mother's past. In *The Kitchen God's Wife,* it is illness this time, not death, that brings mother and daughter together in dialogue. Healing can only take place when they begin to listen to each other and their painful stories. Marie Booth-Foster believes that these two novels are "studies in balance–balancing hyphenation and the roles of daughter, wife, mother, sister, career woman" (209).

As evidenced by Tan's writing, the tension of the mother daughter relationship seems to be magnified within migrant cultures. Not only do the children feel saddled between two cultures, but ultimately asphyxiated by their mothers, who feel it is their role to maintain the traditions and values of their country of origin while at the same time protecting their daughters from the patriarchal system that has brought them to their present condition. Esmeralda Santiago, Judith Ortiz Cofer, Nicholasa Mohr, and others, describe the many times that they had to accompany their mothers to government agencies and serve as their translators/interpreters. The child is immediately thrust into the outside world and into an adult position of negotiating, bartering, sometimes lying, and even begging for the family's well-being. On the other hand, girls are told to be afraid of the "outside world" with all its dangers, especially those posed by men who would try to seduce them, dishonor them, and leave them pregnant. As discussed in the first chapter, one minute the girl is encouraged to study and make something of herself in order to overcome the social and economic status of the family, and the next she is being warned that the only honorable way to move away from home is in the arms of a husband.

In her study of the *bildungsroman* of ethnic writers, Bonnie Hoover Braendlin explains how part of the process of formation is the protest against such oppressive systems as racism and sexism. While Anglo and Jewish women writers denounce gender stereotyping, African-American women recognize racism as an equal problem. In the case of these writers, according to Hoover Braendlin, the text itself is a way for the daughter to overcome the oppression suffered by the mother throughout her life.[6] The daughter's novels have survived long after the mother has succumbed to years of "slaving away."

Like the Jewish, Hispanic culture has two systems in place that promote and perpetuate specific behaviors for both men and women: *machismo* and *marianismo*. Although the two systems can have a positive impact, neither has been much help for mothers or daughters. Indeed, the strict imposition of their norms and expectations has had a detrimental, suffocating, and almost annihilating effect on the Hispanic population of the United States. Rosa María Gil and Carmen Inoa Vázquez have written a self-help psychology book, *La Paradoja de María*, in which they identify the "ten commandments" of *marianismo* and discuss ways for Latinas to strengthen their self-esteem without relinquishing their traditions. Grief, self-sacrifice, and submission are at the core of this feminine system. The model is the Virgin Mary with her virtues of "deber sagrado, abnegación y castidad" ("sacred duty, abnegation, and chastity" 7). Ortiz Cofer speaks of the "admiration and respect" in Hispanic society for *la sufrida* (the suffering one), the "type of woman who has perfected one art—that of self-abnegation, sometimes even martyrdom" ("Woman" 9).

Traditionally, Puerto Rican male writers have perpetuated the image of the mother as self-sacrificing and saintly. Puerto Rican poets in the United States seem to continue this tradition of idealization of the mother figure. In Piri Thomas' biography, the mother remains the one constant source of support, of love, of beauty in a world marred by violence, discrimination, and drugs. Lucky Cienfuegos' poem, "Dedicated to María Rodríguez Martínez, February 24, 1975," is a moving eulogy to the strength of his mother and an acknowledgment of her pain underneath her ever-present smile (Algarín 156–159). Although most Nuyorican poems are about life on the streets of New York, Miguel Algarín recognizes the significant role of the mother:

Mami's evolution has taken her through much despair but the purity of her devotion binds and keeps the worlds of her children together. She is still the central point of reference. (91)

It is against this form of "cultural slavery," of the idealized and romanticized suffering of motherhood, that Nicholasa Mohr writes what Hoover Braendlin calls "texts of protest." The children-protagonists deal with feelings of anger, perplexity, confusion, and pain, typical of adolescence. Juan Flores argues that the main theme of her books is not "childhood, but adjustment. The wrenching changes and consistently expanding awareness of youth serves as the dramatic inner focus" ("Back" 54).

Mohr began her career as a graphic artist, specializing in drawings and etchings. Many of her stories depict women artists exploring their creative talents. Whether the main character is a young girl at the threshold of adolescence or a grown-up woman, they all seem to engage in a search for the expression of self, for a voice that will allow them to rebel against patriarchal norms and explore alternatives to social, gender, and sexual roles.

Mohr gave up her successful graphic arts career and produced a dozen fictional works, several of them for children, and two biographical and autobiographical texts. Her books are crowded with ordinary people struggling for survival. There are families with all of their extended relatives, neighbors such as Mr. Mendelsohn, an old Jewish man, and gay couples, the owners of a candy store, all engaged in struggles against poverty, discrimination, illness, or despair. There are children and teenagers, old relatives going senile, and even cats and roosters trying to stay alive one day at a time. For Mohr, they are the true heroes, the protagonists of her fictional world. Although most of her characters are Puerto Ricans, she insists on the universality of their struggle: "people living and struggling everywhere . . . experiencing pain, joy and most importantly the will to survive" (Flores, "Back" 54).

Her first novel, *Nilda* (1973), begins in July 1941 with World War II as its background. The main character, barely eleven years old, lives in El Barrio with her mother, stepfather, aunt, and three older brothers. The oldest sibling, Jimmy, has left home and is involved in drugs. As the prepubescent Nilda "expands her awareness" of the world outside and embarks on a journey toward womanhood, Lydia, her mother, is constantly reminding her of what she can and cannot do as a woman. Throughout the novel, mother and daughter situate themselves like two axes on an ellipse, in which the umbilical chord that connected them at one time now delineates and limits their movements. Nilda's frustration, anger, and ambivalence toward her mother echo the feelings depicted by Adrienne Rich, Rebecca Wells, and Amy Tan among many, and seem to be a case study of the tensions of the mother-daughter relationship in migrant cultures.

Lydia performs the traditional role of a Puerto Rican mother. When she is not cooking for her family, she is sending packages to the absentee son. Aside from her children, she takes care of her dying husband, her senile aunt, and Sophie, Jimmy's pregnant girlfriend. As a mother, she will defend her children, including Jimmy, in spite of his problems with the law. Her unconditional support is contrasted with that of Sophie's mother, who rejects her own daughter and declares her dead for the terrible crime of running away with a "nigger" (88). But Lydia's main role is that of guardian and teacher of the cultural, social, and moral values. She is constantly telling Nilda to go to church, be careful with boys, be mindful of the way she speaks to adults, etc. Once Nilda begins having her period, Lydia's litanies begin with "A señorita does (not)" and are followed by series of do's and dont's that leave Nilda completely bewildered.

Many of Nicholasa Mohr's characters, whether they are prepubescent girls or grown-up women, think of their first period and the beginning of menstruation as a kind of sacrificial ritual in which the freedom, playfulness, and simple joys of childhood are washed away with blood. In *Powers of Horror,* Julia Kristeva on several occasions relates menstrual blood to the "horrors of maternal bowels" (53). Kristeva goes on to explain how this particular "horror" represents danger to both men and women, but it especially threatens to determine women's identity from within, tying it to maternity and limiting their options. Once a girl has her first period, she becomes a "virgin" whose pure and chaste state has to be protected at all costs and/or a fertile maiden whose prospective pregnancies have to be equally protected and carefully planned to perpetuate the family name and social status. That is the way it is explained to Ana in "Utopia and the Super Estrellas," another story by Mohr.

> Menstruation will make you a woman, Ana, and you'll be ready to bear children. That's when your life will change and your childhood leaves you. No more little girl. You'll become a *señorita*, a virgin. That's also when we all must be very careful to keep a watchful eye on you to make sure the boys keep their distance. (*Matter* 180)

Ana's mother continues to explain how women need to cleanse themselves from "our impure blood."

Adrienne Rich argues that patriarchy has turned this "female experience" into something "sinister and disadvantageous" (106). The "taboo of the menstrual blood" or the "curse," as it was commonly known, seems to hang over Mohr's female characters as a threatening menace to their freedom and potential development as individuals even before it arrives. In *Going Home*, Felita explains that soon after her eleventh birthday, her mother "warned" her about the changes ahead.

> She had sat me down, saying I had to hear about the facts of life so I could protect myself. She told me I must be very careful, and had to guard myself from then on. I could not act like before, and grab my brothers and jump all over them, or sit on everybody's lap like I was still a little girl. That all had to stop. (*Going Home* 15)

In "Utopia and the Super Estrellas," Ana recalls her mother's neighbor, Utopia, a Cuban transvestite who would come over complaining about menstrual cramps. Considering the warnings, the taboos, the long list of prohibitions that accompanies the passage into womanhood, Ana wonders "who and why would anybody want such pain?" (*Matter* 187). As she listens to Utopia narrate his painful tale of being a female trapped in a man's body and beaten by his family because of his "affectation," Ana is baffled as to why he would have preferred to be a woman.

> I thought about my three older brothers, my stepfather, uncles, and all of the *power* and *freedom* they possessed. . . . Ultimately, I never did make any sense out of Utopia's obsession, since there seemed to be no power, no tangible gain or obvious pleasure in his desire to be female, only distress and *precious little freedom in this man's world.* (*Matter* 186–187; emphasis added)

Rita Freedman quotes the old saying, "A boy expands into a man; a girl contracts into a woman," in her discussion of the process of growing up and transformation into adulthood for girls (390). Hence Nilda soon finds out, like Felita and Ana, that becoming a young woman includes a long list of activities that are now forbidden to her. Lydia is constantly telling her daughter what she cannot do, especially once her menstruation starts: she cannot sit in a certain way, she should not play anymore with boys, she cannot play the games she likes so much, she should not be out by herself. Instead of opening up possibilities, her world seems to be shrinking to the confinement of her home, as her mother reminds her: "You are a *señorita* now, and you must help me here at home" (*Nilda* 238). Nilda, on her part, resents her mother's authority and treatment of her as if she were a baby.

What Nilda fails to grasp is that Lydia, in spite of her old age and apparent authority, is equally powerless. Lydia is indeed a strong woman who performs several roles at once. She is nurturing mother who takes care of "everyone" in the family. At the same time, her work at a *factoría* supports all of them, now that her husband has been incapacitated by two heart attacks. Lydia is also the one who has to mediate with the outside world, seeking welfare assistance, legal aid for Jimmy, and camp opportunities for Nilda. Vivian E. Nice warns against the notion of the real power of mothers. The power is really about "setting of restrictions and controlling her [daughter's] behavior; the mother's 'power' over the family in terms of her responsibility to maintain stability" (110). Although Lydia does manage to set the boundaries for her daughter and to maintain some stability within family life, Nilda cannot help but recognize her mother's powerlessness. She recalls the arguments of her mother with Jimmy when he would show up with a new car or cash money. Knowing there was nothing she could say to save her son from drugs, the discussion would simply end with Lydia "wiping her eyes and shaking her head" (31). Moreover, it is the mother's powerlessness to protect her from the prejudices and discrimination of the outside world that frustrates and angers the often hurt child. During a visit to the welfare office, the social worker berates Nilda for having filthy nails and probably for not taking a bath. When they leave, an angry Nilda lashes out against her mother: "Why did you let her talk like that to me? Why didn't you stop her?" (70).

In a constant game of approaching and distancing, Nilda tries to communicate to her mother how confusing she finds the world outside. Unfortunately, her concerns are often dismissed and silenced by her mother. Nilda's questions—whether they are about racism in school,[7] welfare, the police, gang violence and drugs, a distant war that seduces one by one each of her brothers, or about religion (Catholicism, Evangelism, and Spiritism)—very seldom reach an interrogative tone on her lips. When questions escape her mouth, they are only answered with a rude and clipping remark: "Don't be a baby" or "Don't be a sucketa" ("a sucker").

If Nilda's questions are expressed out loud, the mother's thoughts are not even allowed to surface. The writer uses a limited third person point of view that focuses on the story from Nilda's perspective. The reader knows what Nilda is thinking and feeling, and we only get to know the other characters through the child's observations and interactions with them. Hirsch's point about Jocasta is echoed in this novel, where we never learn Lydia's thoughts, fears, preoccupations, and motivations. Only at the end, when the mother is dying, is she allowed to express the turmoil that, as a woman, has been eating at her all these years, and she warns her daughter of the threats, not only against her female body, but also against her mind and soul.

"But we have never, never spoken to each other," Luce Irigaray observes sadly in her lyrical essay, "And the One Doesn't Stir without the Other" (67). The silence between mother and daughter and the suppression of their womanhood within that relationship preoccupies the

French scholar immensely. The essay begins with a reference to the mother's milk and its terrifying effect: "That hot liquid became poison, paralyzing me" (60). She warns that food, whether it is in the form of breast milk or meals, can become a poison that suffocates and paralyzes the daughter. She worries about both of them disappearing "into this act of eating each other" (62). This image of eating each other alive, of suffocating one another is common in fictional depictions of the mother/daughter relationship. In Rebecca Wells' *Divine Secrets of the Ya-Ya Sisterhood,* Vivi complains how "beautiful children can also be cannibals" right before she has a nervous breakdown that sends her to a hospital for several months (261).

Irigaray continues explaining how the daughter begins to assume features and gestures similar to those of her mother. Both engage themselves in games of reflection and reciprocity like a girl mimicking in front of a mirror. Irigaray's essay ends with a plaintive lament: "And the one doesn't stir without the other. But we do not move together. When the one of us comes into the world, the other goes underground. When the one carries life, the other dies. And what I wanted from you, Mother, was this: that in giving me life, you still remain alive" (67).

One could argue that in writing *Nilda*, Mohr is following a train of thought similar to Irigaray's. The writer uses various metaphors throughout the novel to convey the suffocating feelings of Nilda. Her feelings are matched by the summer heat, which forces Don Jacinto to ignore police threats and to open the fire hydrant so that everyone in the street can cool down. The small apartment crowded with siblings, sick relatives, pregnant girlfriends, and babies adds to the feeling of encroachment and suffocation.

Food, on the other hand, is the only way to express love and tenderness from one to the other and Nilda seems never to have enough of her mother's cooking. Even during the school year, the child prefers to walk a long way to eat lunch at home. At the end of the novel, Lydia, on her deathbed, insists that Nilda eat her mother's favorite candies. When the girl eats them, the last food exchange takes place, like a sacramental communion, and the mother dies within a few days.

As she watches her mother, Nilda examines herself in the mirror and wonders if she will look like her mother when she grows up. The girl also searches in the mirror for clues to her father's identity. But it is the "desire of maternity" that attracts Nilda to Sophie and Little Jimmie while at the same time it distances her from Lydia, in what Adrienne Rich calls "matrophobia." In her book *Mothers and Daughters*, Vivian E. Nice discusses the daughter's desire to become a mother herself, the kind of mother she did not have. This time, the daughter has learned what "not to do" from what she has observed in her mother. Mohr constantly warns the reader against the seductive wiles of maternity. In spite of her resentment toward Sophie's presence in the apartment, Nilda becomes obsessed with the baby. She wants to be the one to feed him, care for him, and put him to bed. Even her relationship with her friend Benji is somewhat maternal and protective. But this time, it is the mother who begs her daughter "not to" be like her.

> I only got to the fourth grade; I never had the advantages you got here in this country. You want to be a jíbara when you grow up? Working in a factoría? Cleaning houses? Being a sucketa for other people? (60)

Lydia reminds her daughter that children will only destroy her life: poverty, welfare, and total annihilation will be the disastrous consequences of her attraction to motherhood. Lydia wants her daughter to define herself, not to be defined by her children.

To complicate matters, Nice warns, "We are considering the mother as a *mother* rather than as a woman" (226). Even within *marianismo* and the Hispanic culture that idealizes motherhood, María González clarifies that "the veneration of the mother . . . does not translate into the veneration of womanhood" (156). Hence, what Nilda learns from her mother is what to be and not to be in terms of the maternal function, not necessarily as a woman, as a person, and especially not as an individual. Both Nilda and Lydia speak in metaphors of food, of commandments imposing cultural norms and expectations, of "do's and don't's." As Nilda walks around a summer camp outside New York, she realizes that there are no signs here limiting her movements: "Do not walk . . . Do not pick . . . No spitting . . . No ball playing . . ." and no "Mama always telling me to watch out for . . ." (153). Only on her deathbed is the mother allowed to speak with her body's last breath about the oppression, suffocation, and ultimate anni-hilation of her being. All of Lydia's warnings against men and teenage pregnancy were not to protect the family honor and save Nilda's "pudor"; instead they were intended to extend to her daughter a lan-guage, an existence, an identity that were not defined by the biological function of maternity. In one of the most poignant moments between mother and daughter, Lydia tells Nilda about her impending death and how important it is for Nilda always to maintain a space, a life of her own. The mother explains that she has absolutely nothing. She cannot leave a thing to her daughter because she has nothing. Her life, Lydia concludes, has been in vain because she has only existed and func-tioned in relation to others. The worst part is that were she to recover and have an opportunity to live, she would not know what she would want to do because she can no longer see anything beyond her chil-dren. She does remember that there was a time when there was more to life:

> I remember a feeling I used to have when I was very young . . . it had only to do with me. Nobody else was included . . . just me, and I did exist so joyfully in that feeling; I was so nourished . . . thinking about it would make me so excited about life. . . . You know something? I don't even know what it was now. (277)

Lydia points out that she recognizes that feeling in Nilda and her drawings. She tells Nilda to protect them. Although Nilda has begun to visualize a space of her own, the mother has to die in order to give way to her daughter's life. Literally, the mother's dreams and life have been devoured by her children's needs.

In order to avoid this devastating consequence, Grosz explains Iri-garay's insistence that the mother feed the daughter words that can be spoken: "The gift of language in place of the suffocation and silence imposed by food" (124). Mother and daughter, according to Irigaray, each need to find their own language, their own space in order to find a dialogue outside of the maternal-filial. The search for space and cre-ative expression is at the core of Nicholasa Mohr's fiction. In *Nilda*, the girl constantly struggles to find a space where she does not feel confined by the parameters imposed by her mother. When Sophie, Jimmy's pregnant girlfriend, moves into the apartment and months later has the baby, Nilda has to move her bed to her parents' bedroom, where she sleeps against the wall. In spite of her protest, the girl loses access to a window over her bed, where she would look out and forge a thousand dreams.

Now whenever she wants or needs to escape, she turns to the wall and studies intently all the cracks in it, visualizing the contours of imaginary worlds. During her first summer camp, the absence of doors in the bathroom underlies the total lack of privacy. In her second summer camp, on the other hand, a secluded garden surrounded by trees provides real solace and, in years ahead, an imaginary refuge where she can retreat.

It is finally in the small space of a shoe box, where she keeps her drawings, that Nilda finds her own space. Whenever her mother scolds her, Nilda goes to her room and begins to draw. Minutes later, the protagonist has forgotten her anger and the conflict, and finds herself lost in "a world of magic achieved with some forms, lines, and color" (50).

At the end of the novel, after the burial of her mother, Nilda retires to her new bedroom, which she now shares with her cousin, and she takes out her shoe box with the drawings. When she hears the admiring tone in her cousin's voice because of a talent that is only hers, Nilda realizes that this is indeed her "secret garden," not only a refuge but a place where her spirit can express itself and stretch out in total freedom.

It should be noted that the book is illustrated by the author. It is also of interest that in most of the drawings, the figures that correspond to the protagonist are very light and almost float in the air. These drawings have a fluid quality to them, lacking straight lines and sharp angles, as if they were a universe without boundaries and an atmosphere without gravity. The images are surrounded by words which equally seem to flow like the current of a river.

Nilda's disconcerting realization of what it means to be a girl and to become a woman is echoed in at least two other books by Nicholasa Mohr. *Felita* (1979) introduces the character by that name, a nine-year-old girl dealing with issues of racism, children's jealousy, and the death of her grandmother. One of her constant preoccupations is her inability to talk to her mother. The sequel, *Going Home* (1986), reintroduces Felita at the brink of adolescence and even more bewildered by her shrinking freedom and the increasing boundaries set by her mother. Everyone in the family, including her father, her uncle, and her brothers, seems to conspire in reminding her that "girls do not have the same freedom as boys. . . . That's the law of nature" (20). Faced with these dogmatic pronouncements, Felita can not help . . .

> wondering why my getting older had to make things so complicated. When I was little, life was a lot simpler. But now my brothers were in charge of me. Mami watched me like I was the gold in Fort Knox and someone was gonna steal me! (54)

As her feelings for the handsome Vinny grow, she recognizes the need to hide them because if discovered, her "jail"-like existence will only worsen. "Mami" is less and less perceived as a nurturing figure and more like a security guard at a bank or a warden overseeing the prison.

Nicholasa Mohr also published two collections of short stories depicting grown-up women coping with the same kinds of issues as Nilda and Felita. In *Matter of Pride and Other Stories* (1997), most of the female characters are orphans whose mothers died when they were teenagers. Many of them remember their mothers' advice of accepting their place in society so that they not suffer unnecessary pain. In "A Matter of Pride," Paula is supposed to learn the norms and her place within a Puerto Rican society which allows men to go out on Fridays and have "queridas" (mistresses) while women are expected to attend to their children, cook for their husbands, and consider themselves lucky to have a man that will provide for them. In "Another Time, Another Place," Iris remembers her mother's constant maneuvers to avoid her husband's fury and hand. The mother had tried "to teach" Iris how to avoid a man's wrath and beatings. Iris mentally rejects her mother's advice and decides that she will not put up with it. Rosalina's mother also gives her similar advice: "He won't raise a hand to you as long as you don't give him cause" (112). Rosalina sacrifices her wishes of becoming a nun and later on the love of her life, since as the youngest daughter she is expected to take care of her ill mother.

Throughout these stories, the protagonists recall the lessons of their now deceased mothers. At first glance, it appears that it is indeed the mother who teaches her daughter, and hence passes on to other women lessons on submission, suffering, and silence. Vivian E. Nice explains that "It is not the mother who denies the daughter her value, her rights and control over her life, but a system which treats women as subordinates, taught to service men, devalued and sexualised for men's needs" (154). After all, Gloria Anzaldúa explains, "Males make the rules and laws; women transmit them" (*Borderlands* 16). Having lived long enough, the mother believes that the only way to survive is by conforming to the system imposed within her own culture. In order for the daughter to do the same, she has to be taught "her place" within that society. It is obvious to everyone in Ponce, Puerto Rico, that Paula will have a great deal of difficulty in life unless she learns to accept her role as submissive wife and later on as devoted mother. Her constant demands to go to school, to be heard, to be an equal partner in her marriage to Charlie are perceived as futile challenges, like a child having a tantrum because she has not been taught any better. Both men and women shake their heads knowingly and pity Charlie and Paula because they are doomed to unhappiness as long as Paula continues to challenge "God-given . . . derecho (*right*) because I'm a man" (*Matter* 20). Little do they know that Paula is already planning the ultimate act of rebellion, divorcing Charlie as soon as they get back to the States.

Although the young women in *Matter of Pride* do remember their mothers' lessons, they have reassessed their situations only to realize that indeed they will not achieve happiness if they conform to the system. It becomes then a question of pride to affirm their independence and assert their own places, their own voices, their own rights in society. Indeed, they did learn their mothers' lessons too well, even to the point that they now make a conscious effort not to be like them.

Rituals of Survival: A Woman's Portfolio is a collection of six short stories published twelve years earlier. It introduces what Marianne Hirsch calls "emancipatory strategies" that allow the female protagonists "to subvert the constraints of dominant patterns" (8). As the title indicates, this book is a "portfolio" containing six "samples" of creative work, of creative rituals, of artistic expressions of survival. The name of the main character is part of the title in parentheses, as if to suggest the parenthetical roles of women and/or how their issues are considered to be a mere parenthesis to life. Mohr has expressed on several occasions the importance of writing about "everyday, humdrum, unheroic" events. For these women, these moments are more than just routine; they are indeed a time of confrontation and struggle for survival. For the family around them, including their mothers and their children, these moments are merely of parenthethical significance, a small fire to be put out quickly so that everyone can return to acceptable normalcy.

Although each of the main characters in the stories is unique and distinctive, she seems to be a composite of "*a woman*" (as indicated in the title), an artist, with the need to express herself, fighting the suffocating grip of patriarchal society. Each of them explores alternative ways of challenging the "expectations" of motherhood and daughterhood imposed by that society.

"Aunt Rosana's Rocker" is the story about the commotion and embarassment caused by Zoraida's sexual fantasies. The protagonist is a 28-year-old woman who has had three children, one stillborn, and several miscarriages in nine years of marriage. Casto (whose name means "Chaste"), her husband, is a hypochondriac who believes that aggressive, sexual, and strong women are vulgar. He has invited both his and her parents and his sister to discuss Zoraida's newest obsession, rocking herself into a zombie-like state in a chair that used to belong to Aunt Rosana. As he waits for the parents to arrive, he recalls the nightmare of Zoraida's previous problem of only three months ago: after falling asleep, she began to make love to a "phantom lover." The lewd noises and vulgar movements of his wife were too much to watch and sent him to the kitchen to seek refuge in his medicine cupboard until she would go back to sleep, exhausted by her own ecstasy. The parents took her to Doña Digna, the spiritualist, who had cured her. Casto felt that the wild sex recreated in his wife's fantasies was not the kind of relationship "decent" couples should have. The most shocking part "was her enjoyment" (11). In fact, Casto refuses to touch her in this state of excitement, afraid that he might catch something from her.

The story is narrated mainly from Casto's point of view, through his thoughts. When the family arrives, they all sit at the kitchen table, with coffee and cake served by Zoraida, to discuss the problem. Doña Clara, Zoraida's mother, and Doña Elvira, Casto's, take turns defending their own children and accusing the spouses of not being more sensitive, more caring. Everyone talks about Zoraida in the third person as if she were not there. Except for her mother, they all look at Zoraida with contempt. Even her father is disappointed because he would have preferred a son to carry his name. After many recriminations, it is decided that Doña Clara will take the "cursed" rocker back to her apartment.

The other three women in the story only reinforce the code of behavior acceptable for women. Even Purencia, Casto's sister, who is about Zoraida's age, needs to leave because "my old man doesn't like me going out at night. It's only because of Mami that he let me" (29). Only because of the family emergency is she allowed to break the rules and go out alone at night, but only briefly. After all, she is there to lend her assistance in making Zoraida come back to her proper place in conformity and submission. As the mother, it is Doña Clara's role to give advice to her daughter on how to be a dutiful wife. "All women go through this difficulty," her mother says, reminding Zoraida of the obligation to satisfy a husband's sexual needs (30). She suggests headaches, backaches, or sleep as tactful ways to avoid him. But once in a while, a woman has "to please him . . . make believe you are enjoying it and then get it over with real quick." Doña Clara points out the practical aspect of this arrangement: in exchange for satisfying the husband's needs, the woman gets financial security for herself and her children.

As a daughter and now as a mother, young Zoraida has no needs of her own, much less sexual ones. Her duty, as she is constantly reminded, is to satisfy the demands of others, in this case, those of Casto, her children, her parents, and her mother-in-law. Her pleasure, her enjoyment, her happiness is of no consequence or concern. It is Casto who decides which kind of birth control method to use, a small concession after all of her miscarriages. As everyone talks about her and around her, Zoraida is not allowed to express her own thoughts, feelings, or wishes.

In their role of servitude to others, women's bodies and health become irrelevant. Judith Ortiz Cofer ponders that in a chapter and a poem in *Silent Dancing*. "More Space" describes how her grandmother asked her husband to build a big room in the back of the house with the excuse that she was expecting her eighth child. Soon after the birth, she banished her husband to the new room, claiming her body, her nights, and her freedom to enjoy life before her health was completely ravaged by pregnancies, miscarriages, and children. With quiet defiance, Zoraida resists and insists on rejecting the social expectations imposed on her by others. She had always admired the rocker whose previous owner was a beautiful single woman who entertained many suitors, never giving into any one in particular. It is in this piece of furniture "where she could really be free" (29). It was her escape everytime that Casto approached her at night. After everyone leaves and Zoraida readies herself for bed, she laments the loss of the rocker, where she used to "meet all her suitors and be beautiful" (31). With it gone, she can barely remember who she was dancing with the last time, or what was playing in the background. When she hears Casto come in, she pretends to be asleep. She will use whatever means of resistance is available to her.

Amy and Lucía also use dreams and fantasies as a way of escaping their despair and hopeless circumstances. In "A Thanksgiving Celebration," Amy, a young widow, takes the last few dollars she has left to prepare a feast of dyed eggs, rice, and sweets. As her four young children marvel about the turkey's orange eggs, Amy begins to recount tales of her grandmother's idyllic childhood in Puerto Rico. As the mother seduces the hungry, sickly children with the magic of storytelling, they leave behind the decaying world that surrounds them. In "Happy Birthday," Lucía floats in and out of consciousness and into her small village in Luquillo, Puerto Rico, as she lies in her bed at a hospital in Welfare Island, where all the victims of tuberculosis are sent.

In order to escape, Inez resorts first to the conventional route of marriage and then to her own body. "The Artist" depicts the journey of an eleven-year-old orphan girl who suffers the oppression of her aunt's family and later of her abusive husband, Joe Batista, and ultimately goes to art school. Aunt Ophelia Vasquez is a miserly, avaricious woman who is tight even with the food at the table, denying Inez second servings. On the other hand, she spoils her two children, giving in to all of her daughter's demands and allowing the son to masturbate all around the house, even at the dinner table. As a teenager, Inez meets a much older divorced Joe and jumps at the opportunity to find her way out of such a household. Little does she realize that everyone seems to have a stake in owning her. First, Aunt Ophelia had the responsibility to "watch both her daughter and niece like a hawk" (113), to ensure that "no shame is going to tarnish the Vasquez's family" (114). Later on, Joe points out to her that their engagement gives him permission to her body; after all, "it's my right," her fiancée declares triumphantly.

In the third part of the story, Inez has become a nude model for a painting class at the Art Students' League. While Joe attends evening school, she takes art lessons, which she pays for with her modeling job. Posing gives her long periods of time to ponder her marital situation. Soon after their marriage, Joe demands that she turn over her check from her day job to him. As he begins overturning chairs, cursing at her, and coming on to her, Inez grabs a frying pan and takes a stand. Shocked by his wife's defiant attitude, Joe accepts that she only contribute half of her check to the household finances. Aware of his violent temperament, Inez has learned to anticipate and dissipate his outbursts. Noticing his disinterest in her artwork, she has kept her studies a secret. Now, as her teachers show appreciation for her talent and encourage her studies, she begins to wonder how she can save enough to pay for her classes and art supplies and be able to move away from Joe.

Ultimately, Joe finds out about her studies and assaults her at the school one evening when she is naked and lost in thought. The instructor and the students have to hold Joe until the police arrive. Aldo, another art student, takes her to his apartment, and they become lovers. Years later, she files for an annulment and meets Joe at a cafe. To make sure that he stops obsessing over her and try to bring her back, Inez points out what a total fool he was because he had believed her to be a virgin. The truth, according to her, was that she had been sexually active with her uncle for the longest time, and that it was not the old man who seduced her but the other way around. Devastated by this news, Joe leaves. If it were only her disobedience in going to study or in posing nude, the wife would be brought back and beaten into submission and compliance. But a woman who challenges the social norms of decency and modesty and who, like a man, claims her own sexual prowess, is of no use to a decent man like Joe.

Although Inez has the support of her friends, she does not have her family's support. Aunt Ophelia does recognize Joe's violent temper and the possibility of harm to Inez, but she demands to know "what Inez had done to provoke such a wonderful man" (152). She is willing to welcome Inez back into the apartment if it will lead to a reconciliation with her husband.

Inez had followed the conventions allowed to women and married Joe. When she realized that he would suffocate the artist inside her and ultimately kill her, she decided to co-opt social biases and move away from the confinements of family and marital duties. By exploiting her own body and the harmful notions of female promiscuity, she forges a future where she can be true to herself.

Like Inez, Virginia also entertains the traditional conventions of marriage and motherhood in order to achieve peace and happiness. A "Brief Miracle" describes the brevity and futility of Virginia's transformation from a lesbian to a housewife. Years after eloping with her female high school teacher, Virginia returns to her childhood neighborhood, where she meets Mateo, a man with a "chronic drinking" problem. He has been abandoned by his wife, who took four of their six children. The couple moves to an apartment where Virginia throws herself into her new roles of housewife and mother: "shopping, cooking, even fixing the apartment just the way it suited her" (67).

True to her name, the protagonist follows in the footsteps of the Virgin Mary and all of *marianismo*'s mandates. She becomes the dedicated mother who draws the youngest child from self-imposed silence into speaking. During the day she does all the chores at home, including wallpapering and refurbishing the old furniture. In the evenings, she entertains old friends from school. Even when Mateo begins to drink again and stay out with his friends, she holds the family together. Finally, she can take it no longer and returns to California, where she will stay for a while with Cornelia, her teacher and first lover, and now friend.

"Brief Miracle" introduces several wonders. It depicts a female character challenging the traditional gender roles and sexual orientation in order to assert her own sexuality. As the narrator recalls Virginia's male and female lovers, there are no apologies, no judgments, no attempts at justification. Cornelia is described as a gentle and attractive middle-aged woman who has remained her friend throughout the years. Ironically, the only critical eye is cast on her parents for their traditional views. It is not enough that she has returned home and seems so happy. They have to take every opportunity to talk about marriage and remind the "happy" couple of their sinful state. Because of her parents' archaic notions about dating and sexuality, Virginia finds herself with very little experience and feeling very awkward as a teenager.

The story also denounces the pervasive social notion of motherhood as a sacred institution. It begins with men at the bar where Virginia and Mateo meet, commenting on the miracle and good fortune of the new couple. Virginia has proven to be a better mother to his kids than his first wife and natural mother could ever be. Although they recognize that Bunny and Mateo did marry when she was fourteen and started having babies like "rabbits," there is no excuse for her "neglect" of the children. "I say motherhood is sacred. . . . Anybody can be a father . . . it's being the mother that means a special responsibility," declares one of the drunken men at the bar (57). Soon they are all toasting "motherhood! . . . Para todas las madres" (58). As unforgiving as their criticism is of the maternal shortcomings of individual women, their praise for exemplary motherhood is all encompassing, taking it for granted as the natural way of life. Even Mateo's elderly mother is expected to take care of his children after his wife abandoned him. In spite of Parkinson's disease and diabetes, she has to assume full responsibility for the care of two very young children in her small and unkept apartment. Mateo's only concern is about the impact on the children, not about his mother's welfare.

As a lesbian, Virginia seeks, in the traditional institution of motherhood, "a sense of gratification and peacefulness" to counterattack the "sense of fear and apprehension" that keeps her awake at night, when she is not "performing" for others. Since she ran away with her teacher,

Virginia has been in a series of homosexual and heterosexual relationships, never experiencing a sense of belonging or of home. That is why she, unlike Nilda, feels seduced by the idyllic images of motherhood. But the everyday reality proves to be unbearable: "Winter had brought flus, stomach viruses and colds, keeping the children at home for weeks on end. They had all felt like prisoners" (71). As she waits in the bus that will take her back to her lover in California, she mentally goes through the chores that await her back home: conferences at school about Sammy's behavior, Lillie's lessons for first communion, the errands that Mateo consistently forgets to do, the bedtime routine of getting the children to bed and taking their medications, the dinner party for her parents who incessantly ask about the wedding date (living out of wedlock is, of course, a sin, even if they are relieved at her daughter's more acceptable behavior). Once again, motherhood fails to fulfill the expectations of a woman that so desperately wants to feel completely and fully realized. As Virginia begins to doze off, she cannot help but wonder about the future and what lies ahead of her.

It is the life ahead opening with possibilities that Carmela contemplates in "A Time with a Future." Probably the most unusual story in the collection, it depicts an older woman recently widowed, poised to battle with her children over her right to live her own life. The story opens with her children in the kitchen arguing about "what's best" for their her mother; after all, "at her age . . . she can't be left alone" (35). Carmela is in her bedroom, pretending to rest, listening to them argue about *her* future. As she sneers at her daughters, "grown women . . . acting like children," she begins to recall her life taking care of others, the death of Freddie, her little boy, and more recently caring for her husband, Benjamin, who died of cancer.

It is obvious that Carmela resents her obligation of "caring for others." Even now, after her husband's death, her daughters have insisted on staying with her, resulting in more work for her, that is, setting up beds, cooking, taking care of bathrooms, etc. As a young mother, she had no time to make friends. It was the responsibility toward the family that kept her away from the hospital when Freddy died alone of pneumonia. Her husband had insisted that he could not stay at home and help with the other children. On the other hand, when Benjamin was diagnosed with cancer, he made her promise not to send him away to a hospital, but to let him die at home. Carmela, once again, swallowed her resentment and fulfilled her duties, taking care of him until the end.

Now it is time to inform her children of her plans for the future. But when she goes back into the kitchen, her two daughters and son begin to inform her how everything has been resolved: they have planned to remodel one of their homes in order to accommodate her, they are going to use her savings and social security to pay for some of the expenses, and above all, everything has been graciously approved by their husbands. No longer able to listen to their "nonsense," Carmela opens an envelope and shows them the plan of a co-op where she has purchased a one-bedroom apartment. She will be moving in less than two weeks.

The story is a study of role reversal. While Carmela finally asserts her independence and her right to live her own life, her children are baffled and angered because she did not ask their permission, because she does not act the part of a grieving widow, and ultimately because she refuses to be the loving mother and doting grandmother. Vivian E. Nice explains how the "exclusivity of the mother-infant tie" builds an expectation of the mother's availability to her children: "all-giving, all-understanding and totally selfless, she should immerse herself in motherhood to the exclusion of all else (except being a wife—after all, fathers have needs too)" (31). Carmela's rebellion is her insistence on cutting those ties with her children who are grown-ups and now have children of their own, and with a man who robbed her of her freedom, of her capacity to comfort a dying child, and literally, of her sleep during his illness. The children understand too well what the one-bedroom apartment means: they are welcome to visit, but not to stay! As they begin to protest, Carmela demands "the privilege of taking care of myself!" (50).

The story ends with Carmela standing on the terrace of her apartment, looking at the river and reminiscing about her dreams when she was a girl, of working on freighters so that she could travel the world. Her dreams were quickly put down by her brothers who would point out that "Girls can't join the navy or the merchant marine" (53). But now, here she is in her own place, with the river flowing toward a whole world of possibilities, and she knows that "each day would be a day for her to reckon with, all her own, a time with future" (53).

Vivian E. Nice underlines how "ambivalence is a central concept in writings on the mother-daughter relationship," yet problems stem from the refusal to consider this ambivalence normal (11). Nicholasa Mohr's characters indeed delve into ambivalence and ambiguity as they cope with growing pains and what Juan Flores calls processes of "adaptation." Yet, although a mother herself, seldom does the writer give voice to the woman-mother and her concerns. In her memoirs, Mohr acknowledges that her mother did not leave her anything material when she died, only "her honesty" and "her final words" which "linger on as beacons directing me to honor my goals and to respect my culture" (*Growing* 115). Her mother is the one who encouraged Mohr to be true to herself and to the artist inside her. On her deathbed, the mother, very much like Nilda's, warned Mohr that "a woman cannot live only for others, only for her children" (*Growing* 110). Unlike Nilda's mother, Mohr wants to arrive at the end of her life and see beyond her own children. She wants to remember the "feeling," be able to name it, and above all to own it. Thus, armed with her mother's words and her drawings, Nicholasa Mohr has embarked on a quest to create a fictional world where her mother's advice resonates on every page, where mother and daughter can speak to one another, move with one another, and dance with one another! It is the only way that she can be an honest and true artist!

Notes

1. "And the One Doesn't Stir without the Other," 67.
2. See Cathy N. Davidson and E. M. Broner's *The Lost Tradition: Mothers and Daughters in Literature* (1980).
3. It is not the purpose of this chapter to give a comprehensive summary or a bibliography of all the books, articles, and studies published on the subject.
4. Freud's theory of penis envy and oedipal complex have dominated psychoanalysis throughout the twentieth century. Men's fear of castration helps them surpass the Oedipus complex and develop as active, aggressive, independent individuals. Women, on the other hand, only seem to overcome their frustration of penis envy with the birth of a son.
5. See M. Marie Booth-Foster's article "Voice, Mind, Self. Mother-Daughter

Relationships in Amy Tan's *The Joy Luck Club* and *The Kitchen God's Wife,*" in Brown-Guillory, 208–227.

6. "Bildung in Ethnic Women Writers," 75–87. Unfortunately, Hoover Braendlin's analysis of Chicano literature is very limited and overgeneralized, focusing mainly on the figure of the father and the daughter's acceptance of the family and cultural heritage.

7. Throughout the novel, Mohr relates instances where the girl Nilda encounters other Hispanic children who reject her because she does not speak with the proper Castilian accent. She also overhears teachers criticizing Hispanics' parenting skills based upon their observations on the bus. When Nilda returns to school after a three-week absence due to her stepfather's death, she has to suffer the teacher ridiculing her mother's note and a tirade as to how Hispanics are so irresponsible, all in front of the class.

Chapter 3
The Fluid Identity of Rosario Morales and Aurora Levins Morales in *Getting Home Alive*

From Julia de Burgos' "Río Grande de Loíza" (1938) to Sandra María Esteves' *Tropical Rains: A Bilingual Downpour* (1984) and Rosario Ferré's *Las dos Venecias* (1992), Puerto Rican women writers on the island and in the United States have been navigating the ocean and the rivers and canals of the cities, trying to get ashore alive with their identities still intact. Rosario Morales and her daughter, Aurora Levins Morales, also embark on a similar journey through their poems and poetic journals in *Getting Home Alive* (1987).[1] While Esmeralda Santiago explores the ambivalence and ambiguity of her hybridity, Morales and Levins weave a story of pain, suffering, anger, and celebration of living at the crossroads of Puerto Rican, American, and Jewish cultures. The identity of each is not one, but multiple, fluid, ever-changing, and never fixed.

Because Puerto Rico is a small island, water has been a recurrent image in its literature and music. At the turn of the century, Manuel Zeno Gandía used the image of the stagnant waters of a pond to portray a society that had come to a political, economic, cultural, and spiritual standstill in his naturalist novel, *La Charca* (1894). In the thirties, Julia de Burgos, identifying with the oppressed islanders, sang to the largest river on the island, "Río Grande de Loíza," as the only route to freedom (69–70). In the fifties, the composer Sylvia Rexach further explored the saving attributes of water with frequent metaphors of the sea as the lover who could rescue her. In the nineties, Rosario Ferré utilizes water and the crossing of rivers, canals, and lagoons to signify the crossover between different realities.[2] In fact, Ferré discusses her theories of translation using the metaphor of negotiating a river in her essay, "Destiny, Language and Translation, or, Ophelia Adrift in the C & O Canal" (1991).

As Efraín Barradas observes, Morales and Levins use traditional symbols and imagery of the island (176). Yet, the writers move beyond the traditional and sometimes romantic imagery of the sea to submerge themselves into the politics of body fluids and everyday liquids. They use images of boiling water, *café con leche*, breast milk, blood, sweat, miscarriage discharge, and urine in order to underline their liquid voices that have begun to spill and can no longer be contained in silence. Words stream out like tears, stories spill out of the brain, insults are spit out. Thus they float away from the traditional semiotics of water with its signified notions of birth, renewal, purification, and regeneration to explore the hydraulics of anger, destruction, healing, and above all, *mestizaje.*

Getting Home Alive originated during long-distance phone calls between mother and daughter, who began to read to each other what they had written. With this book, Rosario Morales and Aurora Levins Morales break the dikes of literary genres as their voices flood the pages with poetry, journal entries, and poetic essays to construct an autobiographical narrative. Like their phone conversations, their writing flows easily from one entry to the next, with only a different typeface to establish authorship by one or the other. Lourdes Rojas believes that "by creating this multi-genre literary structure, they are inventing a text that mirrors the culturally multiple essence of their own definitions as Latinas" (175).

In order to understand the myriad emotions and polysemy of this unusual autobiography, one has to understand the family background of the writers. Rosario Morales, the mother, was born in New York during the Depression to recently arrived Puerto Rican immigrants whose marriage was the result of economics and societal rules instead of love. While in college, Rosario joined the Communist Party and married Richard Levins, a young Jewish scientist and activist, whose Ukrainian family were Holocaust survivors. Afraid for their lives during the McCarthy era, the young couple fled to Puerto Rico, where they lived in the isolated mountains of Naranjito in a house without electricity or running water. There, Rosario and Richard had Aurora, their first child. Aurora was a young adolescent when the family subsequently moved back to the Chicago area in the States. Like many other Puerto Rican immigrants, they embarked on a pilgrimage around the country, moving to Oklahoma, New York, and California. It is in the States that Aurora experienced the hate that both her Puerto Rican and Jewish backgrounds aroused in people.

According to Gloria Anzaldúa, the clash of such diverse cultural backgrounds produces "mental and emotional states of perplexity" (*Borderlands* 78). Tolerance is the only way to deal with the "contradictions" and "ambiguities" of the *mestiza's* "plural personality" (79). After all, observes Anzaldúa, "she [the *mestiza*] operates in a pluralistic mode." Morales and Levins' consciousness of their plurality is evident throughout their book. From the first poem, "Wolf," in which Levins encounters a wolf changing into different animals, all endangered species, to the final "Ending Poem," in which mother and daughter collaborate, the notion of an ever-changing reality is constantly present. "Child of the Americas" and "I Am What I Am" have become popular inclusions in Latino anthologies. In "Child of the Americas," Aurora Levins Morales proclaims: "I am a child of the Americas, / a light-skinned mestiza of the Caribbean, / a child of many diaspora, born into this continent at a crossroads. / I am a U.S. Puerto Rican Jew" (50). Rosario Morales, her mother, adopts and subverts a biblical phrase as the title of her poem, "I Am What I am,"[3] where she challenges anyone who might want to take her identity away.

> I am what I am and I am U.S. American I haven't wanted to say it because if I did you'd take away the Puerto Rican but now I say go to hell I am what I am and you can't take it away with all the words and sneers at your command I am what I am I am Puerto Rican I am U.S. American I am New York Manhattan and the Bronx I am what I am I'm not hiding under no stoop behind no curtain I am what I am I am Boricua as Boricuas come from the isle of Manhattan. (138)

The notion of the "multiplicity" of female identities emerges as a feminist response to patriarchal ideals of "sameness." Discussing issues of *méttisage* in the Caribbean, Martinican poet and theorist Edouard Glissant insists that "sameness requires *fixed* being" and diversity is a "pent-up force" "like a *liquid overflowing* its vessel" (98–99, emphasis added). In her essay, "The Mechanics of Fluids," Luce Irigaray asserts that the prevailing culture in contemporary life is organized around the "phallus" and the "solidified form." Elizabeth Grosz explains Irigaray's theories:

> In her [Irigaray's] understanding, patriarchal knowledges represent (male) sexuality by a solidity, stability and identity congruent with the kind of identity constructed for the boy by his oedipus complex. Her aim is to reveal the *fluidity,* the polymorphous multiplicity of the pre-oedipal [i.e. the feminine] which underlies and precedes it. (117)

Grosz underlines how Irigaray's image "stresses the multiplicity, ambiguity, fluidity, and excessiveness of female sexuality" (115). Morales and Levins refuse to define themselves in terms of binary opposition or as complements of masculine subjectivity. Their "I am" repeated throughout the book is constantly fluctuating and changing its copulative link like the wolf in the opening poem. These *Puertorriqueñas* resort to images of body fluids (tears, breast milk, blood, miscarriage discharge, urine, and spit) to inscribe their "I am" that keeps moving from the Ukraine, to New York, Puerto Rico, Chicago, Oklahoma, and California.

For Irigaray, male sexuality restricts language, controlling both grammar and syntax. For women to have their "own" voices, they need "to disrupt or alter the syntax of discursive logic, based on the requirements of univocity and masculine sameness."[4] Arguing that male sexuality is based on a "mechanics of solids," Irigaray proposes an alternative theory of female sexuality and of feminine discourse:

> That it is continuous, compressible, dilatable, viscous, conductible, diffusable . . . that it allows itself to be easily traversed by flow by virtue of its conductivity to currents coming from other fluids or exerting pressure through the walls

of a solid; that it mixes with bodies of a like state, sometimes dilutes itself in them in an almost homogeneous man-
ner, which makes the distinction between the one and the
other problematical; and furthermore that it is already dif-
fuse "in itself," which disconcerts any attempt at static identification. (111)

At the same time, Irigaray warns that the patriarchal economy of
solids is constantly attempting to constrain and solidify the fluids.[5]
Grosz underlines how "The solidity sought by masculinity is the result
of congealing a feminine fluidity. The fluid has no given form on its
own but it can, of course, be given a form: when placed within a con-
stricted space, it takes on the shape of that space" (117–118).

Morales and Levins subvert and reinvent traditional images of
water and body fluids to denounce the containers that constantly bind
a woman's body to keep her "fixed" within the boundaries of socially
(patriarchal) acceptable behavior. Their tears, sweat, breast milk, and
other discharges mix with their liquid voices until they spill over and
break the dikes of confinement.

Containers that congeal the soul

Puertorriqueñas are painfully aware of how both Puerto Rican
patriarchal institutions and American society are constantly trying to
package and label them neatly into preconceived stereotypes. In the
late seventies, Luz María Umpierre-Herrera was denouncing the
"Betty Crocker gringas" and their futile attempts: "Había que coci-
narme y amoldarme, / envasarme al vacío con benzoato y BTZ / y
mantenerme enlatada para que no me saliera" ("They had to cook me
and mold me / package and seal me airtight with benzoate and BTZ /
and keep me in a can so I wouldn't get out" "La receta" *Puertorriqueña* 5). Like Umpierre-Herrera, Morales and Levins denounce
the different containers the women in their families have had to break
and break out of.

Throughout *Getting Home Alive* there are constant references to
enclosed places that threaten suffocation. Levins recounts her grandmother Ruth's journey from Russia to Ellis Island and describes the
place where they slept as "smelly, stuffy, dark" (27). She also describes

the stone house in Oklahoma and the garment factory where her grandmother stitched bras and girdles. Morales is afraid she will "die asphyxiated" with all the shutters closed to protect them from the rain in the mountains in Puerto Rico. Both mother and daughter feel trapped in the city of Chicago, "this brick and cement insane asylum of a city" (Morales, "Sketch" 143). Like Santiago in New York, the violence in the streets keeps them locked in fear inside their apartment (20, 22). Furthermore, the stale air of the University of Chicago's classrooms, where Morales studied anthropology, was such that she was driven to alcohol. Sober, she could not write about Levi-Strauss's and Turner's theories, which she calls "intellectual necrology."

In analyzing the title of the book *Getting Home Alive*, Consuelo López Springfield points out that "'Home' refers to a sense of 'surety,' an experiential focusing that transpires through the act of writing" (303). As López Springfield says, there seems to be a sense of imminent danger and the need to look for refuge, for a hiding place that will protect them from the insults, from prejudice, and even from political persecution. However, such traditional places of refuge as the home, school, and the church/synagogue become sites of confinement, oppression, and ultimately of suffocation.

Gloria Anzaldúa warns against traditional social systems of gender expectation that bind the body more than any physical barrier: "The borders and walls that are supposed to keep undesirable ideas out are entrenched habits and patterns of behavior; these habits and patterns are the enemy within" (*Borderlands* 79). Morales soon recognizes the customs of the Puerto Rican patriarchal society that keep women in their place while superficially maintaining a blissful notion of freedom and power. The writer is puzzled by women who are "strong and independent" but frequently comment apologetically, "'*Mi marido no me deja*,' my husband won't let me" (79). Even she starts using it when she does not want to do something. Unlike her daughter who feels at home on the island, Morales resents the place because for her it is more like an uncomfortable prison:

> this is too much like home for comfort, too many people nagging, harping, pushing you into line, into feminine behavior, into caution and fear, provocativeness and manipulativeness,

full of predatory males who punish you for being female. Little freedom of thought and action, freedom to expand, grow, dare, to do something different, to change. ("Puerto Rico Journal" *Getting Home Alive* 79–80)

The journal starts with an entry written in the plane on the way to Puerto Rico. Morales writes: "I carry my island tucked inside and I'm going home" (76). But within days, she is complaining about the lack of privacy and how she yearns for "stone walls and heavy wooden doors and shutters . . . for the cold, for the closing in and closing off of winter . . . and the deep silence of a northern woods" (77). It is almost as if the tropical environment of her homeland suffocates her, and she needs to run away from it to free herself. Ironically, she seeks refuge in the confinements of her New England apartment. The journal closes with Morales back on the plane to the States staring at the last words written in it: "I'm going home." The contradiction of the initial and final "home" destination echoes "La guagua aérea" ("The Aerial Bus"), an essay by Luis Rafael Sánchez. In it, Sánchez describes the airplane that takes thousands of Puerto Ricans back and forth between the island and the mainland as "el espacio de una nación flotante entre dos puertos de contrabandear esperanzas!" ("the space of a nation floating between two ports smuggling hope" 22). It is only within this space that Morales feels safe. As López Springfield indicates, the writers only feel at home within their writing: after all, the word "home" appears both at the beginning and at the end in the journal. Space then does not designate a geographical area between Puerto Rico and the States, or as Sánchez suggests, the airplane that takes her between the two, but the expansive space of a blank page in front of a writer, infinite in possibilities.

If the island's atmosphere is asphyxiating, Morales' childhood in New York almost congeals her spirit. As she embroiders children's stories, Morales describes an abusive father. The only way of escaping his hands is "standing paralyzed . . . by freezing myself to death!" ("I Never Told My Children Stories" 170). In the story of Zoreida, the writer complains about relatives who constantly demand their children perform for their own amusement. "Why can't they leave little girls alone," cries out the narrator. "You'd think all we were were wind-up toys you pulled out of the drawer and set on the floor to amuse the relatives. Nah. I won't perform on command" (168).

More basic than performance are clothes. For Levins, clothing becomes a metaphor of sexual and gender constrictions, functioning very much like the house and the drawer of her mother's stories: "The point of terror, of denial, the point of hatred is the tight dress stretched across my grandmother's big breasts" (". . . And Even Fidel" 53). Like Santiago, Levins is baffled by the contradictory lessons about a woman's body and sexuality. On the one hand, her relatives warn her against men and the "filthiness" of sex while they check her attire to make sure that she can attract a boyfriend (". . . And Even Fidel" 53). She has witnessed firsthand the effect that societal expectations have had on her grandmother Lola, married at nineteen to an abusive man because "it was my duty to marry him, that it was for the good of my family" ("Immigrants" 23). Levins admires the spirit of her grandmother, who refused to be "smothered in the winter coats and scarves, in my grandfather's violent possessiveness and jealousy" (23). The writer goes on to describe how Lola took advantage of the exciting possibilities of New York in spite of everything. Now retired in her husband's dream house in Puerto Rico, the grandmother only thinks of escaping "out of the stifling air of that house, that community, that family" to "where a woman can go out and about on her own" (23).

Because of Morales' and Levins' political activism, incarceration is not just a metaphor but a very real threat. Morales describes "the fear that we had no future, that Dick [her husband] could be hauled off to jail any day for refusing to fight, that either of us might be arrested and jailed or concentration-camped for being communist" ("Hace tiempo" 29). The fear is much too real as they have friends that have been arrested at home and never seen again. What happens to them is the topic of "For Angel, for Vieques," a poetic essay about a man who dies after having been beaten in jail for protesting the military occupation of the island of Vieques.[6] Levins' idyllic images of "the whitest beaches" with "water so clear you can see fish move through coral reefs sixty feet down" and "low clouds drifting in the sea breeze trail their blue shadows across translucent waves" are violently juxtaposed to the descriptions of the "hot Florida jail cell," where the only colors are the red and blue of "Angel's face, beaten and bruised" (72–73). The signs of "No Trespassing" and "Private Property" are not only metaphors of the colonial status of Puerto Rico but of the asphyxiation and annihilation of the traditions and customs of people whose livelihood for generations had been the sea.

Mother's and daughter's fears of political persecution are intensified by the haunting memories of their Jewish relatives. Morales is afraid to suffer the fate of Jews during the Holocaust: "I am frightened. I know I can be boxcarted off, imprisoned shot gassed like my aunt Tessie, like Samuel of the round face" ("Double Allegiance" 158). As Levins examines photos her grandmother has collected throughout the years, she can see her "pressing her face to the wire of the new camp fences" ("In My Grandmother's House" 184).

More than the physical threats of jail, concentration camps, and boats of deportation, both mother and daughter are concerned about political ideologies used by men to perpetuate traditional patriarchal notions of gender roles that force women into compartments of acceptable behavior even within social activism. Although Morales was attracted to the Communist Party because of its feminist rhetoric, she soon realized that it was "feminism 'mouthed by men.'"[7] She is also suspicious of "Latina women in feminist circles who may 'support the macho line that we needed to fight against imperialism first—only later could we think about women as women'" (Springfield 309).

In "I Never Told My Children Stories," Morales describes her angry disillusionment with the gender politics of marriage: "We were young communists and enlightened and knew about male chauvinism and the household slavery of women and Engels on the family. But I came away with 90 percent of the housework and 95 percent of the emotional mending and ironing any old how" (174). Not only are women expected to take care of the "shopping and cooking and dishwashing and laundry and beds and floors and bathrooms," they are also to provide emotional support to their male revolutionary partners.

Levins echoes her mother's objections in the "Letter to a Compañero," when she accuses a political partner, a *compañero*, of exploiting women sexually (153–156). While he gives speeches, distributes pamphlets, and campaigns, the woman takes care of his wounds, dries his tears, and satisfies his desires. In the title, Levins uses the indefinite article "a" before *compañero,* mockingly insinuating that the letter is addressed to one partner out of many or no one partner in particular. The reader soon learns that the *compañero* had written a love letter with five carbon copies addressed to different women on the island and in the States. Levins berates him for using the word "solidarity" as if it were a credit card for him to get out of trouble. She recognizes that the defeat of women in politics comes "not by foreign policy, but by the sexual politics of solidarity" (155).

Ultimately, mother and daughter reject any political ideology that will constrict their movements and their freedom: "My revolution is not starched and ironed / . . . / It is not ass-girdled and breast-bound" (Morales 161).

Emotional and intellectual containment poses the most deadly threat to the choking voices of Morales and Levins. Irigaray insists that within a masculine discourse of solids, women's discourse is devoid of meaning:

Woman never speaks the same way. What she emits is flowing, fluctuating. *Blurring.* And she is not listened to . . . whence the resistances to that voice that overflows the "subject." Which the "subject" then congeals, freezes, in its categories until it paralyzes the voice in its flow (112).

Morales' and Levins' words have been paralyzed for too long; their stories, Levins tells us, were "stuffed" in an attic "pressing outward on the walls of my head" ("Storytelling" 163). Their memories have equally been stored in "secret reservoirs" and "cubbyholes in the cells" (Levins, "South" 53). Their stories have been contained and silenced for too long, struggling to come out, but mother and daughter have been afraid that once the words started flowing, they would never be able to shut the door/mouth off.

Whether it was due to fear or shame, Morales laments the loss of the Spanish language: "But I'm sad, too. For the English language robbed of the beat your home talk could give it, the words you could lend, the accent, the music . . . I'm sad for you, too, for the shame with which you store away— hide—a whole treasure box of other, mother, language" ("I Recognize You" 145).

Ultimately, Morales' lament turns into outrage at the "silence about injustice" ("Concepts of Pollution" 65). In anthropology courses, marriage customs and puberty rites were discussed but "no one mentioned rape" or talked about the practice of stoning a woman to death because she "pollutes the caste" (62). The Incas were studied, but there was "not a word about how they were despised and killed, infected and killed, tricked and killed, poisoned and killed" (63). Morales denounces the world of academe and its discourse devoid of meaning, where "we write and publish and get promoted, give or receive prizes and grants, and we never mention pain or sorrow or anger or death" (65).

For years Morales and Levins have kept their anger, their frustration, their pain contained. But Morales is tired of trying to be "the reasonable one" (147). She has always appeared to be rational and kind when people made racial and prejudicial statements in front of her. She has tried to keep her anger under control so that she wouldn't become the stereotypical image of a Puerto Rican, "a loud and angry spik" (148). But she cannot and will not contain her anger any more; she will not repress her angry words "under all that crisp english and extensive american vocabulary" (148). From now on, "I will always say *mielda.*" Like her mother, Levins refuses to "keep her accent under lock and key" any longer ("Puertoricanness" 84). She is tired of contracting her body and silencing her mouth so that she can fit into someone else's container: "Now I am angry with years / of stunting my appetite to fit the meal / shrinking my heart to sit conveniently / in someone's back pocket" ("Heart's Desire" 152).

Under the pressure of their repressed anger, the dikes begin to burst and their stories begin to spill over the phone lines and ultimately flood the pages of *Getting Home Alive*. In the poem by the same title, Morales returns triumphantly and stares at the rubble of the houses on her street in South Bronx: "On both sides of the street houses are leveled / Rubble lies on the ground. / . . . / Their bare plumbing showing through the wounds in the walls" ("Getting Home Alive" 17). It is amid the openness and the sounds of those streets of El Barrio, where Morales finally feels safe: "And the first time Dick and I drove back

thru New York past Amsterdam Avenue right thru the heart of Harlem
I breathed again safe brown and black walking the streets safe" ("The
Other Heritage" 56). It is here that she can stop recoiling in the fear of
being congealed.

Fluids that break the dam

In discussing the autobiographical voices of *métis* women writers,
Françoise Lionet believes that it is imperative for them to return "to the
physicality of their experiences, to the racial and sexual characteristics
of their bodies" (33). In *Getting Home Alive*, Morales and Levins
return to the fluids of their bodies in order to shake off, once and for
all, the solidity and rigidity of a monolithic notion of cultural identity.
The constant flow of images, of life-giving blood and breast milk, of
rebellious spit and urine, and of deadly miscarriage discharge inscribes
an identity that is, as Irigaray proposes, "continuous, compressible,
dilatable, viscous, conductible, diffusable," but never the same!

Little by little, mother and daughter allow their stories to seep
through and begin to reconstruct memories, experiences, and emotions until then contained and silenced. Levins puts together the stories of her grandmother Lola with "tears and words spilling slowly"
("1930" 42). She also gets her other grandmother, Ruth, to open a box
of old photographs and to allow the stories to flow: "I get her to open
once again the box of old photographs, to tell me who is who: my
cousin B, her children, my mother's cousins" ("In My Grandmother's
House" 181). Nevertheless, she still fears that once the attic is
opened, there might be no stopping the flood of words: "I almost
spilled them [stories] all right there on the bench . . . loosed the whole
heap of them on to Shattuck Avenue. . . . I imagine them bouncing
and rolling all over the sidewalk, between the legs of passers-by"
("Storytelling" 163).

Morales, on the other hand, is not afraid anymore and is determined
not to be "reasonable" but to let the years of anger spit out of her body
in any shape or form. Annmari Roundberg explains how "magical prop-
erties" that could be "positive or negative, depending on the intent of the
spitter" used to be attributed to spit (37). Still today, he observes, anger
is associated with both boiling and spitting. Thus Morales will spit out

the anger inside of her anyway she can: "cockroaches creeping out of my ears, spitty spanish curses spilling out of my wet lips, angry crazy eyes shooting hate at you" ("I Am the Reasonable One" 148).

Aside from spitting curses, Morales refers to urination and defecation as expressions of anger. Tired of trying to conform to the demands for neatness, cleanliness, and politeness, she is exhorted by her "Other Heritage" to "come out" and assert her own identity:

> que hay de criticar will I do will I pass will you let me thru
> . . . not see me here beneath my skin behind my voice
> crouched and quiet and so so still . . . my spanish sounds muttering mielda qué gente fría y fea se creen gran cosa ai!
> escupe chica en su carifresca en su carifea meáte ahí en el piso
> feo y frío yo valgo más que un piso limpio yo valgo más yo
> valgo cágate en l'alfombra chica arráncale el pelo yo quiero
> salir de aquí yo quiero salir de ti yo quiero salir . . . (57)

> [what's there to criticize . . . muttering shit what cold and ugly
> people they think they are great! spit on their faces, on their
> ugly faces, girl pee there on the ugly and cold floor I am
> worth more than a clean floor I am worth more I am worth
> shit on the carpet, girl, pull out the hair I want to get out of
> here I want to get rid of you I want to get out . . .]

Morales refuses to hide the rhythm of her Spanish accent or the black soil in her feet underneath the clean floors that suggest racial purity.[8] She will no longer be the quiet, clean, polite person that society expects her to be: "how white how upper class refined and kind voice all crisp with consonants bristling with syllables." She spits, urinates, and defecates on the "clean carpet" because from now on she will proclaim her *mestiza* identity: "I come from the dirt where the cane was grown" ("Ending Poem" 212). Her "spitty spanish curses" serve not only to rebel against imposed social roles, but also to assert her worth as a person: "Yo valgo más que un piso limpio" ("I am worth more than a clean floor"), and her angry "unreasonable other."

Traditionally, soiled fluids, such as the putrid creek in Zeno Gandía's novel, have been used to symbolize corruption and social stagnation. Morales exploits the same motif to describe the polluting impact of her alma mater: "the effluvium of the University of Chicago runs through the streets in dirty streams" ("Concepts of Pollution" 62). But she obviously subverts the familiar meaning and uses images of urination and defecation to underline political protest. In "City Pigeons," Morales identifies herself with the birds who, like her, defecate on the same statues:

> You are the same breed as me,
> shitting on the same statues:
> > dead politicians
> > dead generals
> > dead gods (92)

If urination and defecation become expressions of self-assertion and political protest, breast milk is introduced to depict intellectual nourishment. Metaphors of a "totemic repast" are common in Western culture: to spit out insults, to "drink in the words of another," to swallow one's own words. In *Getting Home Alive*, words become a source of nourishment and sustenance for the soul. Irigaray believes that it is a mother's ultimate responsibility to give her daughter, not only the physical, but more important, the linguistic nourishment that will empower her.

> Instead of being the objects exchanged between one man and another, Irigaray advocates the two women taking on an active subject-to-subject relation. It is for this reason that she suggests the mother must give the daughter more than food to nourish her, she may also give her words with which to speak and hear. The gift of language in place of the suffocation and silence imposed by food. (Grosz 124)

It is obvious that for Morales and Levins milk and bread are metaphors for words. Morales describes how her daughter learned at her breast about language and books: "As her tiny rooting mouth sucked my milk, I sucked something from those books I was born wanting. . . . I was hungry for words when she was born" ("Of course She Read" 110). Morales, on the other hand, learned about her parents' poverty and hunger: "Their anxiety was the breath of life to me, their hunger flavored my milk" ("Destitution" 94). Her physical starvation during her childhood will become her intellectual hunger, which will make her a voracious reader devouring books.

Morales and Levins use fluids to underline their diverse identity: spitting, urinating, and defecating to express their angry and political "I," breast milk to express their intellectual life, and ultimately running water and blood to establish their connection to a collective consciousness of cultural multiplicity. Yet, it is the depiction of the grayish discharge of miscarriage floating around the toilet that underscores pain, death, and isolation as an integral part of their existence. In a beautiful moving tribute to her childhood friend, Levins laments how her friend, so curious about life, is now surrounded by death: "In the years since then you've spilled children from you / like wasted blood / half of them dying before you could learn their names" ("Tita's Poem" 59). Unfortunately, both mother and daughter go on to experience the sense of loss that comes from a miscarriage. Morales wonders about her creation looking now like a "dead jellyfish":

> I sat in the cemetery of a bathroom pushed it out with the last of my cramps. I stood there and looked at the blood-stained waters pink against the chill white of the porcelain toilet bowl. And with my heart like a great lead plumb bob hanging on a string from my mouth, I looked down, stared down, at a beautiful soft grey saucer frilled like a sunbonnet, floating like a dead jellyfish, my baby only a small red blob off center, my hopes as dead as my child. ("Birth" 100)

Adding to her pain are her relatives insensitive remarks: "What does she need another baby for? What's the hurry?" (101).

Contrary to their relatives who cannot understand the sense of loss brought by the death of an unborn child, Levins shares in her mother's pain as she describes her own miscarriage in her poem "Heart of My Heart, Bone of My Bone." Here her identification with the dead fetus is absolute, feeling it grow weaker until it grows still: "The fluids of our bodies mingled in one chemical response: I knew *exactly* how you felt, and never, since then, have I been so completely known" (119). Like her mother, she needs to witness the passage into nothingness: "When you floated passive in the salty water and slowly came undone, frilling and fraying at the edges, becoming strands of protein, disappearing into the walls, the glowing cord my flesh—the stillness that followed was terrible, patta-pun *and nothing*, patta-pun *and nothing*" (120).

Ultimately, Morales' and Levins' identity as "a child of the Americas," "a child of many diaspora" finds its expression in the metaphor of liquids spilling and running down the floor until they run into other rivers. Rina Benmayor emphasizes how ascertaining one's multiple identities is not just a question of personal survival but of political integrity as well: "For Rosario and Aurora, the task of reconciling their Puerto Rican and Jewish identities, their allegiances as women of color and as political activists, is painful and imperative" (113). It should be noted that, for the most part, Latina writers identify themselves with the cause of women of color rather than with the feminist movement, which they associate with the white intellectual elite. Benmayor concludes: "For Rosario and Aurora, the point is not to affirm one part of your identity and reject another, rather to convert all your resources into strategies for social change" (116).

In "If I Forget Thee, Oh Jerusalem," Levins identifies with the ideals of the Zionist movement, although she questions the violence in the Middle East. Throughout the book, both mother and daughter embrace the causes of other oppressed groups, such as women of color, Jews, and Salvadoreans, to underline the commonality and yet multiple aspects of their political selves. Levins uses the image of blood to fluctuate among her various ethnic backgrounds. Describing a trip to the Andes, she follows the thread of her blood: Taíno, Arauca, Guaraní ("South" 53). Morales, on the other hand, describes how "Africa waters the roots of my tree" ("Africa" 55).

It is in the kitchen where mother and daughter can finally sit down at the table and commune with all the women before them. López Springfield observes that "Morales and Levins associate food preparation with communal storytelling" (307). The critic goes on to explain how the writers use the kitchen as a "domestic center of women's lives and a conventional symbol of subjugation" and "transform" it "into a metaphor for narrative empowerment" (307). Like Esmeralda Santiago's autobiographies, Morales' and Levins' writings do not depict isolated experiences of two *mestiza* women caught between cultures. On the contrary, they echo the cries of Africans, Taínos, Jews, and many other cultures that have been oppressed throughout the centuries. Morales insists on serving her children dishes that would challenge any *melting pot*: "Jewish chicken soup with cilantro and oregano . . . aceite de oliva and kosher pickles, pasta de guayaba and pirozhni, empanadas and borscht mit sour cream" ("Synagogue" 116).

Similarly, Levins finds her connection to "Puertoricanness" (84–86) through the sharing of "café con leche." She stands in the kitchen, "bathing in the scent of its cooking, bringing the river to flow through my own kitchen now, the river of my place on earth, the green and musty river of my grandmothers, dripping, trickling, tumbling down from the mountain of kitchens of my people" ("Kitchens" 39).

As their words and stories begin to spill onto the blank page, Morales and Levins create a site of resistance against the congealing "masculine discourse." Their fluid images allow for their multiple "I Am" to resonate long after the phone has been put down. After all, Morales explains, "a stew of words . . . could inspire her to self-loving invention" ("I Recognize You" 145).

Rivers that connect our stories / Threads that mend the tears of our souls

In the introduction to *Medicine Stories*, Aurora Levins Morales refers to the years of physical, sexual, and psychological abuse that she endured as a child. The first essay, "False Memories," discusses the effective strategies of the dominant culture for suppressing the voices and the memories of the oppressed. According to the author, "Healing takes place in community, in the telling and the bearing witness, in the naming of trauma and in the grief and rage and defiance that follow" (16). It is appropriate then that her first poem in *Getting Home Alive* is about a chameleonic wolf struggling for survival. López Springfield explains that in Native American culture, the wolf "represents the restorative power of storytelling" (304). The critic goes on to describe the healing power of Morales's and Levins' book: "Their autobiographical writing became, to borrow a phrase from Dick Hebdige, 'a laying on of the hands, and attempt to close the wound, to exorcise and expiate' feelings of isolation" (312). Like Esmeralda Santiago in her autobiographies, mother and daughter spit out their stories, which become the curative saliva that will restore their pained and cramped "I."

As the threads of blood of their multicultural ancestors water their feet, they begin to sew themselves into parts of a quilt that reveal the variety of textures, colors, patterns that make them whole. As foreshadowed by the quilt on the cover of their book, Morales and Levins weave multicolored threads of their poems, journal entries, and poetic essays to form a quilt where Jewish, *Boricua*, America, and *mestiza* coexist in a harmonious design.

Since childhood, Rosario Morales has felt herself being torn apart by Jewish, Black, and Latina women's competing stories of oppression. She feels "the tear starting somewhere behind my left ear" as a sleeve is "ripped off" to show the tattooed numbers on the skin or as a blouse is pulled up to show old whip scars ("Double Allegiance" 157). The more she listens to the cries of these stories, the more her ears tear. She decides it is time to heal her wounds and begin to "sew myself together with the thread we'd spun. . . . I ran small running stitches up my scalp, small chain stitches down my face" (158). If she runs out of thread, she can always make more.

Using the metaphor of sewing, Morales co-opts a traditional role for women and transforms it into a weapon for her own revolution: "My revolution is not cut from a pattern, I designed it/ It's homemade and hand-crafted / It's got seams to let out / and hems to let down / tucks to take in / darts to take out" ("My Revolution" 161). This time she does not sew for her family or the "compañero," but for herself, and she invites other women to create their own designs:

So, when your revolution doesn't fit
           ain't your size
           chokes
           binds
           climbs up your crotch
           bites into your breasts
or rubs your heels raw

Give it back!
[...............................]
and make yourself another
make one of your very own. (162)

This is the challenge presented by *Getting Home Alive*. Superficially, it could be perceived as individualistic, selfish, anarchist. Yet Rina Benmayor explains how both mother and daughter are presented with the question of how to construe progressive politics in which "diversity and difference become rallying points in a common struggle for social equality rather than boundaries that exclude" (108).

Toward the end of the book, Levins confronts this issue in the lengthy essay, "If I Forget Thee, Oh Jerusalem," in which she remembers Psalm 137 and revisits issues of reconstructing the history of oppressed people. As she watches the news of Israel's invasion of Lebanon and the massacre perpetrated by the Jews, Levins expresses her disappointment once again with political rhetoric and the discrepancy between ideology and the images on television. From her meditations emerges the formulation that only an inclusive politics of liberation, not exclusion, can truly succeed: "I want to see a flowering of Arab and Jewish cultures in a country without racism or anti-Semitism. . . . A multilingual, multireligious, many-colored and -peopled land where the orange tree blooms for all" (208). Previously, she had informed the "compañero" about her notion of country: "a rug woven from the rebel threads of a hundred homelands" ("Letter" 155). Morales shares a similar vision, a "glorious pattern and color and warmth and comfort" ("I Never" 172).

They both envision a totemic repast at their kitchen where the guests will carry "all the civilizations erected on their backs" as they commune on a tablecloth "woven by one, dyed by another, embroidered by another still" (Morales, "The Dinner" 51). For Levins, such a dinner is merely a question of survival; after all, it is "the table of the choosers of life" ("California" 195).

Mother and daughter profess a social commitment and solidarity that goes beyond the island, the American continent, or Israel to embrace all humanity in all its multiplicity and contradictions. Rosario Morales and Aurora Levins Morales have filled the nothingness and emptiness of the containers prescribed by society with their fluid images of a multiple identity. They have landed in the *"tierra firme"* of the printed page, where they have embroidered their stories, to provide us with words and images that can never be static, that can never be congealed. After all, their identities are still very much alive!

Notes

1. Hereafter, when discussing Rosario Morales' work, the text will refer to Morales; when discussing her daughter's, Aurora Levins Morales, it will refer to Levins. "Morales and Levins" will be used when discussing both of their work at the same time.
2. See *Las dos Venecias*, 1992, a collection of poems and poetic essays, and her novel, *The House on the Lagoon* (1995).
3. In the episode of Moses and the burning bush, when asked by Moses how to identify Him to others, Yahweh said: "I am who I am" (Exodus 3:14). It should be noted that Rosario Morales changes the relative pronoun "who" to "what," thus objectifying the subject: herself!
4. An explanation given for the French term *"parler-femme,"* "Publisher's Note and Notes on Selected Terms," *This Sex Which is Not One* by Luce Irigaray, trans. Catherine Porter, 222.
5. Although many critics reject Irigaray's theories on the mechanics of fluids because of their simplistic approach to the binary opposition of gender, her notions of solids and containment versus liquids and fluidity seem relevant to the analysis and our understanding of *Getting Home Alive*.
6. Vieques is one of the very small islands that form part of Puerto Rico. The U.S. decided that the island, sitting across from Roosevelt Roads Naval Base, was the perfect location for a practice bombing range. Fishermen all of a sudden were prohibited access to the sea in the area and to their livelihood. Throughout the years and up to the present, there have been protests against the military presence. In 1998, during a military exercise, civilians nearby were killed.
7. As quoted in note 5 of López Springfield's article, 313.
8. Françoise Lionet explains how there is no word for *métissage* in English. According to the Mauritian critic, the somewhat equivalent and often used terms "half-breed" and "mixed blood" "imply biological abnormality and reduce human reproduction to the level of animal breeding" (13). Morales' references to society's obsession with cleanliness and politeness underlines how uncomfortable American culture is with racial impurity.

Chapter 4
"Y si la patria es una mujer": The Political Discourse of Sandra María Esteves

> . . . *Irishmen and Irishwomen fathered and mothered*
> *themselves, reinventing parents in much the*
> *same way they were reinventing the Irish past.*
> *If Ireland had never existed, the English would have*
> *invented it.*
> —Declan Kiberd[1]

For five hundred years, the small island of Puerto Rico has been a colony of two foreign powers. The ideal of *'patria,'* [2] native land, has dominated the literature of the island. The struggle for freedom and the denunciation of the colonial governments has inspired many verses and lyrics. In her collections of poetry, now widely anthologized, Sandra María Esteves goes against this tide. She rejects the idealized and romanticized notions of *patria* and the popular rhetoric of nationalism. With her characteristic militance and aggressiveness, Esteves forges a feminist discourse of collective consciousness and communal and global solidarity. She utilizes Afro-Caribbean, *Nuyorican,* and African-American rhythms to compose a song of liberation to be heard throughout the world, not just in Puerto Rico. Imagery of music and dancing calls for a stepping into action against political, economic, sexual, and racial oppression. A believer and practitioner of *santería*, Esteves uses African religion to create her own "myths" of empowerment and liberation that transcend the objectives of insular nationalism.

In *Inventing Ireland* (1995), Declan Kiberd sets out to examine the relationship between Irish literature and the historical, political, and cultural contexts out of which it emerges, especially the Irish Renaissance, right at the time when "Ireland is about to be reinvented for a new century" (4). Arguing the manipulation and distortion of the Irish past, Kiberd explains how England "invented" an "Ireland" inhabited by "hot-headed, rude and nomadic" people to be the perfect foil to the "controlled, refined and rooted" English (9). As the British empire expanded to India and Africa, the English found the inhabitants of these regions to suffer from the same character weaknesses as the Irish. Kiberd believes that it was in language and in literature that Ireland began to reclaim its past and its culture. He argues that the cultural revival of the Irish Renaissance "preceded and in many ways enabled the political revolution that followed" (4).

Likewise in Puerto Rico, passionate expressions of patriotism found their way into literature long before the formation of national and liberation movements. The quest for the independence of Puerto Rico and for the definition of what it means to be Puerto Rican emerged almost simultaneously under the hegemony of the Spanish government. In 1848, Manuel Alonso y Pacheco published *El Gíbaro*, in which he gives his idealized version of the quintessential Puerto Rican farmer, a romantic image that is still prevalent today. José Gautier Benítez (1848–1880), on the other hand, sang of the delirious ardor and desire of the absent lover for his "island."[3] Cesáreo Rosa-Nieves explains how Gautier Benítez's notion of *patria* (motherland) was not a political one, but a romantic nostalgia for a symbol of the feminine ideal (*Poesía* 104).[4] Both Gautier Benítez's poetry and his sensual imagery of patriotic ardor are very popular to this day.

With the American invasion of Puerto Rico in 1898, the struggle for independence and for a free state intensified feelings of patriotism. Also, an interesting phenomenon gradually occurred: Puerto Ricans, rebelling against the United States and its attempts to Americanize the island, as depicted by Esmeralda Santiago, began to look back to Spain, as *la madre patria* [the mother homeland] and to romanticize and idealize everything of Spanish descent. Hispanophilia, notes Frances Aparicio, "underlies Puerto Rican cultural discourse even today" (*Listening* 6).

As in Ireland, literature became an ideal means of expressing patriotic love and zeal. According to Rosa-Nieves, the two most important themes of Puerto Rican poetry are *patria* and *la mujer* (woman). Such poets as José de Diego (1866–1918) can no longer afford the romantic and idyllic posture of a Gautier Benítez, but write instead to incite people to political insurrection:

Know how to face the angry thrust of storms,
not braying, like a frightened lamb,[5]
but roaring, like a defiant beast.
Rise! Revolt! Resist!
Do as the bull in the face of adversity:
charge
with confident power. (Diego 7)

Rosa-Nieves considers de Diego to be "poeta viril de estro en punta de lanza" ("virile poet with heat at the tip of the sword" *Ensayos* 144), a sword that is ready to defy the Northern invader: "And we have been telling you for a long time, / over and over, / to go to the Devil / and leave us with God" (Diego 26).

Only Lola Rodríguez de Tió (1843–1924), in her efforts to combine Puerto Rico's fight for independence with Cuba's, seems to anticipate de Diego's fiery and passionate call to action. She is best known for her version of *"La Borinqueña,"* which substitutes the lyrics of the national anthem for a cry to arms:

¡Despierta Borinqueño
[..............................]
que es hora de luchar!
[..............................]
No queremos más déspotas. Caiga el tirano ya.
Las mujeres indómitas, también sabrán luchar.
¡Queremos la libertad! ¡Nuestros machetes nos la dará!
Wake up, *borinqueño* / . . . / It is time to fight! / . . . / We want
no more tyrants. May the tyrants fall! / Women, unconquer-
able, will also know how to fight! / We want liberty! Our
machetes will assure it for us![6]

As a political activist, Rodríguez de Tió was exiled three times during her life, and, in fact, she died in Cuba. Yet, most of her poetry, contrary to that of De Diego, lacks this bellicose tone and is mainly characterized by the nostalgia of the poet living in exile and the sadness of watching her land being colonized by a greater power (Rosa-Nieves, *Ensayos* 83).

For the most part, the poets of the first half of the twentieth-century, inspired by the precursory romantic images of Gautier Benítez, depict idyllic features of the Puerto Rican landscape and culture. Virgilio Dávila (1869–1943), Luis Llorens Torres (1878–1944), and Luis Pales Matos (1898–1959), considered among the best poets of this century, sing to "la isla" (the island) as a beautiful woman of great sensuality and voluptuousness. At times, their poems might turn into a lament for the *patria* that is not free. In fact, Luis Muñoz Rivera (1859–1916) calls it "Cinderella" trapped in her ugly cell: "Borínquen, la cenicienta, / no puede romper su cárcel" ("Borínquen, Cinderella, / cannot tear down her prison" Rosa-Nieves, *Ensayos* 105). Years later, Julia de Burgos (1913–1953) would provide the feminine voice that would add her tears "for my people; enslaved" to those of the "Great river. Great weeping" of the "Grand River of Loíza."[7]

Possibly it is the feminine gender of the nouns *isla* (island) and *patria* (native land) that has inspired the fertile metaphor of the *tierra / isla / doncella* (land / island / young maiden) stretched out passively waiting for the tender caresses of her *amado / mar / sol* (lover / sea / sun). Indeed, the lyrics of *La Borinqueña*, composed in 1905 by Manuel Fernández Juncos, is a series of praises to the Edenic island. The national anthem ends with Christopher Columbus arriving at its shores and "exclaiming in admiration": "Esta es la linda tierra / Que busco yo; / Es Borinquen la hija / La hija del mar y el sol" ("This is the beautiful island / That I have searched for; / This is Borinquen the daughter, / The daughter of the sea and the sun").[8] In her groundbreaking study, *Listening to Salsa: Gender, Latin Popular Music, and Puerto Rican Cultures*, Frances Aparicio describes how a writer such as Antonio S. Pedreira points to the recurrent feminization of the island-country in the *danza* as evidence of the docility and weakness of its inhabitants. Pedreira, argues Aparicio, "rereads the danza as a metaphor for the colonizability of Puerto Ricans" (19).

Many other writers and composers are similarly fascinated with the metaphor of the island as a young maiden. Sometimes, the island / damsel awaits with docility to be rescued from violations suffered at the hands of masculine-gendered entities such as *el imperialismo yanqui / el continente / Los Estados Unidos / El Americano* (yanqui imperialism / the continent / the United States / The American). One of the most beautiful and lyrical examples of the feminization of Puerto Rico and romantic notions of liberation is another *danza,* "Verde Luz," composed by Antonio Cabán Vale. The singer speaks of his desire for the "isla virgen" ("virgin island"), "isla doncella" ("young maiden island"), which he wants to possess only after "her sky" is freed and "her star" stands alone.

Octavio Paz immortalized the metaphor of political violation of the woman/land in his essay "Los hijos de la Malinche:" "Si la Chingada es una representación de la Madre violada, no me parece forzado asociarla a la Conquista, que fue también una violación, no solamente en el sentido histórico, sino en la carne misma de las indias" ("If the *Chingada* is a representation of the violated Mother, it is appropriate to associate her with the Conquest, which was also a violation, not only in the historical sense but also in the very flesh of Indian women"[9] 77). In Puerto Rico, that woman/colonized land is embodied in the historical figure of the *Taína* Anacaona. She was chief of her village after her husband had died and, in spite of her ingenuity and leadership, she soon became the mistress of Spanish conquerors. This mythologized union of Spaniard and *Taína* gave birth to the Puerto Rican people. Eliana Ortega explains that the figure of Anacaona becomes then "the mother of a colonized people who lost their mother tongue and their land, stripped from them by the most insidious expressions of patriarchy, conquest and colonialism" (125).

Even though Paz in the 1950s pointed out that the violation was a real one for the Mexican Indian women, it is in the 1970s that Latin American women writers begin to denounce openly the repressive governments and "el lugar desmenguado" ("the diminished place" Mora 160) of women within socially oppressive systems. Sara Castro-Klarén explains how the "Retórica de la Opresión" ("rhetoric of oppression") goes hand in hand with the "Retórica de la opresión sexual" ("rhetoric of sexual oppression"):

La retórica de la opresión sexual tiene su paralelo en la retórica de la opresión racial o mejor dicho La Retórica de la Opresión que se ha practicado a través de la historia contra muchos
y varios grupos. Si la ideología patrista se funda en la presencia / ausencia del sexo para negarle a la mujer un lugar en el
círculo del poder, esa misma ideología, desplazando la mirada
de la zona genital a la jaula del los sentidos, es capaz de encontrar rasgos faciales y mejor aún ausencia/ presencia de la razón
como índice de la inclusión o exclusión del poder. Fue la
capacidad de ser "racional", es decir de articular en más de un
nivel el lenguaje del grupo dominante, lo que se puso en juego
inmediatamente después de la llegada de los europeos al
Nuevo Mundo. (40)

[The rhetoric of sexual oppression finds its parallel in the
rhetoric of racial oppression, or Rhetoric of Oppression that
has been practiced throughout history against many and varied groups. If patriarchal ideology is based upon the pres-
ence/absence of sex organs in order to deny women a place
within the circle of power, that same ideology, shifting its
gaze from the genital zone to the sensorial cage, is capable of
finding facial features, or better yet, the absence/presence of
reason as an index of inclusion or exclusion from power. It
was the capacity of being "rational," of being able to articulate at different levels the language of the dominant group,
that came into play inmediately after the arrival of Europeans
to the New World.]

Puertorriqueña writers do not recognize the divisive lines between
the oppression of women and the political oppression of the island. For
them, the colonial situation of Puerto Rico, the discrimination against
Puerto Ricans in the United States who, in spite of their American citizenship guaranteed by the Jones Law in 1917, are treated as second-
class citizens, and the subordination of the Hispanic women to patriarchal systems and values, are all expressions of socially and politically

oppressive systems. The previous chapter, for example, examines the "Letter to a compañero," in which Aurora Levins Morales denounces the *compañero*'s demagogy of liberation of the island while exploiting women for his own personal gain. Esmeralda Santiago, on the other hand, writes about the anxiety of growing up with contradictory notions of womanhood and gender roles. Sandra María Esteves believes that Puerto Rican women writers in the United States favor both "the autonomy of the nation of Puerto Rico" and "the autonomy of men and women throughout the world" ("Feminist" 175).

The Puerto Rican scholar Efraín Barradas proposes that most *Nuyorican* poets are "heretics" or "myth-creators."[10] In delving into issues of national and cultural identity, a common preoccupation, Puerto Rican writers in the United States seem to be uncomfortable with the cultural notions from the island and reject those imposed from the out- side by Americans. Their reaction, according to Barradas, is either "de apoyo o negación, de aceptación o crítica, ante unos mitos culturales en los cuales creen encontrar su esencia colectiva" ("of support or negation, of acceptance or criticism of cultural myths in which they think they can find their collective essence" 51). In other words, the *Nuyorican* poets might reject the traditional notions of "*puertor-riqueñidad*," and hence be heretics; or they might embrace and elaborate in their poetry the myth of the "island paradise." A third possibility emerges from Barradas' categorization: the heretic/myth-creator, the poet who rejects the traditional discourse of national definition and "invents" stories of political resistance and cultural identity.

Sandra María Esteves distinguishes herself as one of these because of the forcefulness and militancy of her heretical stance. Her works reject both the traditional literary images of the colonization of the island and the popular rhetoric of liberation. While Rosario Morales and Aurora Levins Morales want to sew their own revolution, Esteves raises a cry for freedom using *congas*, *timbales*, and *bongoses*. She stands heretically against the myths of redemption of the Catholic Church, imposed by the Spanish conquest, and searches Afro-Caribbean beliefs for a cosmogony of nature where humans can live in harmony with all creatures. Declan Kiberd believes that "the struggle for self-definition is conducted within language" (11). Thus, it is within the bar notes of musical language and prayers to the orishas that Sandra María Esteves inscribes a rhethoric of reconstruction, of reinvention, of redefinition. Her poetry rhymes with Puerto Rican rhythms such as *bomba, seis chorreao, danza*; with the Caribbean mambo and cha-cha-cha; with the American blues, soul, and rock n' roll; and with Nuyorican *salsa*. She invokes the Yoruban deities of *santería*, the orishas, who "live through and for the community."[11] From this cacophony of rhythms and communal spirits, Esteves composes a harmonious melody of political discourse that reaches beyond Puerto Rican shores to forge a global sisterhood.

Esteves was born in New York, the daughter of a Dominican mother and Puerto Rican father. Her earliest memories of her mother are of a woman working on her feet all day long in a quilt factory, a job she did for forty-three years without ever missing a day. Esteves' first artistic inclination was painting. Growing up "trapped" in the "institutional environment of a convent for Catholic grammar school girls," she wanted to use colors to "turn grey walls into tropical gardens, the way God had created a universe from darkness in seven days" ("Open Letter" 118). She soon discovered words and music. She became actively involved with the Nuyorican Poets Cafe and the Afro Caribbean Poetry Theater, which she directed for several years. She also cofounded *El grupo*, a protest musical group. Esteves has published three collections of her poetry. *Yerba Buena. Dibujos y Poemas* (*YB* 1980), as the title indicates, combines poems and drawings. A cursory look at some of the titles dedicated to such people as Frantz Fanon, Fidel Castro, and Lolita Lebrón[12] reveals Esteves' acute political awareness. In her second book, *Tropical Rains: A Bilingual Downpour* (*TR* 1984), the drawings disappear but not the intensity of her defiance against the cultural and social expectations of women and her cry for "Puerto Rico Libre" (12). Her most recent collection, *Bluestown Mockingbird Mambo* (*BMM* 1990) takes the notes and sounds from the previous poems and, as suggested by the title, makes them into a melodic thread that gives the book thematic unity.

Raising her "machete" against oppression

Yerba Buena (1980) begins with an imperative to her audience: "Óyeme que mi espíritu habla" ("Listen to me 'cause my spirit is speaking" 3). She needs to share what it told her: that everyone is born to be free. With this proclamation, Esteves opens her first collection of poems and attacks the contradictory reality of slavery and oppression in everyday life. Her voice precedes those of Santiago, Morales, and Levins Morales in denouncing the living and working conditions in New York. Manhattan, "grey" and "bleak" is an "isle of spit and hate"; an "Isle of power houses and discount stores / and bargains traded for blood today / for souls tomorrow" ("Manhattan" *YB* 13). Throughout the poems in this book, Esteves describes "people dying in the streets / in houses suspended in cockroach nightmares / waging chemical warfare with their own brains / in factories chained leg to leg" ("Improvisando" *YB* 16). Contrary to the other writers who try to lock out and protect themselves from the violence in the streets, Esteves frequently refers to it and mourns the death of many young minds that "o.d." on drugs. Even hospitals, such as the "butcher shop" of Lincoln Hospital in the Bronx, where she was born, do not provide treatment or healing for the pain and suffering.

For Esteves, there is not much difference between the economic and social oppression that takes place in the streets and factories of Manhattan and the one endured day in, day out within the four walls of the home. Luz María Umpierre analyzes the treatment of domesticity by Puerto Rican women writers, and believes that Rosario Ferré and Sandra María Esteves distinguish themselves for linking the condition of the domestic woman with that of the island oppressed by the United States ("De la Protesta" 139). In "From the Common Wealth," one of the most accomplished poems of this first collection, the feminine voice uses an astute pun to denounce the political status quo of the island, the free associated state known as "commonwealth," and the position of women as common property, "common wealth." The poem begins by confronting the lover/ partner/ political activist who has relegated her to an intolerable position: "So you want me to be your mistress / and find dignity in a closed room" (*YB* 49). The woman / island rejects the roles of domesticity and sexual objectification: "Understanding what a whore sophistication really is / I reject a service role / a position I've truly hated whenever it was forced upon me". Eliana Ortega believes that the *Taína* Anacaona has come to symbolize the sexual objectification of the Puerto Rican woman.[13] She argues that Puerto Rican woman writers have rescued the ingenuity and power of this historical figure. Esteves ends the poem with the feminine voice reaffirming her identity as subject and reclaiming the authority to self-definition:

> And I am a woman, not a mistress or a whore
> or some anonymous cunt whose initials barely left an impression
> on the foreskin of your nationhood
>
> Y si la patria es una Mujer [And if the nativeland is a Woman]
> then I am also a rebel and a lover of free people
> and will continue looking for friction in empty spaces
> which is the only music I know how to play.

The woman in this poem refuses the traditional Anacaonian myth and will not be reduced to a genital part that begets the Puerto Rican race; she, with an anonymous identity, inspires many a poet and composer on the island. Esteves wants to compose her own music out of "contrary chords and dissonant notes / occasionally surviving in mutilated harmony." The frictions of empty spaces, like the dissonant chords of her poetry, are metaphors of the blank page and the constant creative struggle to inscribe herself through writing.

Esteves is aware of the tension between the etymological and morphological gender of *patria*. The noun comes directly from Latin meaning "fatherland," because of its root *pater* meaning father. Amy Kaminsky insists that the noun is "gendered masculine" because of its etymology but also "because of the emotional, historical, and interpersonal charge it bears" (5). Yet, in Spanish, *la patria* is without question a feminine noun. Esteves appears to recognize the term's dichotomy and decides to appropriate its ambiguity. "*Y si la patria es una Mujer,*" it is no longer, then, the historically passive "island / young maiden," the object of admiration and oppression, but an "I, rebellious woman, lover of freedom," a subject in search of new spaces and new expressions of liberation and affirmation.

Equally in "Who says I can't," the rebel "I" affirms her right to raise her voice in defiance. By repeatedly posing the question "who says?" the female voice seems to challenge social and cultural conventions that insist on not allowing her to "scream," to "be who I am," to "take a stand," to "save my earth," etc. (*YB* 53). She warns that whoever "says I must be . . . sweet . . . soft . . . barefoot . . . & helpless" will receive a response of "RAGE!!! with revenge." There is no subtlety in her rebellion.

The repeated use of the interrogative pronoun "who" is more an expression of defiance, a daring, rather than a request for information. Esteves has learned the lessons of "a tennis racket enforcing the law against every word she spoke in spanish" and "the contradictions of being traded from one 'master' to another, from spanish to english, from the Caribbean to the mainland" (Louis Reyes Rivera, "By Way of" *YB* xv). And she is, indeed, very clear about who the master / oppressor is. The poet can see her mother "walking to the white man's factory / so she could catch sunsets" ("Ahora" *YB* 67). As she questions the irony "of brown men subduing brown men / while the invisible perpetrators go free," she painfully realizes "that when too many rabbits occupy a small space / they will turn on each other and kill" ("Report: for National Record" *YB* 64). From the beginning of the book, the poet warns the reader against a systematic and organized form of oppression: "Now the oppressor has an international program / and we sit precariously within the monster's mechanism / internalizing anguish from comrades" ("From Fanon" *YB* 4). It is important to recognize the layers of hypocrisy within government and social institutions, such as charitable organizations like "the ford foundations of the world / who control the government / which hired the meter maids / . . . / who forever rip us off / and charge us rent for being born" ("Capital" *YB* 83).

As part of the process of colonization, Esteves writes: "we lost identity / assimilating our master's values" ("From Fanon" *YB* 4). Like the Irish, colonized people are convinced that they are deficient in some way and in need of the civilizing influence of the outsider, in this case, the British. Frantz Fanon explains how "the settler" believes "the native" to be "lacking in values" (41). Accordingly, "the customs of the colonized people, their traditions, their myths . . . are the very sign of that poverty of spirit and of their constitutional depravity" (42). After the American invasion of Puerto Rico, U.S. officials, trying to decide the future of the island, insisted that Puerto Ricans were not yet capable of self-determination and self-government. It was decided that a period of "tutelage" was necessary to teach "the children" about democracy.[14] Fifty years later in 1952, it was deemed that "the pupils" had learned enough to be allowed to govern themselves, and the constitution of the Free Associated State established a Puerto Rican government. However, to the present, Puerto Ricans still do not have the power of self-determination.[15]

From the beginning, Puerto Ricans demanding social justice and political independence were perceived by Americans as "ungrateful emotional children" (Morales Carrión 237). Like Aurora Levins Morales' "For Angel, For Vieques," Sandra María Esteves denounces the abuse in prisons where Puerto Ricans are beaten to death: "They killed you / called you slave / . . . we watched them kick your face / and break your neck" ("Eulogy for Martín Pérez" YB 28). The struggle for the independence of Puerto Rico unfortunately has many such bruised faces, many heroes. Among them, Lolita Lebrón stands out. According to Esteves, she is "the warrior, the martyr, the woman who takes on the challenge for the sake of liberation and who refuses to acknowledge defeat" ("Feminist" YB 172). The poet recognizes that Lolita Lebrón might have been "released from your cell / yet prisoner on your island," since the political situation that put her in jail for more than twenty years has not changed at all ("For Lolita Lebrón" YB 33). The poem goes on to ask Lebrón to teach her people, to "Write us books," to "Explain the process," to "Unlock the walls of ignorance," to "Stock the young" with "Visions, alternatives / circles" that will inspire new generations of Puerto Ricans to action.

However, it is the imprisonment of "mind and soul" that seems to concern the author the most. In her poem "Esclavitud" (slavery), Esteves elaborates on the intellectual death that comes from the silencing of her voice (YB 18). The next two poems, "Pienso en los momentos" ("I think about the moments" YB 19) and "Here" speak of "the theft of my isla heritage" as she poignantly depicts the years of living between cultures: "I am two parts / a person / boricua / spic" (YB 20). And to think that she spent years thinking in another language and in a culture that was not hers: "Pienso en los años que pasaron / en cosas inglés y blancas / cosas del pueblo no-tropical / cosas que no eran / de mujer, Latina, Africana, India" ("I think on the years that went by / in things english and white / in things of non-tropical people / things that were not / of Latin, African, Indian, woman" *YB* 19). Like many other Puerto Ricans in the United States, Esteves grew up not knowing about the history of her people. As Fanon and many others have observed, part of the colonization process is to silence and, if possible, erase altogether the culture and history of the colonized people. "The settler," explains Fanon, "makes history and is conscious of making it . . . he constantly refers to the history of his mother country" (51). In her thorough examination of *Gender and Colonialism*, Geraldine Moane points to the threat of "internalized oppression" and its devastating consequences, such as "self hatred, sense of inferiority, helplessness and despair, mutual distrust and hostility, and psychological distress and madness" (20). Nevertheless, she observes, "oppressed groups have developed methods for confronting internalized oppression."

Against this systematic political, economic, social, and cultural menace, Sandra María Esteves astutely develops military strategies for protest. As her poems cry for "Freedom," she invokes the figures of Fanon, Castro, and Lebrón, as well as such contemporary artists as Jesús Papoleto Meléndez, Louis Reyes Rivera, and the Losaida poets, to inspire people to revolution. In his introduction to *Yerba Buena* (pepper mint), Louis Reyes Rivera describes the book as a series of "herbal cantations" with medicinal powers to awaken "the strength we claim and, in having, recognize within ourselves" ("By the way" *YB* xvii). For Esteves, that strength resides in language: "A poem is a simple truth that blows up like a bomb in your head" ("Open Letter" *YB* 120). Thus, she reaches into her cultural past and seeks the "truth" of Julia de Burgos' poetry, which embodies "the hopes and aspirations of emigrating Puerto Ricans" ("Feminist" *YB* 171). "A Julia y a Mí" is a poignant dialogue between the contemporary Nuyorican artist and the poet who was found dead in the streets of New York in 1953. Esteves identifies with Burgos' cry for liberation, but reproaches her because "you let the dragon slay you" (*YB* 50). Unfortunately, things have not changed much: "it is the same world that has not moved / . . . / women still tend fires that men burn" (51). Esteves insists that it is time to do more than just denounce the oppression; it is time to grab the machete and fight. Luz María Umpierre examines the poem in detail and how it responds almost line by line to the poetry of Burgos ("Ansiedad" 139–147). Although they are both combative in tone, according to Umpierre, Esteves' hand becomes a weapon: "my fist is my soul / it cuts into the blood of dragons"; while Burgos' hand only carried the torch: "Contra ti y contra todo lo injusto y lo inhumano, / yo iré en medio de ellas con la *tea* en la mano" (emphasis added; "Against you and against everything unjust and inhuman / I will go in front of them with a *torch* in my hand" 144). Esteves' poem ends with a series of verbs that throw the speaker into action: "Yo vivo! / y grito si me duele la vida / y canto con la gente / y bailo con mis hijas" ("I live / and if life hurts I scream / and I sing with the people / and I dance with my daughters" *YB* 51).

Both writers recognize the parallels between the domestic oppression of women and the colonized situation of Puerto Rico. Yet Burgos, like the poets at the turn of the century, sees in the sea / river the ideal man that will come to rescue her / the island from all iniquities.[16] Esteves, on the other hand, rejects the romantic notions of *patria*: "Nada de ti encuentro / en las esquinas de valores muertos" ("I find nothing of you / in the corners of dead values" "Homeland" *YB* 47). The idyllic island paradise becomes a wounded body crying in defiance: "Isla jardín de lluvia / derramas sangre, . . . / . . . / Isla con voz de trueno / . . . isla trigueña / Isla manos de fuerza" ("Island garden of rain / you spill blood . . . / . . . / Island with voice of thunder / . . . brunette island / Island hand of force" 47). Instead of the "sola tu estrella" (your lone star) in the free sky of Cabán Vale's *danza*, the poet identifies with an isolated enslaved country: "Isla solitaria pearla [sic] / en mi cadena de sufrimiento" ("lonely island pearl / in my chain of suffering" 47) . No longer passively awaiting to be rescued, the thunderous voice proclaims both her racially mixed background and her right to fight for her liberation with her own strong hands.

Tropical Rains: A Bilingual Downpour is a brief shower that comes down with a forceful discourse of rebellion and resistance, hoping to wash away the iniquities of oppression. No drawings are included in this book, only twenty-six poems in English and Spanish, a flood of words that breaks the dikes and, with militancy in its current, raises the levels of revolutionary waters. It is fitting then that the collection starts with "It is raining today," "each droplet" is a "tear," each "contains our history / . . . / of the past / Murdered ancestors" (5). The poem ends with a series of imperative verbs: "give me back," "return," "bathe me," "identify," "invocate," "recreate," "reunite," claiming back the "power" from her "ancestors" and "rituals."

This poem and "Boycott" (*TR* 28) are calls to mobilization and action, echoes of de Diego's "virile," bellicose rebellious spirit. "Boycott" wants to "Mobilize the brothers and sisters" and commands them once again to rise, this time not "against" oppression but to defend the "power" of their cultural identity: "Don't sell your power / Instead produce your power / Reproduce it / . . . / Liberate it / . . . / Advance the Caribbean African identity" (28). "The prize," according to the poem, will be "an island in the crossroad/center."

Like *Yerba Buena*, *Tropical Rains* denounces the oppression that kills her people, whether it is with drugs, hunger, poverty, or despair that drives ultimately to death. The poem "Lil' Pito" tells the story of a five-year-old who falls to his death through a rotten window gate, which the landlord had promised to fix but obviously never did (30–31). It poignantly depicts the indifference of doctors, nurses, security guards, even the landlord, in dealing with the enormous grief of the mother.

Behind the lights and rhythms of a nightclub, Esteves reveals in "Nuyoricos" a world of drugs, death, and suicides (*TR* 10–11). "San Juan is dying butterfly wings," cries out the poet while "Cursing the Yankees for whoring the island." She reminds "Nuevayorquinos" that while they dine at elegant places, "North Americans still bomb Vieques," and that they are closing their eyes to the "slow death torture / Of Espiritu Borinquen" ("Borinquen Spirit" 11). Like "Boycott," "Nuyoricos" ends with a call to rebellion: "Despoja! / . . . / Sensual liberación / Libre Huracan, fist, puñio pegao [sic] / . . . / Levanta / Despierta / Camina libre / . . . / Despoja!" ("Strip! / . . . / Sensual liberation / Huracan Free, fist, sticky fist / . . . / Get up / Wake up / Walk free / . . . / Strip!" 11). Verbs in the command form are frequent in the poems of *Tropical Rains*. Although a short collection, the frequent use of the imperative adds to the intensity and the urgency of Esteves' rebellious voice. Like Morales and Levins Morales, Esteves urges the reader to strip off the binding clothes of oppression and to step into a sensuous dance toward freedom.

The political struggle goes hand in hand with sexual liberation. "Transference" echoes the warnings and defying tone of "From the Commonwealth" from the previous collection. Here, the female voice warns her lover once again not to expect her to conform to traditional roles: "Don't come to me with expectations / Of who you think I should be" ("Transference" *TR* 14). The poem follows with the anaphora, "I am not your" and a list of relational, social, even political functions: "your mother," "your sister," "your girlfriend," "secretary," "judge," "colonizer," etc. It concludes by asking for the "chance to be / Myself and create symphonies" and invites him to "a dialogue of we." (15).

Like Esmeralda Santiago, Esteves also feels caught between two cultures, "A once removed Borinqueña" ("Puerto Rico, I" *TR* 25). In the first half of the poem, the poet poignantly depicts the romantic longing of the Nuyoricans "to smell your turquoise beach" in contrast with the "stench" of her everyday surroundings. Yet, in spite of her idyllic notions of *patria,* Esteves harbors feelings of alienation from the island: "How you tried to deny me / Said I was not yours." It is not uncommon for Puerto Ricans on the island to ridicule and reject outright those living on the continent because they have been "Americanized," as Santiago is accused by her own mother. Unfortunately, short stories like "Pollito Chicken" by Ana Lydia Vega have helped promote a caricature of the "Nuyorican." Thus, Puerto Ricans in the United States, like many other immigrants, feel that, in spite of their citizenship, they are not fully American, while they are told by those on the island that they are not really *Boricuas* either!

"Not Neither" continues to evoke these feelings of ambivalence and ambiguity already examined in *When I Was Puerto Rican*: "Being Puertorriqueña Americana / Born in the Bronx, not really jíbara / . . . But yet, not Gringa either" (*TR* 26). The frequent use of conjunctions such as "but yet," "ni . . . ni" ("neither . . . nor"), "y" ("and"), both in English and Spanish, calls attention to the place of those brief linguistic forms which are supposed to "join together," to link two clauses.

Except here, the link fails to be established, only to be left in that space of cultural limbo: "We defy translation / Ni tengo nombre / Nameless, we are a whole culture once removed." Once again, it is the connection with the past, in this case the blood spilled for "the independant star" by "Lolita" Lebrón and many others in "Daily transfusions into the river of La Sangre Viva" ("The Blood Alive").

Six years later, with the publication of *Bluestown Mockingbird Mambo,* the discordant notes of previous poems, such as "From the Common Wealth" (*YB* 49), become a thematic motif that keeps the beat throughout the book, as indicated by the title. One by one, the poems in this collection become a manifesto of social activism and "sisterhood" awareness that defies racial, economic, and political boundaries. Sandra María Esteves recognizes that the strangling arms of social and economic oppression extend far beyond the island of Manhattan.

From the beginning, the text establishes the commonplace oppression of women. One of the major criticisms of the feminist movement has been its narrow concern with the issues of mainly white, upper-middle-class women. bell hooks, for example, discusses the problematic of the feminist movement and its ideology and the need for a more inclusive political struggle against racial, gender, economic, and religious oppression.[17] Chandra T. Mohanty, on the other hand, warns against the "homogenization and systematization of the oppression of women in the third world" ("Under" 54). Like Morales and Levins Morales, Esteves sees the need for a global sisterhood that will fight against all forms of oppression. After all, she reminds Luz María Umpierre and others in "So Your Name Isn't María Cristina," "We all get the same kick in the ass" (*BMM* 33). As a poet and as a woman, it is important to understand the various ways that repressive systems operate throughout the world: "Discovering new meanings for old worlds / listed in the encyclopedia of colonialism. / Each day becoming reference volumes, / forming bridges of correspondence from old to new worlds" (32). As "one Borinqueña within our universal identity," the important thing is that she "watched, and studied, and learned, / awakening into womanhood" (33). Armed with an understanding of colonial government and its manifestations throughout the world, women can begin to fight back.

Her verses lament and mourn the suffering of oppression, whether it takes place in "South Africa, New York, / South Bronx, Soweto, Harlem, East Harlem, Namibia, / Lower East Side, Sharpville, Williamsburg, Watts, Johannesburg" ("Fighting Demons" *BMM* 65). "What is the difference between here and there?" Esteves demands to know:

What is the difference in the name of the bank
that funds the weapons of racism?
That suppresses nations of builders into limbo / drug / depression / regression, oppression on a master scale? (65–66)

On the one hand, there are cities ravished by drugs, "watching pushers / pushing nightmares into their dreams" "While in Guatemala / fifty thousand dreams are shattered / . . . / produced by slaves of the neonazichristianrepublicanstates" ("Love Affair With A Welfare Hotel" *BMM* 41).

Esteves is not trying to establish a hierarchy of oppression; on the contrary, the masters may have different faces, but their imperialist and/or fascist features are painfully familiar. If "Common Wealth" denounces the colonization of Puerto Rico by the United States, "Who is Going to Tell Me?" accuses Spain of the same kind of sexual and economic exploitation: "España, golden father of my ancestors, / who captured my mother as slave, stripped her naked, / plowed treasures from her shores" (*BMM* 57). Barradas observes correctly how in this poem, Spain, a feminine noun in Spanish, is depicted as the masculine father, with aggressive and imperialist traits (171). Although the faces and the accents may differ, the oppression and exploitation throughout the centuries taste bitterly the same.

Esteves continues to develop motifs introduced ten years earlier. Like Aurora Levins Morales, she, too, writes a letter, this time to Congress, denouncing the enormous military buildup. How many people could be fed with "just one space flight," she asks in her "Open Memo to the Congressional Appropriations Committee and the Military Department of Defense" (*BMM* 61). "What if we could exchange an M-1 rifle for a solar reflector / so that our building could have heat all the time," or what about "a decommissioned aircraft carrier to relieve tight housing problems," continues the inquiry. The sender, "The People of the Rest of the World," knows too well that, as the "rest," the other, the outsider, they are not "in" the committee with the power of decision-making that ultimately impacts them. In "Gringolandia," one of the last poems in the book, Esteves criticizes the imperialist and arrogant demagoguery of intervention proclaimed by "north american intellectuals" (*BMM* 72). She denounces how they use language and "brutalize communication," "commanding the copywright [sic] of thought communication / with presumptuous ownership." At the same time, the poet reminds the reader that there is an alternative discourse of fighting and strength: "How I love to listen. / Remind myself there is more to the world. / The whole of it. / The multinational ethnicity of it. / . . . / Then establish the rhythm of counterbalance / the offbeat note of discovery at the crossroads / where montuno comes alive" (72).

Stepping into rebellious movements

While Rosario Morales and Aurora Levins Morales manipulate liquids into metaphors of rebellion, Sandra María Esteves plays with different beats to compose new rhythms and dances that will step out of the oppressive circle. While Irish writers use language to "invent" an Ireland of their own, Esteves taps the rhythms of *salsa, guaguancó,* blues, jazz, mambo, rumba, *bomba, décimas,* rock'n roll, soul, and *cha-cha-cha* in order to find an alternative discourse of resistance. In *Listening to Salsa,* Frances Aparicio eloquently discusses how music becomes a locus of the sexual and racial biases of a society. She points to the European origins of *danza* and the adoption of this dance not only for the Puerto Rican national anthem but also as the island's national dance. On the other hand, *bomba* and *plena,* popular rhythms of the African population on the island, are dismissed by writers such as Manuel Alonso who, while living in Spain, pretends to give a complete portrait of Puerto Rican customs and traditions of the nineteenth century. In addition, Aparicio points out that musicians playing instruments that were not of European origin would get arrested.

With its origins in New York, Aparicio identifies salsa as "the music of the immigrant and the urban working class. It is also the music produced mostly by black and mulatto musicians" (81). The critic goes on to explain the importance that music, specifically salsa, has for the Puerto Rican migrant:

> The repeated melodies, rhythms, riffs, and instrumentation provide a sense of familiarity to the displaced community of listeners and an auditive, sensorial instance for reconstructing the cultural self and collective memory. . . . As transitory as this experience may be, it counteracts the colonialist fragmentations with the past, with nation and homeland. (90)

With the repetition of different beats, Esteves begins a dance of rebellion against the colonization of her country, her culture, her body. The poetic incantations of *Yerba Buena* set out on a search for the appropriate pitch that will carry out her defiantly militant message. The same poem, "Óyeme que mi espíritu habla," that begins by claiming her right to speak and to be heard, also ends by proclaiming her right to movement: "Y mi espíritu baila mucho aquí / en un ambiente colectivo" ("And my spirit dances a lot here / in a collective environment" *YB* 3). Likewise in "Who says I can't," she challenges anyone who dares to tell her she can't "speak my language / in my rhythm" dance or "play my drums any time of the day" (*YB* 53).

Her mind is constantly "beating," searching for sounds of universal comprehension. The poet recognizes the universality of music and its soothing and healing effect: "Weave us a song for our bodies to sing / a song of many threads / that will dance with the color of our people and cover us with the warmth of peace" ("Weaver" *YB* 23). In "I am looking," she searches for the center, for the "womb," for the core of her being, where she ultimately finds "vibrating music" (24).

The second part of the first collection of poems, appropriately titled "Marcando Quinto" ("Marking the Beat"), includes several poems that speak of the search for the harmony and resonance of different rhythms and sounds, "not one isolated beat" ("Fill my world with music" *YB* 41). She rejects the passivity and docility of "Ay benditos" (Oh, poor me, bless me) for sounds that will "wake me up / and work me out." "Windchimes" seeks in nature the reconstruction of both a national and individual identity that has long been silenced by the dominant culture. The speaker wants to go "back into time / before the colonizers came / and stole away the land / before the yankee erased our names" (*YB* 60).

She is "trying to find you / with words that are eyes / and eyes that are sounds." Only then, with the "melodic sighs" of "rainfall," of "roses blooming," of "windchimes," of "rivers flowing," and of "cascading waterfalls" can she reinvent not only herself but her island.

Music also becomes a locus for the struggle against oppression. In "Some people are about Jam" is a moving elegy to a man "who tried to jam on the subway / the police arrested him for disorderly conduct" (*YB* 42). The man no longer jams "because he is dead," but many others continue to do so, "hoping that people would follow his example" in establishing a community of cultural reaffirmation (43). The verses of "Canción de Martín Tito Pérez" seek in the rhythm of *guaguancó* some kind of redemption for the people ravaged by drugs, by hunger, by poverty. In response to the rhetoric of sexual and political oppression of the lover in "From the Common Wealth," the speaker proclaims ". . . I too am music / the sum total of contrary chords and dissonant notes / . . . / and will continue looking for friction in empty spaces / which is the only music I know how to play" (*YB* 49). Ultimately, Esteves insists that Puerto Ricans should "fight for the land with *machetes* and songs" ("Take the hearts of children" *YB* 77) or that "we take the hammers in our hands / we build / a place called home" ("A pile of wood" *YB* 90).

If *Yerba Buena* is a search for sounds of rebellion, *Tropical Rains* begins to pour them out. The first poem in the book convokes an "Areyto," an ancient Taíno ceremony in order to get "back my rituals," which will allow her to reconnect with "my ancestors who have existed suppressed" ("It is raining today" *TR* 5). To this celebration, the book extends an invitation to musicians and poets to bring their "conga," "maracas," "timbales," "bajo," to play the "octaves" of dissonant and rebellious notes that will ultimately provide an "escape from the madness" ("If words could be" *TR* 34). As in the *Bible*, Esteves goes to the origin of the universe, except this time the Word is not at the center of it, but sound:

In the beginning was the sound
Like the universe exploding
It came, took form, gave life
And was called Conga. ("In the beginning" *TR* 6)

And the Conga and the Quinto begin a new creation, a new Edenic landscape, where instead of fruits and animals of sin, there is an abundance of "Maracas y Claves / Chéquere y Timbales" that proclaim the power of music, of people, of racial identity.

As Frances Aparicio suggests, music becomes the "medium" that allows Esteves to reconnect with her Afro-Caribbean heritage. Like many other Latino writers in the States and Puerto Ricans on the island, Esteves reacts against Hispanophilia by identifying herself with her Afro-Caribbean roots. Efraín Barradas calls this process one of "*recaribeñización*."[18] In Esteves' case, Barradas observes, she seems to reject anything Spanish (i.e., related to Spain), and insists on "asociaciones" ("associations") with anything and everything that *is not* Spanish, *not* European, *not* white.

In "Puerto Rico, I," the "I" of "A once removed Borinqueña" claims back her "black mother who teaches" her "There exists only music / In light and shade" (*TR* 25). "Dame mi número" ("Give me my number") once again echoes the poetry of Julia de Burgos, specifically a poem by the same title (*El mar* 53–54). Instead of de Burgos' pessimistic tone begging to die, Esteves' poem is a loud demand, a defiant reclamation of her ancestry, her culture. With the repetition of the imperative "Dame" ("Give me") at the beginning of every stanza, the poet presents a catalogue of the instruments (i.e., *conga, clave, maracas, bongoses, campana*), the rhythms (*décima, danza, bomba, cha-cha-cha, bolero*, rock n'roll, disco, *guaguancó*, blues, and *salsa* soul), and elements of *santería* (santos de palo, agua buena, orishas, baños de flores) that she demands in order to live because they are "mi cultura y mi identidad / mis sonidos caribbeños[sic] y costumbres antillanos" ("my culture and my identity / my Caribbean sounds and my Antillean costumes" *TR* 29). She invokes the musicians that inspire many of these rhythms: Willie Colón, Ismael Rivera, Celia Cruz, El Gran Combo, los Pleneros de la Ciento-Diez. To be devoid of these, to be robbed of these means nihilism: "Y si no puedo vivirlo / Bueno, entonces, no quiero nada más" ("And, if I cannot live it / Well, then, I do not want anything else" 29).

Ultimately, music carries with it the rumbles of rebellion. "Nuyoricos, From the Nuyorican Poets Cafe" depicts a common scene in a nightclub with the lights, the glitter, even the drugs; but above all it carries the sounds of Esteves' contemporary poets, such as Tato Laviera, Miguel Algarín, Lucky Cienfuegos, and others. She also invokes the spirit of the Puerto Rican comedian Freddy Prinze and asks him to "return with machete in hand" while "Cursing the yankees for whoring the island" (*TR* 11). The poem ends with a list of verbs in command form, reminiscent of de Diego's poem, that exhort the reader to rise up. Previously in the poem "Yerba Buena," Esteves uses the format of a song with the repetition of a chorus to invoke the spirits of pro-independence activists, such as Ramón Emeterio Betances and Pedro Albizu Campos. It is almost as if the poet wants to conjure the spirits of her ancestors to rise and lead everyone into revolution (*TR* 8–9).

Indeed, the poem "Candumbé" describes a "ceremony" of preparation for rebellion:

> We chase dragons at noon
> machete the paths where their footprints lie
>
> . . . .
> We drink their blood of dreams
> digest the magic
> shit out the waste
> absorbe [sic] the nourishment. (*TR* 27)

Although at times readers shy away from the militant tone of Sandra María Esteves' poetry, they should understand that more than advocating violence, she is searching for a break from the cycle of oppression and an alternative path to world harmony. The last poem in the 1984 collection speaks of the responsibilities of a poet. The writer of poetry should be a speaker of the truth and is in charge of "nourishing the hope, seed and future of the eagle" ("To be the poet" *TR* 35). Ultimately, the poet is a composer of "Healing songs for its nation divided."

On the other hand, *Bluestown Mockingbird Mambo* introduces the metaphor of the poet as "architect," "deciphering cosmic symphonies" ("Affirmation #2, There is a Poet Inside You" 37). Armed with the familiar sounds of the "soneo," the "clave," and the "conga quinteando," Esteves wants to draw a new landscape "the way Betty Carter can deliver a blues" ("I want to paint" *BMM* 20–21). Her canvas is not only filled with "trees, rivers, thunderstorms, mountains," but also with "tunes," "poems," and "songs." To paint, to create, is to "Be / the sounds that make me come alive, / . . . / bringing forth the birth of our own voices, / bursting with melodies of our own songs." And like God / the creator on the seventh day of the creation, she too wants to sit back and "listen to them . . . / . . . as they sing."

The musical notes of a mambo make up the palette that traces the graceful movements of Carlos y Rebecca on the dance floor "As coconuts fall from imaginary palm trees / ancient to Borinquen souls" ("Mambo Love Poem" *BMM* 24). To the beat of African drums, "two become one in the land of salsa" and they are transformed into "jíbaros in eagle wings." As the lovers step in and out of "palm trees," "the rooftops of El Barrio," a "fiery desert" evoked by African congas, "Shangó—Cabio Sile—enters their bodies, / they flow magically into one" (25). This mystical experience of being possessed by a spirit, typical of *santería*, transcends the gray walls of El Barrio, the voluptuous shores of the island, and the distant coastline of Africa, to reconnect the lovers in a collective "circle of tropical love."

While Irish writers borrowed from the Cuchulain legend to reconstruct a non-Anglo-Saxon Ireland (Kiberd 25), Esteves resorts to the musical registers of the bomba, plena, salsa, blues, and jazz that emerged from marginalized nonwhite communities both on the island and in the United States to compose symphonies of global force. In "Who is going to tell me?" she acknowledges the cultural heritage from both Spain and Africa: "Whose court inspired our danzón, corrido, and gracious bomba" that originated from the "African drumbeat" (*BMM* 57). "What melodies will evolve from our mixings?" ponders the poet. Will her cultural "mettiságe" find expression in the cacophony of such disparate sounds?

The artist / composer continues to search for the "occult melodies from our work songs" that will carry her, her sisters, her brothers, beyond "our nearsighted vision" "into the voluminous ocean, spread / across the seven seas," ("From the Ferrybank" *BMM* 77–78). In "Resurrections," dancing, even if it is with our "pained" exploited bodies, might provide "cures for self and the world's diseases" (*BMM* 79). The poem insists that we will continue on this maddening quest, "desperate for the naked sounds" that will allow us to "partake in the treasured secrets of our ancestors." In order to rise and achieve this transcendental moment of communion with the world, the poet invokes the assistance of Nina Simone, Celia Cruz, Billy Holiday, Bessie (Smith), Aretha Franklin, La Lupe, Diana and the Supremes, Ronnie Scepter, Gladys Knight, and Roberta Flack—her "Sistas all the way" ("Sistas" *BMM* 19).

Inventing a new paradise

It is this sense of community that attracts many to the practice of *santería*. There is a "reciprocity between community and spirit" (Fernández Olmos et al. 3). Miguel Barnet explains how this religion "is linked to the notion of family":

> Out of this system of tribal or family lineage emerges a religious brotherhood involving a godfather and godchildren in a kinship that transcends blood connections to form an all-inclusive and compact horizontal lineage. . . . The godmother or godfather becomes mother or father of a brood of children, forming a group popularly known as a *línea de santo*, a line or lineage of initiates. (81)

La línea de santo or line of the saint has nothing to do with blood lineage but with communal bonds established through the ceremony of baptism. As a group, they are under the protection of an *orisha,* a deity with some specific attribute. The orisha emerges at a moment of violent emotional crisis during which its concrete being disappears, leaving behind the *aché,* "power in a state of pure energy" (82). During ceremonies that combine music and dancing, the *padrino* ("godfather") and/or the initiates can be "mounted" like a "horse" and be possessed by one of the deities. At that moment, describes Barnet, "the possessed can dance or sing with formidable virtuosity" (86). Through these communal rites, people find protection and a spirit of tolerance in Santería, also known as the *Regla de Ocha* or religious system of the Ocha.

Esteves invokes the *aché* of her Afro-Caribbean ancestors as she "invents" her *patria* and tears apart old myths. The "herbal incantations" of *Yerbabuena* introduce the seeds of metaphorical subversions of traditional religious discourse. In the poem "Oración" (prayer), the reader may recognize the familiar words of the "Hail Mary" only to realize immediately that the invocation is addressed to "Changó y Oshún / Obatalá y Ogún / Yemayá, Elegua y Oya" (*YB* 61).[19] It is a prayer for "the crucified christians"; "May we, the third world, first world brothers and sisters / be delivered from democracy's prisons" (61). According to Barradas, this is not merely a substitution of one religion for another, but a deliberate "rechazo de las ideas y los ideales de la sociedad opresora por los oprimidos" ("a rejection by the oppressed of the ideas and ideals of an oppressive society" 160). Frantz Fanon warns that "the Church in the colonies is the white people's Church" (42). Evangelization and the conversion to Catholicism were an integral part of the conquest and colonization of Latin American countries by Spain. Faced with this "repressive imposition of the Catholic Church," explains Miguel Barnet, "African blacks set into motion a most complex sociological phenomena when they syncretized their divinities [the orishas] with the Catholic saints" (87). Like her Caribbean ancestors, Esteves rejects the myths imposed by institutionalized religion and seeks both spiritual and cultural syncretism. "The ignorant laugh" suggests that religious eclecticism echoes the multiethnicity of her ancestry. Why not believe, asks the poet, "in magic / witchcraft / brujería / la religión / santería / meditation / chanting / astrology (*YB* 38)," which ultimately reflect the "many colors" of life? Esteves reaches into nature to dig out her roots that will free her creativity and imagination in her poem "Fertile woman is moon": "Is ocean of our father's land / . . . / Tree digging roots deep / Into the soil of Obatala / . . . / Creator of destiny / . . . / With natural creativity / Motion of majesty" (*YB* 69). There is nothing forced in this cosmogony; woman communes with the elements (be it ocean, fire, thunder, sky), and her fertility finds expression with an ease and simplicity that is ultimately majestic.

It is amidst the baptismal waters of *Tropical Rains* where Esteves begins to explore the rituals of her ancestors, both Taínos and Africans, in order to construct a new paradise of freedom. In the first poem, "It is raining today," the poet demands to "Give me back my rituals / . . .

/ Recreate the circle of the Ayreto [sic]" so that the "candles of wisdom" of her ancestry will speak forever. *Areyto* was a Taíno ceremony of religious and secular significance. Similarly, she invokes the Afro-Caribbean ceremony of "Candumbé" in the poem by the same name. Like the *areyto, candumbé* combines music and dancing. For Esteves, the ceremony will allow "to merge greatness of being / with the spirit of the people" (*TR* 27). It is in this communion with the past, that "We drink their blood of dreams / digest the magic / shit out the waste / absorb the nourishment" that will feed the revolutionary spirit.

If the "Word" is at the core of Catholic Messianic beliefs, sound is at the center of the Esteves' cosmogony. "In the beginning was the sound" ("In the beginning" *TR* 6). In this, the second poem, a musical "genesis" of Esteves' opus, "música," "gente," and "raza" (music, people, and race) was created, and "So it was written" (6). Against biblical genealogies that trace Christian lineage all the way back to Abraham and David, the poem "Boricua" establishes a descendency from pharaoh, witch doctors, *espiritistas,* warlords, etc. (*TR* 24). Previously in the poem/chant "Yerba Buena," the poet ends by establishing her descent from Puerto Rican patriots and poets, such as Pedro Albizu Campos, Ramón Emeterio Betances, and Julia de Burgos, as well as from African "orishas" "De Oya, Ochún y Yemayá / De Elegua, Changó y Obatala" (*TR* 9). From all of them, Esteves can proclaim the divine within humanity. At other times, she invokes a blessing from "Ra, Sun, Amen, Allah, Alam" to make her one with nature ("Alam, Allah, Blessing" *TR* 17).

Esteves recognizes the responsibility of the poet, not only as myth-creator and/or heretic, as Barradas would say, but as a warrior with divine powers who can redeem oppressed people. Although she had introduced this motif before, it is in the last poem of *Tropical Rains,* "To Be the Poet" where she equates the artist with the ultimate deity of creation: "Mother Earth" (35). Like the Holy Grail, "To be the poet is to be / The crystal goblet of burning truth," carrying "Healing songs for its nation divided." The poet is to be a listener, an informant, a wanderer, a creator, but above all, a healer who soothes the "abused child" and brings "resolving calm that follows the path of the hurricane."

Ultimately, it is amidst the songs of *Bluestown Mockingbird Mambo* that Sandra María Esteves is fully possessed by the *aché* of her rebellious and subversive spirit. First, the traditional Bible stories and history as construed by the white dominant culture have to be challenged:

And within these verses is history,
since before the age of many-hued-man,
even before that ol' wives' tale 'bout some woman
an' some man's rib.
I tell you, these folkloric pictures must be questioned.
("Affirmations #1, Life Shopping in Ma Becksy's Deli"
BMM 12)

Second, the assistance of her "Sistas" is invoked to provide the strength of their musical notes "always by her side, no matter what" (*BMM* 19). The poet goes on a quest, "A gradual rise towards a turbulent horizon. / a sanctuary for strayed eagles" ("This is a Hill that Climbs" *BMM* 38). Instead of the Edenic island of traditional Puerto Rican poetry and songs, Esteves seeks "a canyon cut of stone," "a river which smooths the surface of rock," "a sky of restless motion," "a silent haven," "a rainfall washing fertility dust," "a hill rising from the earth."

The third and final section of the book, appropriately titled "Batarumba Autonomy," referring to the *rumba* and the *bata* (African drums used in ceremonies of initiations in *santería*), beats in celebration of the "baptism" of a new self. The first poem, "Rumba Amiga, Amiga," conjures the *aché* of "mi hermana" [my sister] that fills with hope the entire community: "de familia hasta familia, / de persona hasta persona, / de mujer hasta amiga" [from family to family, / from person to person, / from woman to girlfriend]. At the end, the poem includes a brief reference to typical altars set to the *orishas:* "Tu pasión es un lindo baile / al lado tu mesa blanca / que sirve un trópico fresco / de madamitas y santos" ("Your passion is a pretty dance / next to your white table / that serves a cool tropic / of godmothers and saints" *BMM* 71).

"Padrino" praises the significant role of the godfather within the community. According to the poem, Padrino is charged with interpreting "visions / sent by caring saints," with "Choosing to guide our steep awkward climbing," with "setting our spirits free," and with "causing our rebirth," so that we may "return to the house of our ancestors"

(*BMM* 83). It is again through the rhythms of "pulsating precise cosmic music / vibrations consuming darkness," that we will be able to enter "the mystical playground of our Great Grandfather's garden." "Bautizo" [baptism] might no longer liberate them from the sins of Eden, but it will allow the padrino to initiate his children into the protection of the saints while freeing them "of solid lead shackles" ("Bautizo" *BMM* 84). This poem describes the simple ceremony that takes place on an "Early Brooklyn morning":

> Full of aché
> Babalorisha[20] invokes the ancestors,
> family of one-hundred-thousand names,
> to join this rebirth,
> sing and feast in prodigal victory,
> reaffirming linkage
> to bloodlines woven like luminous veils
> over walls and windows of their souls,
> opening to reveal the precious landscapes
> and inherited panoramas of our connected intelligence.
> (*BMM* 84)

With the crescendo of words such as "invokes," "ancestors," "family," "linkage," "bloodlines," "inherited," and "connected," Sandra María Esteves underlines the urgency for a global sisterhood in a *patria* where the landscape does not include fences, borders, or frontiers. Only then, total communion with the *Regla de Ocha* can be achieved.

In the next to last poem, "Ocha," Esteves sings with elegant poise to this mystical transformation captured in terms of the "metamorphosis of the butterfly" (*BMM* 86). Like the caterpillar in its "sealed coffin, / finding need for its own rebellion, / heaving its liberation song with calculated force," we, too, need to fight against "annihilation in the war of loneliness". We, too, need to stretch our wings "with beauty blazing mantle adorning its back" so that we can begin "invisible, perfumed, / trailing a direct spiral into heaven."

Ultimately it is with words that Esteves begins to tear down the deadly prisons of the colonial ideology and composes a national anthem of cosmic freedom. As she declares in "101st Poem for My Husband," the last entry in *Bluestown Mockingbird Mambo*, "these shallow words / are all I have" (87). Thus, Sandra María Esteves writes incantatory poems that raise a prayer for the liberation of the oppressed masses, for the communion of all "hued souls," and for an Edenic *patria* of free life everlasting.

Notes

1. *Inventing Ireland* (Cambridge: Harvard UP, 1995) 7, 9.

2. *Simon and Schuster's International Dictionary* defines *patria* as "country, native land, fatherland, motherland." In Spanish, it is common to speak of the homeland as *madre patria*, referring to it as a mother. For this reason, "motherland" will be used for *patria*.

3. See his poem "Ausencia" where he writes: "Y si brotas a mi deseo / como espléndido miraje . . . Y yo, patria, que te quiero, / yo que por tu amor deliro, / que lejos de ti suspiro, / que lejos de ti muero. / Tengo celos del que mira / tus alboradas serenas, / del que pisa tus arenas . . ." ("And if conjured by my desire / you appeared as splendid mirage . . . Homeland, I, who loves you / I who suffers in delirium for you / who, far away, longs for you, / who far away for you dies. / I am jealous of whoever looks / at your serene dawns, / of whoever steps on your sand . . .") 10.

4. In this sense, Gautier Benítez echoes the romantic movement and the poetry of Gustavo Adolfo Bécquer in Spain.

5. The image of a lamb, symbol of St. John [*San Juan*] lies at the center of the Puerto Rican coat of arms (San Juan used to be the name of the island, and Puerto Rico referred to the port in the capital city). For many, the lamb represents the passivity and docility of the island's inhabitants. Frustrated with that association, De Diego rejects it and invokes the bull, a significant component of the agricultural industry which sustained the economy at the time.

6. English version by Aparicio in *Listening to Salsa*, 21–23.

7. English version of "Río Grande de Loíza" included in Santiago, 43–44.

8. English version by Aparicio in *Listening to Salsa*, 20–21.

9. "The Sons of La Malinche," *The Labyrinth of Solitude and The Other Mexico. Return to the Labyrinth of Solitude. Mexico and the United States. The Philanthropic Ogre*, translated by Lysander Kemp (New York: Grove Press, 1985), 86.

10. See his essay, "Herejes y mitificadores: Sobre poetas puertorriqueños en los Estados Unidos," *Partes de un todo*, 41–57.

11. In their introduction to *Sacred Possessions: Vodou, Santería, Obeah, and the Caribbean*, Fernández Olmos and Paravisini-Gerbet explain how both

the practices of Vodou and Santería "are group phenomena" (6). In his chapter, "La Regla de Ocha: The Religious System of Santería," Miguel Barnet insists on this communal aspect as he describes the "religious brotherhood involving a godfather and godchildren in a kinship that transcends blood connections to form an all-inclusive and compact horizontal lineage," 81.

12. In 1954, Lolita Lebrón, together with three other militant members of the National Party, opened fire from the gallery of the House of Representatives. They were all sentenced to prison and became instant heroes of the pro-independence movement. They were pardoned by President Jimmy Carter in 1979 (*U.S. News & World Report*, September 17, 1979, 56).

13. Ortega quotes the chronicles of Fernández de Oviedo and, more recently, the songs of Tito Curet Alonso and Cheo Feliciano to demonstrate the diminution and sexual objectification of the historical figure of the *Taína* woman. ("Poetic Discourse" 122–135).

14. See Arturo Morales Carrión's historical review of the development of tutelage in his book, *Puerto Rico: A Political and Cultural History* (New York: W.W. Norton & Co., 1983), 144–172.

15. In spite of all the highly publicized plebiscites that have taken place on the island during the nineties, it is up to the U.S. Congress to decide whether Puerto Rico becomes a state or a free nation.

16. In his introduction to the complete works of Julia de Burgos, José Emilio González discusses the significance of the recurrent image of man-sea-river (*Obra Poética*, comp. Consuelo Burgos y Juan Bautista Pagán, San Juan: Instituto de Cultura Puertorriqueña, 1961).

17. See *Feminist Theory: From Margin to Center* (Boston: South End Press, 1984).

18. *Partes*, 168–171.

19. These are all *orishas*, deities of *santería* based upon "the Yoruba pantheon of Nigeria as identified with their corresponding Catholic saints" (Glossary 288). For a detailed analyses of Afro-Caribbean religions, see *Sacred Possessions. Vodou, Santería, Obeah, and the Caribbean*, edited by Margarite Fernández Olmos and Lizabeth Paravisini-Gebert (New Brunswick: Rutgers UP, 1997).

20. A priest or priestess who presides over ceremonies of initiations and liturgies of Santería.

Chapter 5
"I Just Met a Girl Named María": Luz María Umpierre-Herrera and the Subversion of Sexual/Cultural Stereotypes

On a bus in Oxford, a young man saw Judith Ortiz Cofer, walked up to her, dropped to his knees, and began to sing "María" from *West Side Story* (*Latin* 148). On another occasion, as she was trying to return to her hotel room, she was blocked by the father of a bride whose reception was taking place there. Obviously intoxicated, the man exclaimed, "Evita," and proceeded to sing "Don't Cry for Me Argentina" (*Latin* 151–152). Encouraged by the round of applause from his daughter and friends, he next sang "La Bamba." But this time, the lyrics were changed to something about María, and the end of each stanza rhymed with gonorrhea. Unfortunately, these incidents are not an oddity but are commonplace in our society, as they reveal stereotypes associated with a person's appearance and/or ethnic background.

Ortiz Cofer feels fortunate that her education and fairness of skin have saved her for the most part from such incidents. On the other hand, she also believes that for many Hispanic women, career opportunities are limited: societal expectations prescribe that they will become either a hardworking domestic with a family to support or a prostitute. As Umpierre-Herrera points out in her poem, "La Receta" ("The Recipe"), hot, moody, and temperamental are assumed to be the basic "ingredients" of Hispanic women.

Luz María Umpierre-Herrera came to the United States in the mid-seventies to conduct graduate studies at Bryn Mawr University in Pennsylvania. Aside from seeking professional growth, she was hoping to find refuge from a suffocating, authoritarian father and Puerto

Rican oppression of women, especially of lesbians.[1] Always an out-spoken child, always a maverick, she was not ready for the onslaught of racial, ethnic, and sexual discrimination to be encountered in what was supposed to be *"el país de las maravillas"* ("wonderland"), the land of freedom and opportunities. Even within the world of academe, the idea of a Puerto Rican doing graduate work was unheard of. Not only were her intellectual capabilities questioned but her linguistic skills as well. After all, she did not speak "Castilian Spanish." As a result of these challenges, Umpierre-Herrera's poetry is controversial for its razor-sharp verses and her attacks against everything and every-one that obstructs her progress down the "yellow brick road." In her distinct, deliciously rebellious style, she co-opts the discourse of prayers, the law, academe, even children's stories, to tear down the oppressive institutions that are the pillars of American society. In the end, the reader is left with a bouquet of "Margarita Poems" (Daisy Poems) that scents the air with the lyrical tenderness and vulnerability of a woman.

Luz María Umpierre-Herrera's expectations of and disillusion-ment with life in the United States are not unique. With the American invasion of Puerto Rico, the agricultural economy of the island was supplanted by an industrial one. In order to alleviate problems of over-population and rising unemployment, government-sponsored emigra-tion programs were implemented. The loss of their agricultural base coupled with the promises of the lottery and recruitment programs for agribusiness on the continent promoted mythic notions of an American *El Dorado* or Shangrila, the land of opportunities, the land of the free. The reality was that displaced farmers were shipped to the States, where they worked in subhuman conditions. One of the most famous short stories in Puerto Rican literature is "La Carta" (The Letter) by José Luis González. The story is the letter itself written by a young man to his mother to tell about his newfound job in New York, his salary, and his apology for not having sent anything yet because he hasn't had time to go to the better stores to ensure the quality of the products. Finished with the missive, the young man folds the paper, puts it in his pocket, and stands in front of the post office with one hand hidden in his shirt, pretending to be maimed, in order to collect the five cents needed for the stamp. This dichotomy between the misery of the lives of Puerto Rican emigrants and their desperately proud attempts to give hope to their relatives in the island is prevalent in the literature of the forties and fifties.

Equally disappointing has been their odyssey across the sea in search of the civil rights and equality that was denied the island's inhabitants during the colonial rule of Spain. Encouraged by the Jones Act of 1917, which granted American citizenship to Puerto Ricans, many of them came to the United States seeking refuge from the discrimination and oppression they had known under the Spaniards. The memoirs of Bernardo Vega, a cigar worker in New York during the first half of the twentieth century, record the experience of many Puerto Ricans who soon found out they were second-class citizens in the United States, "little brown brothers" in need of "tutelage" (see Andrew Iglesias). Vega cites the newspaper articles at the time waging a campaign that depicted the Puerto Ricans as a primitive tribe, inferior to Anglo-Saxons, with a predisposition to crime and with intellectual deficiencies that rendered them incapable of being educated or holding a job.

The movie *West Side Story* (1961) only helped reinforce these stereotypes. Nicholasa Mohr calls these pernicious and yet persistent images the "María's syndrome," "immortalized in that great American musical classic. . . . Beautiful music, exquisite dancing, the entire production conceived, arranged, choreographed and presented by successful white males" ("Journey" 82–83). To this date, when people hear of Puerto Rico they have images of the popular Broadway musical and its movie rendition with young men in violent gangs and hot-tempered women lifting their skirts as they danced seductively. Esmeralda Santiago describes how people would expect her to break out dancing, like Rita Moreno in the role of Anita, when they found out she was Puerto Rican.

The Women's Liberation Movement of the sixties and seventies also failed in its promise of equal rights for all women. By the end of the seventies, it was obvious that those feminist thinkers were for the most part upper-middle-class white women and that the plight of the poor, Black, Asian, Latina women remained brushed under the rug of white women's manifestos. Lesbianism became "a political response to male aggression" rather than a question of sexuality and sexual rights (Moraga 119–120). With the writings of Audre Lorde, Toni Cade Bambara, Barbara Smith, and bell hooks, the voices of African-American women, many of them lesbians, began to be heard toward the end of the seventies. In 1981, with the encouragement of Barbara Smith and Toni Cade Bambara, Gloria Anzaldúa and Cherríe Moraga published *This Bridge Called My Back: Writings by Radical Women of Color*,[2] a groundbreaking collection of writings by Black, Chicana, Latina, Indian, Asian, and Jewish women proclaiming the commonality of their radicalism and their experiences as "women of color." Almost ten years later, Anzaldúa responded to the need for a sequel to this volume by editing *Making Face, Making Soul. / Haciendo Caras: Creative and Critical Perspectives by Feminists of Color.* The first collection, *This Bridge*, brought attention to the isolation and the silence suffered by "women of color" who also happened to be lesbians. To be a female homosexual is seen by men of color as a betrayal of one's own people. Moraga explains how lesbianism is perceived by Chicanos as a "disease" introduced by white men to undermine the proliferation of the Indian race (*Loving* 105). Similar claims can be made by other minority groups.

Encouraged by her work with *This Bridge,* Moraga published in 1983 *Loving in the War Years*, a collection of journal entries, essays, and poems, which traces the painful journey of a Chicana lesbian, who for the longest time was afraid of words. If spoken, they would become a threat to her, to her family, to her culture. She tried everything to deny who she was, from turning to religion in her teen years, to heterosexuality, and ultimately self-exile in the white community of lesbians, artists, and intellectuals. Moraga examined herself closely in the mirror of her cultural background, that of an Anglo-Saxon father and a Chicana mother. She wrestled with the demons of her heritage: La Malinche and la Virgen de la Guadalupe. Ultimately, she was able to pronounce "*lo que nunca pasó por sus labios*" (what never crossed her lips), an affirmation of her sexuality, her identity as "woman of color," her love for women and her right to be equally loved, her love for her mother, and even the recognition of her own learned patterns of oppression.

Like Anzaldúa and Moraga, Umpierre-Herrera's journey through the murky rivers of silence, marginalization, racism, and sexism has been long and painful. Seeking refuge in the United States from the authoritative figure of her father and the incipient harassment at the school where she was teaching, she only found racial and more sexual discrimination in Pennsylvania for being Puerto Rican and a lesbian. But as she proclaims, she has had long years of experience in speaking up and protecting herself so that "her point of view would not be squelched."[3] Thanks to the sacrifices of her parents, Umpierre-Herrera attended a very prestigious private school in San Juan, where as a poor child, she did not fit in with the daughters of doctors and lawyers. Scholarships facilitated the completion of her bachelor's degree. As she was about to graduate from law school, she decided to go to Bryn Mawr to pursue doctoral studies in Latin American literature.

She then went on to teach at Rutgers University, where she became the first Puerto Rican woman to be granted tenure. Soon after her difficult tenure case, Umpierre-Herrera lent a hand to other women on campus so that they could organize and bring a class-action suit against the university. Labeled a "troublemaker," Rutgers tried to "detenure" her. Umpierre-Herrera became chair of the department of Modern Languages and Intercultural Studies at Western Kentucky University in Bowling Green and later at the SUNY in Brockport, where she again found herself involved in a lawsuit. Throughout her professional career, the labels, the racism, the prejudices, the homophobia have followed her relentlessly.

Growing up with a dominant father, Umpierre-Herrera learned from early childhood to use words to challenge his authority and to defend her own point of view. Words once again would become her refuge and her weapon against the dominating and authoritarian institutions of academe and American society. In 1979 while still a graduate student in Bryn Mawr, Umpierre-Herrera published a short collection of "writings" entitled *Una Puertorriqueña en Penna*. *Penna*, a pun referring to Pennsylvania and to *pena*, the Spanish word for sorrow or pain, immediately suggests in the title the content of the book, the sorrows of a Puerto Rican woman in that state. These poems were incorporated into her next publication, *En el País de las maravillas* (1982, *In Wonderland*). This time there is no pun, just complete sarcasm because what the reader is about to encounter is anything but wonderful.

. . . *Y Otras Desgracias / And Other Misfortunes* . . . came out in 1985 and records the misfortunes generally encountered by women. Inspired by the honesty of Moraga's *Loving in the War Years,* Umpierre-Herrera published *The Margarita Poems* in 1987, in which she records the blooming of her lesbian identity. *For Christine: Poems and One Letter* appeared in 1995 after a terrible lawsuit that left her completely destitute and led to her hospitalization for depression. *For Christine* is a beautiful tribute to the people who helped her survive what she considers "one of the most horrifying experiences" for an academician.

Umpierre-Herrera has also published several books and articles of literary criticism. As a scholar, her writing is deeply rooted in canonical texts and literary theory. In her scholarship, she recognizes the "anxiety of influence" in the works studied. Yet, she utilizes Mallarmé's graphic style, Quevedo's satirical sonnets, Julia de Burgos' imagery, and Virginia Woolf's and Sylvia Plath's anguished tone to raise her accusations against oppression and raze the institutions and the traditions that perpetuate a society in constant tension between the dominant culture and its colonized people.

As a Puerto Rican poet, Umpierre-Herrera recognizes the geography of oppression, the specific location of authoritarian and biased norms. Her initial work pinpoints these infamous sites on a map and traces the roads of rebellious discourse. Once identified, she attacks the racial and sexual stereotypes embedded in cultural iconography and traditional literature. *The Margarita Poems* are a cartography of the female body as the locus for the decolonizing process and the affirmation of an identity that is female, lesbian, poet, survivor— a whole with all its different parts intact.

Alice in Wonderland No More

Historian Eric Hobsbawm noted the fact that living in exile confronts the emigrant with questions about national, cultural, and even individual self-identity that might not have been considered in the homeland. For example, when Jane Doe from the United States travels to another country, her name is no longer sufficient to answer inquiries about her identity. Now, she has to explain her national origin, the purpose of her presence in foreign territory, etc. In the United States, these questions seem to multiply with the bubbles on applications and forms to be filled out. For immigrant cultures, the questions can pose overwhelming conflicts of identity and questions of allegiance. If one fills in the bubble Cuban-American, does that mean one is less Cuban, less American? And for bilingual writers, does the choice of language reveal a political agenda? Judith Ortiz Cofer, like many Latino writers, finds herself having to answer these kinds of questions in her essay, "And Are You a Latina Writer?"

For Puerto Ricans, the politics of geography become excruciatingly painful. In spite of their American citizenship, those still on the island do not have a vote in presidential elections and do not have congressional representation. They have no representation in Congress, aside from a Commissioner-in-Residence in Washington, who has no real power. By the same token, as American citizens, they can move to any place in the United States without any documents, get a license with a new permanent address and register to vote in any state of their residence. Due to the ambiguity of its commonwealth status, Puerto Rico is in both a literal and figurative limbo. Even airlines have a hard time deciding if a trip to the island should be considered a domestic flight or an international one.

At the same time, Puerto Ricans in the States are confronted with a barrage of questions they never had to answer before. Are they citizens? Do they have a Puerto Rican passport? Contrary to forms in Puerto Rico that would never dare to ask for race, religious denomination, etc., they are forced to come up with answers that they often do not have. Where is the bubble for *trigueño*[4]? "I was born a white girl in Puerto Rico but became a brown girl when I came to live in the United States," begins Judith Ortiz Cofer in her essay "The Story of My Body" (*Latin* 135). She examines issues of skin, color, size, and looks as she attempts to convey the bewilderment of a little girl who thought she was pretty, only to start school in New Jersey and to discover a new "hierarchy for popularity": "pretty white girl, pretty Jewish girl, pretty Puerto Rican girl, pretty black girl" (*Latin* 143).

All of a sudden, because of a transcendental process of coloration that apparently takes place in "la guagua aérea" ("the air bus") during their migration, Puerto Ricans become people of color, regardless of the complexion of their skin. In spite of having fair skin like her father, Ortiz Cofer knows that she is a person of color in the States. Likewise, Umpierre-Herrera declares that ever since she arrived in this country, she considers herself a woman of color. Cherríe Moraga chronicles this painful journey of self-identification that for white Americans might seem totally arbitrary and senseless. In a segment of her essay, "The Dying Road to a Nation: A Prayer para un Pueblo" ("A Prayer 'for the People'"), Moraga speaks of the heart-wrenching decision to break her longtime relationship with a white American woman so that she could raise her son as a Chicano (*Loving* 195–213). Although her skin is as white and fair as her father's, she constantly affirms that the faith that sustained her is that of her Mexican-Indian mother. Her partner for eight years cannot comprehend why Moraga "chooses" to be Indian, to proclaim *La Raza* (The Race), to choose not to be white. Moraga calls it "concientización," "a consciousness born of a body that has a shade, a language, a sex, a sexuality, a geography and a history" (203).

Like the term "third world women," "women of color" designates a political alliance between women that suffer oppression in specific ways. Chéla Sandoval summarizes the debates about naming a political sisterhood in her report on the 1981 National Women's Studies Association Conference. At the time, "Women of Color" was the term suggested because it represents "both the nature of our oppression and the basis of our political solidarity."[5] This identification allows for the inclusion of Jewish, Asian, Latin American, African-American, Asian-Pacific, Native-American, and other women who are marginalized, pushed aside by the centers of power, and it speaks for social and political activism against institutionalized racism.

In her analysis of the tensions between feminist studies and third world women, Chandra Talpade Mohanty observes that "racism is often the product of a colonial situation, although it is not limited to it" ("Introduction" 24). Thus, the American invasion of Puerto Rico forced the inhabitants of the island to confront issues of race up until then ignored or previously expressed as questions of social and economic class.[6] The increasing numbers of Puerto Rican migrants to the

United States has only heightened the consciousness of racial prejudice. Although there has always been racism in Puerto Rico, it was never expressed in the physical segregation and violence that took place in the United States.

Luz María Umpierre-Herrera, like Sandra María Esteves, is very much aware of the duality of oppression from both the colonial status of her island and the patriarchal institutions everywhere that insist on controlling a woman's body. As a child, she soon learned to balance herself delicately between two worlds: her modest house in Santurce and the rich private school she attended during the day. But according to Umpierre-Herrera, at least no one questioned her right to be in that school as long as the tuition was being paid and rigorous academic requirements were being met. In Philadelphia, she experienced everything but "brotherly love," and her *pena* finally emerged from the bowers of Bryn Mawr to denounce the geography of "gringolandia" as opposed to "wonderland."

Una Puertorriqueña en Penna (*PP*, 1979) is indeed a lament with all the fury of the pain inside, lashing out against everything around it. Its anger, intensity, and rage at times takes the reader aback. Umpierre-Herrera does not mince words. There are no lyrical metaphors to soften the punches. Her words are in your face, and there is no place to hide. In the introduction, Umpierre-Herrera reveals a very clear notion of space, of physical location, when she speaks of prejudice, pain, sorrow. She refers to the "insensitive microcosm" and to the "little world of Bryn Mawr College" as the theme of the poems included in the collection. There is a desperate need to "desecrate" what up until then has been considered sacred land, sanctuary of intellectuals and ultimately of civilization. The collection repeatedly refers to specific places that suggest a very conscious cartography of this woman's journey into the black hole of dementia and back.

"Conversación telefónica," the second poem, simulates a phone call from a Puerto Rican in the United States to a friend back on the island. The speaker immediately situates herself in the spatial dichotomy of two worlds: the here and the there. The here is "gringolandia," "Bring Mal diaki" ("Bryn Mawr here" *PP* 6). Here she is "entre loh blanquitoh," "en la cuna del elitismo," in "el espanish diplamen" ("among the whities," "in the cradle of elitism," "the Spanish department"). Here she is described as "jodida, jodona, y jodienda" (screwed up, screwing up, and a nuisance). Here she has become "luzmaraya," a phonetic transcription of her name as pronounced by English speakers. The there is "mi pueltorrico." There is her name "Luz Mar." There is the sunlight (*luz*) and the sea (*mar*) of her island. There are the other Puerto Ricans, *pueltorro* whom she hopes will still recognize and understand her Spanish. To them, she insists "Is mi," "Soy yo" ("It's me"). She begs them to listen to her sorrow: "te jablo del penna" ("I am talking to you about sorrow/ Penn(sylvania)"). That is why she is calling.

The poem that follows expands both the tone and the content of that conversation. "Rubbish" (*PP* 9) enumerates all the rules that are so alien to many Hispanics. People are to stand in a straight line when boarding a bus, to walk on the right side of the street, to speak softly as opposed to the loudness of Spanish speakers. She feels as if she is living among trained animals who do things automatically. Against the fake politeness of "Excuse me" and "I'm sorry" in English, the poet juxtaposes Spanish expletives that correspond to the reality of a toe stepped on, people bumping into each other, and the onomatopoeic sound of a crash, "acángana."

At the end, she mocks the verbal amenities, such as "I b-e-g yul paldon, escuismi," and declares that as a Latina she finds it all to be just "RUBBISH," and she will not stand for it. By capitalizing the word, she enhances the nonsense and worthlessness of these social expressions that are repeated without meaning, and she denounces a society that insists on vacuous etiquette. The poet, like many immigrants, expresses her shock and disappointment not only with the bitter winters but with the coldness and insensitivity typical of highly industrialized and urban places. "Vivo en el país de los amaestrados" ("I live in the country of the tamed"), begins the poem, a country where the automatization of many services creates the impression of a robotic, impersonal environment in which no one cares for the individual.

A previous poem, "El trabajo escrito" ("The Written Work", *PP* 7) uses the onomatopoeic sounds of a typewriter to decry the senselessness of writing term papers ("¡El telmpeipar!"). "Taip taip taip,"

"Clink," "tip tip," are repeated and printed on the page (an obvious influence of Mallarmé) to echo the mechanical repetition of the process and the emphasis on the format, not the meaning of the words. The corrosion of this world comes to full term in "Dios se muda" ("God moves away" 11). Disgusted with *el barrio latino*, God, she writes, is moving to the white suburbs of Philadelphia. Like the geographical opposition of "Conversación Telefónica," this poem is also organized with the polar tensions between *el barrio* and North Philadelphia. Throughout her writings, Umpierre-Herrera uses capitalization very deliberately, and it is no accident here. North Philadelphia is indeed a superior local to the "low cap" neighborhood. The antithesis between the two areas is literally and figuratively black and white: "El Señor se marcha hacia blancos suburbios" ("The Lord departs to the white suburbs") because "ya no soporta las caras trigueñas" ("[he] can no longer stand the dark faces").

El barrio is the place of rats and roaches, dirty walls, and trash. It is crowded with crying children, drunk men, hunger, and early death. North Philadelphia has beautiful houses, lawns, and trees. "Dios Padre" ("God, the Father") prefers to see the faces of healthy children, their smiles, their opulent tables. The food from *el barrio* "stinks" while he dreams of "pancakes," "bagels," and "juicy steaks." God prefers the soothing sounds of a waltz played on the piano as opposed to "salsa" that beats from "African bongós" and "congas." The end of the poem is very clear: God will not be back to *el barrio latino*. His former apartment has a sign on the door: "DIOS SE HA IDO / GOD HAS MOVED" (*PP* 12). The verb "leemos" ("we read") is the only time the first person plural form is used. The speaker includes him/herself in the group of the abandoned and forces the reader to become part of that anguished "we." Marginalized, Puerto Ricans not only feel abandoned by the government and its institutions that are supposed to protect their interests, but ultimately by God, who no longer answers their prayers. By choosing "Father" and "Lord" to refer to God, the poet insists on the poignancy of the betrayal of that paternal figure and all the biblical promises of unconditional love.

"Jaculatoria in Nomine Domine" (*PP* 16–17) co-opts the discourse of prayers or litanies uttered at the end of the rosary to underline the despair of Puerto Rican people. The traditional prayer is a series of invocations to Biblical figures and icons, such as the Arc of the Covenant, the Tower of David. To these invocations, the congregation responds "Rogad por nosotros" ("Pray for us"). "Jaculatoria" interjects more specific petitions between the invocations and responses. The petitions reflect the harshness of everyday life, such as praying for the bus to arrive on time, for the line for food stamps to be short, for the garbage truck to come soon. There are also more serious requests: that they may not die waiting at the hospital, that their loan be renewed, that their wallet not be stolen. The last part of the prayer clarifies who is doing the imploring: "LA HIJA DEL MAR Y EL SOL," "BORIKEN," "HONOR DEL CARIBE" ("The daughter of sea and sun," "Boriken" [name given by the Indians to the island], "Honor of the Caribbean"). Although many of these concerns could be those of any poor person, the poet wants to make it clear that these are the litanies repeated by Puerto Ricans every day to no avail.

The next to last poem is "Patria de Nadie" ("Homeland of No One"), a clever game with "om," "ombliguito" ("little navel"), [h]"ombre" ("man") and "am," "[h]ambre" ("hunger") to signify the hunger for men of vision, for her people, for her country. Four words are capitalized: "PATRIA," "PUEBLO," "CENTRO," and "CERDOS" at the end ("Homeland," "People," "Center," and "Pigs"). The capitalization of these words emphasizes the search for a homeland, for her own people, for a navel / a center of her own being. The ambiguity of location of "CERDOS" within the syntax of the last verse directly under "PUEBLO" suggests the duality and the ambivalent feelings that stem from it. Pork is a staple food for Puerto Ricans. But "pigs" is a common insult, criticizing the living conditions of the poor. At the center of her search for nationhood there is the food that feeds Puerto Rican bodies and/or tears their human dignity to shreds.

Umpierre-Herrera's second book, *En el País de las Maravillas (Kempis puertorriqueño) (PM* 1982) goes further into this very fictional world because Alice/Luz María has found out that there is absolutely nothing wondrous about it. The collection incorporates all but one of the poems published in *Una puertorriqueña en Penna,* obviously intending to expand on the sorrow of a Puerto Rican not just in

Penn(sylvania) but in "wonderland." The book is divided into three
parts: "Exodo" ("Exodus"), "Jueces" ("Judges"), and "Lamentaciones
de Luz María" ("Luz María's Lamentations"). Asunción Horno-Delgado also finds three levels of referentiality:

> 1) the allusion to situations that call forth the Puerto Rican
> experience in the United States; 2) reclaiming the Island
> through memory and by juxtaposing that memory with her
> present situation; and finally, 3) those poems that consciously
> reconstruct the tension between the two worlds and concretize
> a solution. (*Breaking Boundaries* 138)

Aside from the allusion to Lewis Carroll's work and to the idealized view immigrants have of the United States, the title also contains
a reference to Thomas A. Kempis' *Imitation of Christ*, a medieval manual for Christian living. But Eliana Rivero reminds the reader in her
introduction to the collection that this is a Puerto Rican Kempis: "no la
imitación de Cristo adobada a la criolla, sino el rezo de una creyente
iconoclasta que rechaza lo establecido y usa el sarcasmo irreverente
para sacudir la conciencia" ("not the imitation of Christ sprinkled with
local seasonings, but the prayer of an iconoclastic believer who rejects
the status quo and uses irreverent sarcasm to jolt the conscience" *PM*
i). This time, Umpierre-Herrera uses Spanish, English, and Spanglish,
sarcastic humor and poignant lyricism to give the reader a manual not
for living in *wonderland* but for tearing down the walls of a world constantly divided between presence and absence, between the continent
here and the island there.

"Oración ante una Imagen Derrumbada" ("Prayer before a fallen
image") follows the structure of the traditional Catholic Apostles'
Creed, except here the beginning line is "No creo" ("I do not believe").
The poem proceeds to throw off their pedestals a series of classical
icons of American culture. The speaker does not believe in the Donald
Duck who occupies the White House, nor Mickey Mouse, nor Bonzo
the Clown, nor the "American Dream of Oz." Instead of the traditional "begotten, not made" and the references to the virginal birth,
Umpierre-Herrera begins the second stanza with "Fornicó y fue forni-
cado, / . . . / y subió al pentágono" ("He fornicated and was fornicated,

/ . . . / and ascended to the pentagon" 17). Once again, Umpierre-Herrera subverts a well-known prayer and renders it with the crudest physicality to tear away the power of the "almighty" in politics. By combining the references to the White House and the Pentagon with the Disney characters, she reduces American politicians to mere caricatures. While the traditional Apostles' Creed affirms the belief in heaven and eternal life, this creed absolutely denies the American Dream and its rose-colored glasses. Ultimately, as the next to last verse states, she does not even believe in Alice in Wonderland ("ni en Alicia en el país de las maravillas").

This wonder/wasteland is a cold industrialized society, far from her warm tropical island. "Pase de Lista" ("Roll Call") is indeed an attendance checklist to verify who or what is present. The poem is organized in two columns in Spanish. The one on the left itemizes such things as "people walking in a hurry," "my language which is my voice," "grey skies," "footprints in the sand," etc. The right column marks them present or absent. Present are the "white faces," "grey skies," "naked trees," "cold civilization," "faces without smiles." Absent are "my language," "the sun, brown faces, human warmth," "the green." The last item in the checklist is Puerto Rico. The reply on the right is: "todo está ausente" ("everything is absent"). Umpierre-Herrera is like many other Latino writers who do not find anything of their own culture around them, only the muffling of their voices, the erasure of their culture.

The automatization of an industrialized society completely devoid of human life is cleverly depicted in "Alumbramiento" ("Childbirth" 24–25). In this poem, the process of childbirth is equated to a Xerox machine. Put in the coin, put in the original, wait for the "mechanic orgasm," and out of the "mechanic uterus" hundreds of papers will come out of an orifice. The "zap zap" and "ting ting" on the margins of the poem emphasize the technological aspect of this reproductive system. In a society that at times treats its machines better than the human inhabitants, Umpierre-Herrera's sarcasm is as loud as any engine. At the end, the poet warns the world, "La raza de papel hoy se levanta" ("The paper race is uprising today" 25).

Against the satirical tones of these poems, Umpierre-Herrera introduces a very lyrical, intimate voice that explores the pain of living in wonderland. Toward the end of the collection, the speaker in "Kansas" (37) wonders if someone will understand what "picking a flower in the snow," or seeing the "Sun on an icy day," or "finding a memory lost in a wave" means to her. How can anyone out there in Kansas, which Dorothy calls home and where the writer spent two years, begin to comprehend the significance of these things to her? The "what if" interrogatives are posed in a plaintive tone as opposed to the sarcasm and the irony of the other poems. "Y si encuentro una navaja fina entre hilachas de azul y rojo?" ("And if I find a thin razor amidst the threads of blue and red?" *PM* 37), can the reader then understand her pain cutting deep down into her bruised soul? The last question, "¿Responderás?" ("Will you respond?") remains unanswered. The silence of the two-thirds of empty page speaks loudly of the anguished search for answers down a brick path that may lead to Kansas, to Oz, to wonderland, or ultimately to nowhere.

In this wonderland of modernization and industrialization, American universities remain one of the last bastions of intellectual freedom. But nothing prepares Puerto Ricans and other Hispanics for the racism and discrimination encountered within the ivory towers. It is not until the nineties that studies, articles, and books appeared describing the subtle and not so subtle biases existent in the classrooms, in the faculty lounges, and in tenure and promotion procedures. Raymond V. Padilla and Rudolfo Chávez-Chávez's *The Leaning Tower: Latino Professors in American Universities* brings together a collection of narratives and essays about the shocking and frequently short lives of Latinos in academe.[7]

Umpierre-Herrera was among the first writers to launch an attack against the solemn institution of American academe. Her satirical renditions of scholars are sometimes hilarious but always acerbic and right on the mark. "Los Intellectuals," a poem included in both *Una Puertorriqueña en Penna* and *En el País de las Maravillas*, describes academicians as pretentious, petty people whose world is that of articles, lectures, and meetings. These "know-it-alls" wear glasses to hide the emptiness of their gaze and their ignorance. They spend their days on senseless matters, such as "diacritic dialectics," "marasmus," "rhetorical, empirical, scatological questions." The abstract complexity of their work contrasts with the mundane details of their "asses" growing as they sit at their desks (*PM* 5). In order to sound even more intelligent, they exaggerate their pronounciation of Spanish, "usando veinte latines / y pronunciando hasta las comas" ("using twenty Latins / and pronouncing even the commas" 6). What the poet laments the most is their lack of understanding of "mi gente" ("my people") because they live in a "cloister" surrounded by "un casticismo anglicano" ("Anglican purity"). In teaching foreign languages and literatures, professors tend to emphasize a notion of standard Castilian Spanish found only in textbooks and a canon dominated by Peninsular works which alienate them from the culturally diverse reality of the worldwide Spanish-speaking population.

This preference for Castilian Spanish has given way to the phenomenon that Ana Celia Zentella calls "chiquitafication" or "the belittling of non-Castilian varieties of Spanish" (1). Renowned for her studies on bilingualism in Latino populations of the United States, Zentella explains the prevalent notion that "real" or "pure" Spanish is only spoken in Spain. The American public believes this and many teachers of Spanish endorse it, promoting the idea that the language spoken by the immigrants from Latin America is inferior (4). According to Zentella, these false assumptions are part of the biases and discrimination against Latinos. Puerto Ricans are totally taken aback to find out that there is a hierarchy of Spanish accents, with the Castilian leading the way and their own ranking at the bottom of the scale. Umpierre-Herrera's experience of being corrected for her pronunciation or diction is not uncommon even among educated Puerto Ricans. She uses her poetry to express her indignation.

In the poem "Conversación Telefónica," Umpierre-Herrera purposefully utilizes "Spanglish" and exaggerated accents of the *jíbaros* (people from the Puerto Rican countryside) to emphasize her feeling of alienation. "Pointing Marginals" (*PM* 8) lists the professor's comments on a Puerto Rican student's paper. However, the corrections, all in caps in the poem, have nothing to do with grammatical structure, the content, or the organization of ideas, but instead with specific choices of words: "COCHE NOT CARRO," "CENA NOT COMIDA."[8] The professor objects to: "ANGLICISMO," "PUERTORRIQUEÑISMO," "REGIONALISMO," "ARCHAISM."[9] He suggests the student "FAMILIARIZE YOURSELF WITH THE CASTILIAN WORD!" The comments on the margin represent the professor's frustration, intolerance, and disdain as well as his imperious tone. His final grunt of disgust is "UF!"

To the authoritative discourse of the academic, the marginalized Puerto Rican student responds in lower case, in parentheses and with an expletive that is repeated in both languages: "(¡mierda!) / (bullshit!)." The student clearly places herself outside the standardized institutional style and uses what she is accused of, slang, to stand, like her island, isolated in the margins, in a parenthetical limbo. Horno-Delgado believes that this interaction echoes "the tension between the Puerto Rican context and that of the colonizer" ("Señores" 142). Interestingly enough, Puerto Ricans have to deal with two separate linguistic systems of colonization. English, of course, is the language of Academia, of the Establishment, of Authority. If Spanish is to be spoken, Horno-Delgado observes keenly, "it is only possible to pronounce a Spanish that is allied to power. It is a way of once again taking on the discourse of the Conquest" ("Señores" 143). The Puerto Rican student refuses to use either and resorts to vulgarity to challenge any further attempts to subordinate her.

The hostile atmosphere in Academia does not change much, whether Umpierre-Herrera is a student, a colleague, or a poet. "Colleagues," published with her third collection, . . . Y Otras Desgracias / And Other Misfortunes . . . (YOD 1985), echoes the resentment and anger of "Los Intellectuals." Written in English, it repeats many of the mocking images of the previous poem with some minor variants. Instead of their "growing asses," it refers to their "coccyx" levitating; their "casticismo anglicano" becomes "their yankee Spanish" (YOD 7). Once again, her American colleagues see themselves as superior, both in their language ("their torrid gringo Spanish / is all there's to be taught" [emphasis added]) and everything else they do:

> They'll speak of studying "languages"
> they'll write "cultural" texts
> they'll levitate in their digress

their tumored brains will indicate:
THEY ARE GODS

The poet uses hyperbole and images of physical deformity to underline the large egos of scholars in academe and the twisted notions that inform their prejudices. Ironically, the poem's title, "Colleagues," suggests a work relationship of equality, but the poet only finds the familiar interaction of colonizer and colonized.

There is no doubt about the identity of the so-called colleagues; they are white Americans. The references to their "yankee" or "gringo" accents, together with the physical description of "their blondie heads," makes it clear. They are the ones who will climb "the ladder / of national success." Under their "civilized" demeanor, the speaker warns, "Suppression will occur / harassment will jerk off." The constant use of the third-person-plural pronoun and adjective, "they" and "their" positions the speaker and the reader outside of that group, making them "the other." "They" are the ones with the power, as signified by "their enthroning chairs," "the yellow aureolas," "their seats of power." As the verse says in capitals, they are the gods. Against that third person, there is an implied "we," never spoken, except when it speaks of "Temptations will crop up / wild thoughts will be incurred / to dynamite their seats of power. . . ." However, these "anonymous" thoughts of rebellion are quickly squelched by the threats of "suppression" and "harassment" subtly conveyed under their "enchanting" politeness.

If a Puerto Rican student and a Puerto Rican colleague provoke such hostile reactions, to be a Puerto Rican poet in 'gringolandia' is ultimately a nightmare. "La muerte de la inspiración" ("The Death of Inspiration") and "Entrevista" ("Interview") explore the terrible anxiety of the artist. She is very much aware that she will be judged by these so-called intellectuals who will tear apart and criticize everything, even her pronunciation.[10] Included in *En el País de las Maravillas*, the poems reveal that there is nothing wonderful about being an artist, a writer in this country. Written in Spanish, not in English, the poems denounce the critics' expectations of conformity to norms and paradigms that are culturally alien and totally irrelevant to her as a Puerto Rican. Several times, Umpierre-Herrera denounces publishing houses that discriminate against women, especially when they are "non-traditional hispanic." She laments the fact that such writers as Sandra María Estevez can only get published by small presses that do not have the means of distribution and the marketing capabilities of the big houses. She also objects to people questioning the value of her manuscripts based upon the number of poems included.[11]

"La Muerte de la Inspiración" (*PM* 29) recreates a poetry reading where the audience demands the poet recite a given poem. Umpierre-Herrera includes the audience's response in quotation marks; the poet's reactions to their shouts are stated in parentheses and without capitalization. She feels cornered and rejected as the public screams, "A ti NO, que eres puertorra, criticona y absurda" ("NOT you, who are puertorican, so critical and absurd"). She knows that the cutting satirical tone and thematic tension of her poetry is alienating to them. As their shouts grow louder and threaten to silence her soul, the poet ends in a cry of total despair raised above their voices, in capital letters, using expletives and exclamations typical of the island: "PERO CARAJO BENDITO SI NO ME QUEDA NADA" ("But Blessed Hell, I don't have anything left"). The poet is totally depleted of inspiration, of words; she has given her best, but that is not good enough.

If "La Muerte de la Inspiración" depicts the public aspects of a poet's life, "Entrevista" examines the intimate struggle of the writing process. Reminiscent of Gloria Fuertes' poetry, there is no tension here between the mundane reality of writing and the esoteric poetic subject. She writes at night with a nineteen-cent pen or during the day while traveling on the turnpike. She does it while she watches cars on the asphalt or the roaches on the apartment walls. The inspiration, the impulse to write is described in terms of "el deseo de masturbar / a algún papel blancusino" ("the desire to masturbate / any whitish paper" *PM* 36). As she contemplates the brand of paper, she looks into the future, when "algún profesor asexuado / con culo almidonado" ("an asexual professor / with a starched ass") will present a paper about her poetry. Hopefully, the scholar will make the following pronouncement about her work: "SEÑORES, la poeta se ha orinado" ("Ladies and Gentlemen, the poet has urinated"). By insisting on these physically crude metaphors, the poet subverts the traditional notions of poetry as being about lofty feelings, heroic actions, sublime matters. Like Rosario Morales and Aurora Levins Morales, who use bodily fluids to reach "home alive," Umpierre-Herrera opens the floodgates of her body to allow her most intimate feelings of desire, of pain, of rage to wet the page, which is the only space where she can be herself, Alice-Luz María-Luz Mar-Luzma.[12]

Whether it is with urine or with the cheap ink of her pen, the poet traces the images of two places that she feels safe and at home. Umpierre-Herrera uses calligrams to depict these wonderful sites. "Título Sobreentendido" ("Understood Title" *PP* 10) and "Sol Boricua" ("Boricuan Sun" *PM* 38) use words placed on the page to create "GHETTO" in the first poem and a sun with its rays in the second. In "Título Sobreentendido," the clever repetition and organization of the words such as "la clave" ("rhythm stick"), "one two three," "bongo," "conga," "salsa," and "happiness" form the "GHETTO." This place, usually considered to be at the margins of society, provides a safe haven for *Una Puertorriqueña en Penna*. It is with this salsa beat and its instruments that this sorrowful Puerto Rican finds happiness.

"Sol Boricua," placed at the end of *En el País de las Maravillas*, plays with the "sol" ("sun") and the musical notes, do-re-mi-fa-sol, to create an irridescent planet. Like the "GHETTO," it brings music and light to the bleak world of "wonderland."

Amid the specificity of such a place as Philadelphia, Pennsylvania and of such institutions as Bryn Mawr, academe, and the Church, Umpierre-Herrera shreds the fancy language of politeness to expose in all its crudity the geography of sexual and racial stereotypes. Once she has dismantled the myth of the American Dream and traced the coordinates of wonderland, the ugly grimaces of discrimination and the prejudice begin to appear.

I just met a girl and her name is NOT María

In the Western world, no other name is so synonymous with virtue, holiness, and absolute maternal devotion as Mary, *María*. It conjures up images of the Madonna and child; of Michaelangelo's *La Pietá* with its quiet but moving expression of grief, of a pretty girl in a Broadway musical with a tragic ending reminiscent of the romantic *Romeo and Juliet.*

In "A la Mujer Borinqueña" ("To the Boricuan Woman"), Sandra María Esteves proclaims: "My name is María Christina" (*Yerba Buena* 63). The poem is an attempt to claim an identity for the Puerto Rican woman that recognizes both her Caribbean and Nuyorican background. "María Christina" tries to "respect their ways / inherited from our proud ancestors" and admits to doing the cooking and the child-rearing, as is expected of her. Although she also declares herself "the mother of a new age of warriors," whom she will teach to be strong, the poem still endorses the female roles of keeper and teacher of traditional cultural values. In spite of her admiration for Esteves' work, Umpierre-Herrera could not resist raising her objections to this model of "Boricuan woman." Thus "In Response," included in . . . *Y Otras Desgracias / And Other Misfortunes* (*YOD* 1985), she insists that "My name is not María Cristina" and she will not "accept their ways / shed down from macho-men ancestors" (*YOD* 1). This María Cristina (with the spelling in Spanish) is "no cooking mama" and no doting mother. The poetic repartee between the two writers did not stop there. Five years later, Esteves published *Bluestown Mockingbird Mambo*, in which she included an apologetic explanation dedicated to Luz María Umpierre. "So Your Name Isn't María Cristina" admits that the girl was young and naive "with no definitions of her own / No recognition of her vast cultural experience" (32). Now she understands words like "colonialism." Now she knows that she is not the only one suffering from "forms of enslavement." By now, that little girl has "awakened" into "womanhood."

This intertextual dialogue that went on for ten years reveals two important points. One is the evident adoption of "María" as the name for the mythic "Puerto Rican" "Boricuan" woman. Second, and of more significance, it underlines the ongoing polemic of what it means to be a Puerto Rican woman, born in El Barrio or on the island. Most of the writers discussed in this book search for a definition of womanhood that stands on its own with dignity and respect. Somewhere between the tropical rain forest and the cement jungle, there has to be a space for a Puerto Rican woman to be herself, embracing the cultural cacophony of her background, while rejecting the subordination and suffocation of traditional patriarchal roles in Puerto Rico and in the United States.

Ever since arriving in this country, Luz María Umpierre-Herrera has realized that, as a tall, big-framed woman, as a lesbian, as a serious intellectual and honest writer, she could never fit into the stereotypes and expectations people have of a Latin woman. *Una Puertorriqueña en Penna* begins with "La Receta" ("The Recipe"), one of her most popularly anthologized and quoted poems. This recipe begins with an italicized list of eleven ingredients, such adjectives as "Moody," "Hot-Tempered," "Difficult." As the recipe gives the instructions, according to "gringas" like Betty Crocker and Julia Childs, the verbs are accompanied by the first-person-indirect-object pronoun "me." What they are cooking, preparing, and ultimately packaging and labeling is "me," a female Puerto Rican. In the last three verses, the subject shifts from the third-person-plural of the American cooks to the first-person-singular of a woman who does not want to be labeled, concocted, and defined by others. Against *their* canned label, "EXPLOSIVE / HANDLE WITH CARE," the "I" of the poem wants to wrap herself in her own flag on which only one word will be printed: "HUMANA."

Umpierre-Herrera, like many others, laments the fact that Puerto Rican women have become an exotic popular product to be found on the shelves of the "International Aisle" of American stores. Frances Aparicio and Susana Chávez-Silverman discuss the phenomenon of what they call "tropicalization," the process of infusing "a particular space, geography, group, or nation with a set of traits, images, and values" (8). The result is an appropriation by mainstream America and its translation into something akin to the Spanish-speaking Chihuahua in Taco Bell commercials. For women, it has meant "racialized and gendered representations of Latina subjectivity—variously encoded as tropical, exotic, hyper-eroticized sexuality" (Chávez-Silverman 101).

Julia Alvarez, Judith Ortiz Cofer, and Esmeralda Santiago speak of the painful impact these representations had in their dating lives. In *How the García Girls Lost Their Accents*, Alvarez narrates the protagonist's first romantic relationship in college. Soon after Yolanda García meets Rudolph (Rudy) Brodermann Elmenhurst III, they begin dating. When his parents realize Rudy is dating a "Spanish girl," they encourage him to learn more "about people from other cultures" (98). Although Yolanda resents being reduced to a "geography lesson for their son," she does not have the words to express her feelings. Ortiz Cofer describes a similar sense of uneasiness, of not being treated as an equal, when she goes out to a dance with a boy and he uses adjectives to characterize her as a ripe fruit ready for the taking. In her first book, Esmeralda Santiago discusses how she was perceived by a Jewish man and a Texas millionaire as an exotic fling, the perfect means for a minor rebellion against family traditions. Notwithstanding the humorous tone of some of these narratives, the bewilderment and the confusion caused by these men are always the same: the young women are left to ponder the cartography of their bodies, to figure out what signs elicited their dates' demeaning behavior.

Umpierre-Herrera realizes that there is no geography of sexual prejudices, no specificity of place either in American cities or in the female body, but an assimilation of cultural and sexual stereotypes so pervasive, so reinforced by media, religion, and other social institutions, that the "tropicalization," the erotization of Latin women, is acceptable. She uses her poetry as a blade, or as Mireya Pérez-Erdélyi puts it, "a palabra como bisturí" "the word as a scalpel," to cut through and expose the rotten bones of sexism (61). It is not an easy task being a woman, Hispanic, and the defender of Hispanic women in a world that is less than wonderful.

In *En el País de las Maravillas*, Umpierre-Herrera has already acknowledged the difficulty of her mission. "Una Defensa" ("A Defense" 18) tells her sister, "mi pana" (colloquial Spanish for friend, pal, or buddy), what a nuisance it is to be a woman and to defend her cause. The reader soon finds out that the difficulty stems from non-conformity: a woman who is not "decorous and quiet," who does not speak her "Yes, yes, Mister," in soft tones is a pest. To be a radical woman of color is, indeed, to be a nuisance. In other poems, Umpierre-Herrera also echoes the notion that scholars, teachers, and critics find her a difficult "trouble-maker."

On the other hand, the second part of "Una Defensa" decries the difficulty of defending "la mujer de mi raza!" ("the woman of her race"). But why, asks the poet, should it be so objectionable and controversial to defend the woman who takes care of the children and the home while maintaining a subservient role to a sometimes abusive husband? The last three verses are an invitation to "mi pana" to raise her voice and rise up in rebellion. After all, she and her female friends have suffered enough "en este mundo de mierda" ("in this shitty world").

. . . *Y Otras Desgracias / And Other Misfortunes* . . . (1985) expands on the tribulations of a sorrowful *puertorriqueña* in wonderland, already introduced in the previous two collections. In what Nancy Vosburg considers to be "a landmark of Umpierre's development as poet," Alicia-Luz María expands on the use of phonetic games, sarcastic irony, and the subversion of traditional discourse "now reinforced by a lucid feminist consciousness that allows the poet to begin to create a new female archetype as old myths are humorously pulverized" (553). The book is divided into two parts: "Mishaps," with poems mainly in English, and "Poemas Malogrados" ("Ill-fated Poems") mostly in Spanish. Both parts finish with the poem "Creation" or "Creación," in English and Spanish versions. Here, the writer uses children's fairy tales as well as Biblical stories to subvert sexual stereotypes.

. . . *Y Otras Desgracias* . . . begins appropriately enough with "In Response," briefly discussed at the beginning of this section. In answer to what Esteves deems "A Boricuan Woman," Umpierre-Herrera fully rejects the traditional roles associated with her gender. She will not be subservient, submissive, or silent before men; after all, she does not seek permission "from dearest *marido* / or kissing-loving papa" (1). She acknowledges with pride that "they call me pushie," "they call me bitchie." In many ways, the poem introduces what will be the ultimate goal of this collection:

> I do complain
> I will complain
> I do revise,
> I don't conceal,
> I will reveal,
> I will revise.

This is, according to her, "the only way to fight oppression." She is determined not to conceal anything, but to reveal and complain about every single "misfortune," "mishap" encountered.

The poem that gives title to the collection, "Y otras desgracias," reveals other misfortunes faced by women, especially those like Umpierre-Herrera who want to be artists in their own right. In the outside world, there are critics trying to dissect her belly and look inside at what she is writing. They examine her entrails, her mouth, her tongue. On the other hand, she sits at her desk surrounded by phantasmagorical apparitions of monsters, witches, and Alice—ghosts that are trying to populate her writing—while at the same time, she contemplates the empty refrigerator and the phone bill. The poem concludes, "Estas son otras desgracias. / En el país de las maravillas y otras desgracias" ("These are other misfortunes. / In wonderland and other misfortunes." *YOD* 31) The book goes on to "reveal," to "revise," and to "complain" against the aesthetic norms and societal expectations imposed on women both at home and in the workplace.

"La Jogocracia," a poem published in her first collection, already denounces an American aesthetic of beauty based on dieting and exercising. As the title suggests, society is governed by the "rule of jogging," and the aristocracy is made up of the "urban tenniscrats" whose intelligence "is measured in blocks, miles, and Adidas" (*PP* 8). Under this ruling system, life is about latex suits, anorexia, and ultimately, about annihilation. Here is a warning to those who do not conform: they will be attacked by those who "descargan con raquetas su racismo inhumano" ("discharge their inhuman racism with tennis rackets").

. . . *Y Otras Desgracias / And Other Misfortunes* . . . raises the voice of rebellion against this inhuman, prejudicial, sexist rule. Within the women's liberation movement of the sixties and seventies and the feminist movement of the eighties, Umpierre-Herrera recognizes the same patterns of oppression. "The Astronaut" condemns the phenomenon of the "Superwoman," who has a career and a family, an office, as well as "a man and a family wagon" (*YOD 5*). She has bought into the aesthetics of "la jogocracia" as she walks "hermetically tightening her thighs." "You have seen her," "we have seen her," insists the poem, making the reader a witness to this phenomenon of the successful woman, the product of a highly industrialized society, who has become "a patriarchal tool / a matriarchal break up." This combination of Super-Mom and career woman is too busy conforming to modern societal expectations to recognize her own oppression and that of other marginalized groups: "she loathes the word sister." "The Statue," published in *The Margarita Poems*, similarly denounces the assimilation of the flower girl of the sixties, who went from "hip to yup," from "messy hair" to "face lifted fully," from "glossy bead droplets encircling her neck" to "flowered blazer from Saks on her back" (*Margarita* 23–24). There are no statues in this poem, just the stifling of the young girl's free spirit into the "fully galvanized, / fully modernized" "symbol of the U.S. of A." (24).

In order to avoid this choking transformation, Umpierre-Herrera sets out to revise even the most rigid forms of discourse. With this in mind, she dismantles traditional fairy tales. In "A Rizos de Oro" ("To Goldilocks"), the poet tells Goldilocks that she will no longer be tolerated nor allowed to intrude in someone else's land: "venías a robarnos la sopa de la mesa; / soñolienta corrías a jodernos las camas" ("you came to steal the soup from our table; / sleepy, you ran to screw up our beds" *YOD* 47). The first-person-plural speaker represents the voices of three female bears from Bolivia, El Salvador, and Puerto Rico. They do admit that initially they were seduced by her whiteness, her golden curls, her "gracious fainting." They also recognize that beneath the feigned gestures of friendship, Goldilocks was trying to "ponernos al cuello la cadena / y en el pie, el grillo" ("put a chain on our necks / and shackles on our feet").

Umpierre-Herrera does not distinguish the oppression of colonialism from the pernicious impact that American culture has had on the colonized people to the point of erasing their own values. The use of the first-person and the second-person-familiar "tú" when referring to Goldilocks creates the intimacy of a dialogue spoken with frankness, strength, and conviction. At the end, in that same "matter-of-fact" tone, the three female bears describe what happened to Goldilocks: "te mandamos a casa, / a ser nuevamente común en vez de mito" ("we sent you back home / to be common again instead of a myth"). Bolivia, El Salvador, Puerto Rico, among many other countries, will not allow Americans to choke the people of Latin America with their myths, fairy tales, oppressive discourse. No longer will they permit Goldilocks, Betty Crocker, or Alice in Wonderland to set the standards of beauty and gender.

"Cuento Sin Hadas" summarizes this theme of disillusionment with the world of wonderland, already introduced in Umpierre-Herrera's previous collections. In Spanish, fairy tales are called *cuentos de hadas*. The preposition *sin* (without) signals the lack of fairies, the void of enchantment in the familiar stories of our childhood, myths that have informed our moral and ethical understanding. The protagonists, a male and a female doll, reverse the traditional gender roles. *La muñeca* laughs, scares, pees, speaks, walks, and moves around. *El muñeco*, on the other hand, is described in terms of what he does not do: he does not laugh, he does not speak. In her analysis of this poem, Teresa de San Pedro explains how the "woman-doll" breaks away from two characteristics traditionally associated with the heroines of fairy tales: beauty and passivity. Yet, according to San Pedro, what is ugly and scary about this "woman-doll" is her conduct (93). Her actions are in "grotesque" opposition to her gender. Using the dolls, the poem describes the perfect marriage, the expected happy ending of fairy tales. Indeed, it is the perfect "tin" marriage, in which everything seems to shine on the surface: an expensive dollhouse with porcelain figurines, a beautiful table set with silver utensils, social debuts, memberships in the right clubs, write-ups in the newspaper, servants, and even the fashionable visits to the psychiatrist.

But behind this image of perfect bliss, the reality is that the marriage and family are crumbling. All the verbs in the fourth stanza indicate disintegration: "se destripa" ("disembowels"), "se desbarata" ("falls apart"), "deshilachan" ("unravel"). Instead of the traditional formula that ends children's stories in Spanish, "Colorín, colorado, este cuento se ha acabado" (an untranslatable expression saying that the story has ended), the poem ends with a variation of it: "Y el colorín, colorado ya no sirve, ya no encanta" ("And the 'colorín, colorado' does not work anymore, is not charming anymore"). The old formulas, old myths and tales are no longer effective. According to San Pedro, Umpierre-Herrera is rebelling against "poemas que cantan a una belleza inexistente, una perfección imposible, unos valores ya podridos y unas instituciones sociales que lo único que conservan de su ideal inicial es el nombre" ("poems that sing of non-existent beauty, of an impossible perfection, of values already rotten and of social institutions which only preserve the name out of their initial ideals" 98). Subsequently, in *The Margarita Poems,* Luz-Mar/garita searches literally for a new language that will allow the expression of her true self. The old paradigms of linguistic formulas, of signs and signifiers, of Castilian Spanish, of academic discourse, of institutional hierarchy, of editorial censorship, and of behavioral patterns are no longer acceptable in the marginalized space of this Puerto Rican writer.

One of the most powerful social institutions in Latin American is the Church. The Catholic Church has a tremendous influence on such issues as divorce, abortion, and homosexuality. *Marianismo*, a descriptive system of behavior for Latin American women, is based on the Catholic devotion to the Virgin Mary. Another Biblical figure of great importance in female behavior is that of Eve, the cause of original sin, who, like Pandora, opened the garden to all sorts of evils, illnesses, and ultimately, to death. The opposition of these two figures has led to a dualistic tension in women's societal roles. Woman is either perceived to be a mother, the most holy of figures, capable of absolute devotion and self-sacrifice, or, she is a *femme fatale*, a seductress who will bring about man's destruction. La Malinche, Hernán Cortes' Indian mistress, is solely to blame for the conquest and colonization of the great Aztec civilization. Moraga calls this "the legacy of betrayal" and insists that it is not limited just to Mexican and Chicano culture (91).

With her characteristic humor, Umpierre-Herrera satirizes this perennial blaming of women. "El Original" (*YOD* 35) reconstructs a casual conversation about a piece of clothing that has been taken to the "clinar" (cleaners) because of a stain that won't come out. The female speakers wonder if it is "salsa criolla" or "gelatina." As they argue about whether "clorox" or "Viva," a new product, will take care of it, it becomes important that the garment returns absolutely clean. If not, people are going to speculate about the "snake," "the apple," or "Adam's dirty trick" when he "came" that day. They all know what is going to happen if the stain persists: "la penintencia de 20 siglos encima" ("a sentencing for 20 centuries upon them"). The last two stanzas sound almost like a popular proverb, carrying words of wisdom and a warning:

—Cuando se trata de manchas, si no sale con el clinar nos toca
ser lavanderas hasta que nos llegue el día—BUENA SUERTE
(*YOD* 35)

[—When it is a matter of stains, if it doesn't come out at the cleaners we are going to have to be laundry-women until judgment day arrives—GOOD LUCK]

The irony of this wish for good luck at the end is obvious; everyone knows that we are all born with the mark of original sin. In fact, the Catholic Church insists on the purification of baptism as soon as a baby is born to wipe away original sin. Everyone also knows that Eve is to blame for this curse, and that women have been "cursed" with menstruation and childbearing as fitting punishment. The casual tone of the conversation contrasts with the seriousness of the subject matter. The contrast between genders is also noteworthy. The use of feminine adjectives and the endearment terms "hija" and "m'ija" (daughter, girl) reinforce the point that this is a woman's concern, a woman's problem, her ultimate responsibility. "El" (he) is only used to speak of the consequences: "he" has the authority to determine what will happen to the female "them."

Although there is a light attempt to blame Adam, it is not taken seriously. After all, men are expected to be promiscuous and to prove their virility. Women, on the other hand, under the precepts of *Marianismo*, are to stay pure, chaste, and without stain. Like the images of the Virgin Mary, women are perceived as bodyless, void of physical needs and sexual desires. In her previous collections, Umpierre-Herrera had co-opted the discourse of prayers to tear down the suffocating religious dogmas of gender roles and sexual behavior. "¿Sacrilegio?" ("Sacrilege") is not a prayer, but as the note in parentheses states, "a petition." The poem depicts the speaker's anguished search for a Virgin, for an icon that will represent the reality of women. As the title indicates, her quest is sacrilegious: instead of the traditional veneration of kneeling in front of the statue and kissing its feet, the speaker wants to masturbate, to bring orgasms and pleasure, to make the figure "menos piedra, menos niña" ("less stone, less child"). After all, she insists to the Virgin, "Soy mujer de carne y hueso / . . . / y en este país de hombres" (I am a woman of flesh and bones / . . . / and in this land of men" *YOD* 37). The poem ends with the speaker giving up, feeling that her words are childish, just like her petition for "una virgen encinta, immaculada y sacrílega" ("a pregnant, inmaculate, and sacrilegious virgin" 39).

In her analysis of popular representations of the lesbian body, Yvonne Yarbro-Bejarano underlines the "blending of the sensual with the spiritual, bare flesh and sexual desire with the power of religious iconography" (187). Umpierre-Herrera refuses to submit any longer to patriarchal religious dogmas that insist on the virginity and purity of women, but not of men. Her poetry rejects the traditional sacraments and the notion of virginal conception by the Holy Spirit, and instead uses verbs like "fornicar" and "masturbar" to speak of sexual desire, of physical beauty, of love. As she begins her journey in *The Margarita Poems,* she seeks to transcend the world of iniquity, misfortunes, and denial of the female body.

Toward the end of the collection, the poem "Transference" anticipates *The Margarita Poems,* with its use of puns in the search for names, an identity that will "label" her lesbian "I." The speaker invites "tú" (the familiar you) to engage in a game of naming; one will say "La Margarita" while the other will say "Sister" (*YOD* 55). Hesitantly, they will try on other labels, such as "Bliss" or "Eve," even "M . . .," not sure if it stands for "Mierda" ("Shit") or "Mine / Mía." The poem moves away from the cynical criticism of "torrid gringo Spanish" and recognizes the difficulty "en tu acento de español de principiantes" ("of your beginner's Spanish accent"). The use of phonetic terminology to describe the pronounciation of certain words and the positioning of the tongue in the mouth reveals both the complexity of articulating an identity of her own and the sensuality that words have for Umpierre-Herrera. Words are very sensual, and she likes the way they feel in her mouth, as she repeats them and changes them. As the "tú y yo" of the poem continue exchanging nouns, they end "sweaty" and exhausted from this erotic game in which they ultimately "scream in ecstasy": "Amante," "Amada," "Hija" ("Lover," "Loved one," "Daughter"). "Transference" begins the process of conveying her most intimate feelings and desires that will come to full bloom in her next collection, *The Margarita Poems*.

But in order for this transformation, and transference, transcendence to take place, Umpierre-Herrera has had to tear down the walls, the fences, the borders that have confined her sexual and ethnic identities. The process that began in *Una Puertorriqueña en Penna* and in *En el País de las Maravillas* achieves lyrical expression and poetic balance in . . . *Y Otras Desgracias / And Other Misfortunes*. . . . In her introduction to this collection, Nancy Vosburg insists that its central theme is "creation and destruction" (*YOD* xi). Indeed, the last poem in both sections is the bilingual version of "Creation," in which Umpierre-Herrera examines "the paradox of creation in language which is both comic and tragic" (xii). Sometimes, the artist is afraid of what the words might say and she does anything "in order not to write poems" (*YOD* 27). She will maim herself, she will devote her days to inane routines, such as "combing her hair," she will drink Coca-Cola in order to give herself both physical and mental constipation, or she may simply not buy anymore paper. But all of these efforts are not enough. Ultimately,

> for her to arrange not to write
> she penetrated the sea
> > without leaving a trace
>
> > > or
>
> she deposited her head
> > on the rack in the oven. (*YOD* 29)

The references to Virginia Woolf's and Sylvia Plath's suicides are obvious. According to Vosburg, Umpierre-Herrera is aware of "the absurdity of living and creating on the edge of nothing" (*YOD* xi). The Puerto Rican poet laments the fact that these two brilliant writers gave up in their struggle with the absurd and silenced their voices forever. Like them, she, too, has suffered the madness, the suicidal impulses of trying to escape the suffocation of her gender, her sexuality, her creativity. In the poem "To a beautiful illusion / Bella Ilusión (danza)," the speaker contemplates Sylvia Plath's grave and expresses the desire to bring her remains back to life to give her love and hope, to bring her back home (*For Christine* 5–7).

"Creation" "Creación," placed at the end of both sections of *Y Otras Desgracias*, serves as the wake-up call for the poet, who immediately begins to write the poems to be published in her next book, *The Margarita Poems*. In the introduction to this volume, Umpierre-Herrera acknowledges the need to speak "that which I had not uttered, and which was being used as a tool in my oppression by others" (*MP* 1) the words that up until then had been spoken in accusations and legal suits against her. If she continues her silence, she realizes that she will bring about her own destruction, like Woolf and Plath. Thus, this time she lets the words fall from her lips like daisy petals directly onto the page. *The Margarita Poems* and *For Christine* transcend the labels, the gossip, the insults pronounced in an attempt to package and stamp her with sexual stereotypes.

On the transcendence of being Luz Mar/garita

Having survived the sorrows and misfortunes in wonderland, Umpierre-Herrera embarks on a journey that takes her across the river of madness, racism and sexism, only to emerge as a survivor with her identity intact. As she rejects the sexual and cultural images associated with "María," she searches for a name that will subvert all of the traditional discourses of oppression. *Margarita* emerges as an alternative only to pose the question of its identity. In her introduction, the author explains:

> Margarita is an intoxicating drink, a flower back home in Puerto Rico, the title of a traditional "danza" that was a favorite of my mother and the name of a woman I love. Margarita is all of these and none. Margarita is my muse, Margarita is my poetry, Margarita is my imaginary lover, Margarita is my Self. (*MP* 1)

But *margarita*, in the hands of this clever poet, becomes a pun on the words *mar* (sea) and *garita* (garret, tower). These sentry boxes can be found all around El Morro Fort in Old San Juan, built by the Spanish in the sixteenth century. *Margarita* is also used as a symbol of the colonization and the oppression of the island, as the walls of the fortress built by the colonizers stand four hundred years later.

In an interview with Mireya Pérez-Erdélyi, after a poetry reading in 1985, Umpierre-Herrera explained how for the longest time she had felt divided, as if living between two worlds (66). Afraid that she, too, would end like Plath and Woolf, living in this schizophrenia, the writer spoke of what would become *The Margarita Poems* (*MP* 1987). The principle behind these poems, she explained, was her realization that the "ultimate liberation" can only take place when a woman "looks at herself" and begins the process of self-identification (67–68). For Umpierre-Herrera, this means allowing the different voices inside of her to speak.

In his analysis of this collection, Roger S. Platizky believes that these poems are a fine example of how "redemptive art is a communal act."[13] Against the idealized inspiration of a "Beatrice" or a "Laura," Umpierre-Herrera invokes the names of real women, such as Sor Juana Inés de la Cruz, Julia de Burgos, Sylvia Plath, Marge Piercy, and Marjorie Agosín.[14] *The Margarita Poems* contain four short introductory essays (by Julia Alvarez, Carlos Rodríguez, Roger S. Platizky, and the author herself) and nine poems "written in movement" (*MP* 2), proclaiming her lesbian identity and her love for other women. Ultimately, the book is an affirmation of self-love, proclaiming who she is as a lesbian woman and her right to love and be loved by other women.

The journey begins with the first poem, "Immanence," in which the "I" is crossing the "MAD river in Ohio," struggling not to drown under the weight of all the names others have called her: "sinful, insane and senseless, / a prostitute, a whore, / a lesbian, a dyke" (16). Thus starts the quest for that which is immanent in her, that which only exists in her consciousness. Most of the stanzas begin with the present progressive: "I am crossing," "I am traversing," "I am transferring my Self," making the reader a witness to the transformation that is taking place right in front of us. She invokes "armies of Amazons," she rejects traditional roles by "changing my clothes," "clicking my heels," and she arrives at her own "lustful / kingdom, / in sexual lubrication / and arousal" (17).

In order to get to what is essential in her being, the speaker has to search deep inside her body, reach "my clitoral Queendom," in order "to unfold my margarita, / my carnal daisy / that buds between / my spread out legs" (18). Only then is she able "to bring my Julia forth / lesbian woman." Traditional, patriarchal religions have denied the female body because it is usually associated with sin. As discussed in chapter two, women are to become mothers without ever being considered sexual beings, with their own passions and desires. One might call it "sexless maternity," as does Yvonne Yarbro-Bejarano, epitomized in the asexual pregnancy of the *Virgin* Mary. Cherríe Moraga argues that "if the spirit and sex have been linked in our oppression, then they must also be linked in the strategy toward our liberation."[15] Throughout this collection, metaphors are graphically erotic and physically sensual. Like Sandra María Esteves, who uses *santería* and salsa to find her own *paradise*, Umpierre-Herrera invades her own body to expose a sacred "queendom," a holy land, an Edenic garden where "the rosie colored lips / covered with hair / of Margarita, / my yellow margarita" can blossom (18).

At this point the poem stops and the reader is told there is a "(pause)" before the verses resume. Umpierre-Herrera inserts this word in several poems in this book. "(Pause)" suggests a parenthetical instruction for a recital or for an actor on stage. Added to the sense of movement of some of the poems, the collection reads like monologues of characters entering and exiting the stage. With her pervasive sense of physicality and concreteness, Umpierre-Herrera insists on a dramatic performance of her quest for self-assertion.

This dramatic pause signals not only a change in verb tense but also the success of the transformation. "I am Julia / I have crossed the river," affirms the second to last stanza. The present perfect in "I have crossed" and "I have come forth" announces the completion of the process and the achievement of an identity rooted in the present "I am," reminiscent of Morales' and Levins Morales' self-affirmations. Now that, like Plath's "lady lazarus," she has survived the turbulent waters of oppression and has emerged alive, "Julia" can "touch my petals" and proclaim the love for herself: "I love me, / I love me not" (18).

Having established her own identity, the next two poems deal with the assertion/insertion of that persona back into the city. "Transcendence" describes her reentry into society, but this time, on her own terms (*MP* 19–20). She has returned "a soltar a Julia" ("to let Julia loose") and to break all social conventions. This time, she will dishevel her hair, both on top and between her legs; she will take off her clothes and "dress of Spring during the winter"; she will rub her breasts against people and let others touch her buttocks. She will transcend the norms and expectations of society, so that she can be true to her "yellow sex," her daisy. She knows what will happen: people will want to imprison her for not conforming.

"No Hatchet Job" begins every stanza with "They would like" and goes on to describe how society "would like" to deal with her (*MP* 21–22). If "they" fail to change her and are unable to proclaim, "We have domesticated this unruly woman," "We have saved, we have cured this vulnerable woman," then they will "have her OD on the carpet" (21). Like Julia de Burgos and Sylvia Plath, they can bury her and make her into a myth: "We have glorified this poet woman" (22). But the reader already knows that Luz Mar/garita Alice does not like to be canned and labeled, and the poem's last stanza proposes a different set of adjectives from those "they would like" to assign to her. She is "headstrong," "intractable," "unrestrained, unshielded / willfully / WRITER / WOMAN" (22). The capitalized words at the end remind the reader of Umpierre-Herrera labeling herself "HUMANA" in "La Receta."

This "woman / writer" will not conform to any preconceived notions of womanhood, sexuality, or poetry. Even in her introduction, she defies those who have questioned the validity of this volume because it only has nine poems (*MP* 2). According to Roger Platizky, *The Margarita Poems* challenge "patriarchal and heterosexist assumptions about female sexuality, power, and desire."[16] Like Sandra María Esteves, Umpierre-Herrera recognizes the oppression of both her colonized island and the female body and sexuality. In their introduction to *¿Entiendes? Queer Readings, Hispanic Writings*, Emilie L. Bergmann and Paul Julian Smith explain that the "agenda of repressive political regimes includes gender conformity and, specifically, persecution of homosexuals" (7). Colonial governments are not only interested in political and economic power, but also in exerting control over every aspect of daily life, be it cultural, sexual, or psychological. Only then can the colonizer ensure the total subordination of the "natives." An important consequence is the internalization of oppression, where the oppressed begin to assimilate similar patterns of racism, sexism, homophobia, etc.[17] Moraga and Anzaldúa both recognize the fact that sometimes women of color, and especially lesbians, will silently conform to patriarchal norms, afraid of being accused of betraying their own culture and consequently becoming totally alienated.

The problem is compounded for gay and lesbian Puerto Ricans. Arnaldo Cruz-Malavé examines the traditional metaphors of effemization of the island that have silenced all homoeroticism in the country's literature during the first half of the twentieth century.[18] Both Antonio S. Pedreira and René Marqués insist on the faulty character of Puerto Ricans and argue for a return "to the paternalistic rhetoric of the nineteenth-century *hacendados*" (Cruz-Malavé 140). Marqués often uses the parable of a boy growing up and achieving "manhood" and "independence." The failed struggle for nationhood is often symbolized in the character of a "feminized man," sometimes even crossdressing. Cruz-Malavé will not allow for the irony of this argument to go unnoticed by underlining the fact that Marqués was himself a homosexual.

The search and affirmation of a lesbian identity has never been easy. "Madre" and "Ceremonia Secreta" speak of the resultant anguish and despair of losing the "mother" in one and "Margarita" in the other. "Madre" is not only about the lost mother, who has died, but also a quest for that which is maternal in her, for that which provides nourishment and strength within (*MP* 28–29). It will be in "Letter to Moira," included in *For Christine*, that Umpierre-Herrera will finally delve into the notion of lesbian motherhood. For now, "Madre" depicts the desperate tasting, touching, groping, of different flowers, muscles, caverns, in order to achieve self-knowledge. "Ceremonia Secreta" traces the long, painful journey of discovery of her lesbian self (*MP* 30–32). The question, "¿Dónde estás Margarita?" ("Where are you, Margarita?"), is followed by references to previous poems and collections in which the "she" was absent. Like many homosexuals who try to conform, she, too, admits to "lying" and to "calling out masculine names," but to no avail. She also recognizes that, in spite of all her efforts, Margarita remains elusive and will always escape her verses. After a "(Pausa)," which again enhances the theatrical quality of this collection, the verses begin to speak of a witch, magic, incantations, and riddles, all the necessary ingredients for the "secret ceremony" that is about to begin. The reader is invited at the end of the poem to turn the page literally so that the sacred ceremony, the incantations of "The Margarita Poem" can begin.

Probably one of Umpierre-Herrera's most accomplished writings, "The Margarita Poem" depicts the epic struggle for the liberation of the poet's muse, her poetic voice, her lesbian being, and, ultimately, herself. The first part, written in English, describes the drowning and almost total annihilation of "Self the Muse/ The Sea" and of "her language" (*MP* 33–34). The repetition of the monosyllabic "glu, glu" not only recreates onomatopoetically in Spanish the water bubbles made by a person submerged but also the deterioration of the language. She "must invent a language / to heroinely save hers" (*MP* 34). Only with new metaphors will she be able "to dismember the patriarch, / to destroy the colonizer's tools," and to rid herself of "dogmatic lies / and religious guilts." She will have to find her own words, her own spells in order for her to perform her own miracles and resurrect Lady Lazarus. At first she tries "Jeringonza," a nonsense language. But ultimately, she returns to her mother tongue, Spanish, to rescue "los dos símbolos isleños: / el mar, mi mar, verdoso, azul, / y la garita, el puente del vigía, del colonizador" ("the two island symbols: / the sea, my sea, greenish, blue / and the garret, the sentry box, that of the colonizer" *MP* 35).

The poem goes on to explain the need to rescue "la garita" ("the garret"), a silhouette that usually decorates tourist advertisements for the island. It is as if sign and signifier have to be rescued from one another. *La garita* is indeed part of the fortress of El Morro, and is commonly known as *la garita del diablo* (the devil's garret).[19] El Morro was an essential military facility for the defense of the island by the Spaniards. After the American invasion, it was occupied by U.S. armed forces who found its strategic position on the Caribbean of great use during World War II. Thus, as the poem indicates, the fortress is associated with "rifles, canons, and nuclear bombs." It has become an emblem of the presence of the colonizer on the island "of prejudice," "of the English language." With its huge walls that surround the old city of San Juan, it signifies the imprisonment, the isolation of that island that is not even allowed to be touched by *la mar* (the sea).

Here the next section of the poem begins with the transformation and the transcending of all barriers to achieve the reunification of *mar / garita*, of the sea and the island, of "LUZ Y MAR," of Luz María with her muse / Self. Only the words spoken from within the female body, from the mouth and the vagina, from the esophagus and the rectum, from the fallopian tubes and the uterus—words, letters, syllables, they all have to be spit out, vomited onto the page. Imperative verbs command the transformation. Another "Pausa" signals the last part of the poem. The repetition of the adverb "ya" ("already") signals the completion of the process of liberation: "La isla ya está libre" ("The island is already free" *MP 38*). The poem ends with the recognition of the muses that came before her, de Burgos, Agosin, Piercy, and the proclamation of her love for her island, for language, for freedom, for "wise women," and for self.

The ultimate liberation takes place within her own body. She is not a fool; she does realize that:

Hay un pueblo isleño
esclavo en el Caribe
pero una isla amazónica libre
en el exilio:
aquí en mi cuerpo,
que hoy se llena de libertad y de luz (*MP* 39).

["There are island people / slaves in the Caribbean / but a free Amazonic island / in exile: / here in my body, / that today fills up with freedom and light."]

The poem ends with a date (December 10, 1985), which one might assume is the date of composition. Appropriately, it is called "Día de la libertad" ("Day of Freedom"). *The Margarita Poems* are composed of petals of courage and intelligence, poetic maturity and emotional vulnerability, the strength of a woman's body and the fragility of her heart. The author acknowledges in the introduction the warning of her friends that some of these words, these poems, may be "hurled against" her. But in order to survive, Luz María has to transcend the labels, the walls, the prejudices, and the stereotypes raised by others. She has to perform her own miracles, to raise her own Lady Lazarus, and call it by name: Luz Mar/garita.

Umpierre-Herrera is very much aware that once she has spoken the words of her sexuality and her identity, the struggle only begins: the miraculous resurrection of her muse / Self will have to be repeated again and again. *For Christine: Poems and One Letter* (FC 1995) is a delicate bouquet, a humble offering to those who, dead or alive, inspired the Puerto Rican poet "to survive." The introduction describes the terrifying circumstances that led to these poems, a lawsuit that left her destitute, at times without shelter and without food. When she was hospitalized, her doctors would not allow her to participate in group therapy out of fear of her open lesbianism. These poems differ from her previous collections because of the raw emotions and intimacy of suffering that are depicted.

The "one letter," mentioned in the title, is a missive to Moira, the young daughter of a colleague with whom the poet had fallen in love. While at the hospital, a woman asked Umpierre Herrera if the little girl in the picture was her daughter. The question left her baffled and led her to consider her feelings. As the letter unfolds, the writer realizes that she indeed would like to think of Moira as her daughter. But can a lesbian woman be a mother? As she ponders these questions, she comes to similar answers as those of Moraga: "I am a Lesbian because my primary relationship in my life was with a woman—my mother" (FC 34). She is a lesbian because she loves women and she cares for their rights and their dignity. She can then proclaim her lesbian relationship, which has less to do with sex than with her love for her colleague and the child. To be a lesbian mother is indeed about "calling things, finally, by their true name in life." Hence she finishes the letter declaring that "Tía Luzma would be floored but honored to have you [Moira] as her child," and she begs the girl to "always remember our Lesbian relationship" (FC 38).

It is this honesty, this integrity, this absolute sense of truth that makes Luz María Umpierre-Herrera and her poetry so controversial, so difficult at times, but also so absorbing and so essential for the survival of women of color, lesbians, and the Alice / María / Margarita / Julia that lives in every one of us. . . . *Y Otras Desgracias / And Other Misfortunes* . . . opens with an epigraph from Franz Kafka about the kind of books that are needed: "A book should serve as the axe for the frozen sea within us." Like a captain of a shipwreck, Umpierre-Herrera has set the course for her poetry to cut through the "frozen mentality" of people in Bryn Mawr, in Philadelphia, and ultimately in "wonderland." The scathing critical assault on traditional ideologies of race, sexuality, and gender, make us feel, as Kafka says, "as though we were on the verge of suicide." But right when we are about to drown forever in this maelstrom of racism and sexism, Umpierre-Herrera's tender and lyrical affirmations of love for self and other women cut through the fog as a beam of hope. Her poems emerge like *margaritas* amid the frozen sea, as tools of survival amid "cultural schizophrenia." Luz María's verses empower all women to find names of their own.

Notes

1. Agnes Lugo-Ortiz describes the laws passed in 1974 that specify homosexual relations as criminal acts and dictated harsher sentences (up to ten years of imprisonment).
2. Originally published by Persephone Press in Watertown, Mass.; all quotes here belong to the second edition published by Kitchen Table in Latham, N.Y. in 1983.
3. The biographical information was obtained from an interview with the author published by Mireya Pérez-Erdélyi, "Luz María Umpierre—Poeta Puertorriqueña," *Chasqui* 16.2 (November 1987), 61–68; and Nancy Vosburg's biographical entry, "Luz María Umpierre-Herrera," in *Contemporary Lesbian Writers of the United States: A Bibliographical Critical Sourcebook*, ed. Sandra Pollack and Denise D. Knight (Westport: Greenwood Press, 1993), 549–555.
4. *Trigueño* designates a person of darker complexion. It can refer to a person of light olive complexion or very dark.
5. "Feminism and Racism: A Report on the 1981 National Women's Studies Association Conference," in *Making Face, Making Soul / Haciendo Caras: Creative and Critical Perspectives by Feminists of Color*, ed. Gloria Anzaldúa (San Francisco: Aunt Lute Books, 1990), 62. She also sum-

marizes the arguments for "Third World Women," but most of the *Puerto-rriqueñas* discussed in this book prefer the term "women of color."

6. See Eileen J. Suárez Findlay's *Imposing Decency*, a study about sexuality and race at the end of the nineteenth century in Puerto Rico; and Winthrop R. Wright's *Café con Leche*, a book about race in Venezuela, which in many ways reflects the attitudes in Latin American countries without the factor of an American colonizing government.

7. (Albany: State University of New York P, 1995). Other groundbreaking studies were Sarah Nieves-Squires' "Hispanic Women: Making their Presence on Campus Less Tenuous" (Washington, D.C.: Association of American Colleges, 1991); María de la Luz Reyes and John J. Halcón's "Practices of the Academy: Barriers to Access for Chicano Academics" in *The Racial Crisis in American Higher Education*, eds. P. Altbach and K. Lomotey. (Albany: State University of New York P, 1991, 167–186; and Guadalupe Valdés's "Minority and Majority Members in Foreign Language Departments: Towards the Examination of Established Attitudes and Values" (*ADFL Bulletin* 22.2 [Winter 1991]: 10–14).

8. *Coche* and *Carro* both mean car, but different countries give preference to one term or the other. *Carro* might be considered an Anglicism, but it is fully acceptable. *Cena* means supper while *Comida* refers to a meal, regardless of the time of day. Some countries use *comida* to refer to the main meal of the day because it is considered to be the one complete meal. The choice of words would depend on nationality, on preference, on context. There is not an inherently incorrect usage.

9. As one of the last colonies of Spain, Puerto Rico has retained many words from the nineteenth century that have already disappeared or were never used in some of the other colonies that gained their independence in the early 1800s.

10. One of the characteristics of Castilian Spanish is the pronunciation of the "zeta" (z) as a "th" sound. In Latin America and especially the Caribbean, people do not make a marked distinction between the c, s, and z.

11. In her introduction to *The Margarita Poems*, she responds to readers who question the validity of a poetry "volume" with only nine poems, 2.

12. "Luzma" is Umpierre-Herrera's nickname, an abbreviation of her first two names, Luz María.

13. "From Dialectic to Deliverance: Luz María Umpierre's *The Margarita Poems*," *La Escritora Hispánica*. Actas de la decimotercera conferencia anual de literatura hispánicas, ed. Nora Erro-Orthmann and Juan Cruz Mendizabal, 265.

14. Sor Juana Inés de la Cruz was a renowned poet of the seventeenth century who became a nun so that she could devote her life to her studies and her writing. Marjorie Agosin and Marge Piercy are contemporary writers.

15. *Loving,* 123.
16. "From Dialectic . . . ," Erro-Orthmann and Mendizabal, 265.
17. See Geraldine Moane's *Gender and Colonialism.*
18. "Toward an Art of Transvestism: Colonialism and Homosexuality in Puerto Rican Literature" in *¿Entiendes?,* 137–167.
19. Legend has it that, during the Spanish occupation of the fortress, soldiers assigned for night duty to the most remote garret kept disappearing. Superstition gave way to stories about devils and/or seducing *Taínas.*

Chapter 6
Kissing the Mango Tree: Judith Ortiz Cofer and the Ritual of Storytelling

Nicholasa Mohr speaks of "kissing the mango tree" and beginning to tell stories.[1] Judith Ortiz Cofer describes countless afternoons when her grandmother sat underneath the "mango tree" and entertained the whole family with her narratives, until she could not distinguish between her Mamá's and her own voice. For these writers, writing was not a choice, but an urgent need. The conclusions of the previous five chapters articulate with different rhetoric the same notion: for these *puertorriqueñas,* writing becomes the tool, the weapon, the magic wand enabling them to authorize themselves in a literary tradition that up until the second half of the twentieth century denied them access. It is through writing that these women can create a space of their own, can rescue themselves from the borderlands of literary canons and stand at the epicenter of their own imaginary community. They will use any means to give expression to their voices, muted for so long. So, they co-opt literary genres, such as the *bildungsroman*, traditionally associated with masculine characters; they subvert traditional political discourses; they revise old myths and children's tales; they use music, fluids, drawings, religion, and even *santería* to create a homeland somewhere between the island and the continent, where their authorial "I" stands erect with dignity.

Perhaps because she always wanted to be a teacher, or perhaps because she became an English professor, conducting workshops on creative writing all over the United States, Judith Ortiz Cofer seems to be keenly aware of this process of creation through writing. She speaks of writing and the art of storytelling in many of her own works, including an autobiography and an essay. As she consciously examines her own craft and that of others, she begins to realize its sacredness. Visions of a temple appear before her where she recognizes her *"comadres,"*[2] high priestesses of storytelling that have opened and shown her the mystical road. The cosmogony is mixed and varied, from Virginia Woolf to her own grandmother, from books at the library to old folktales, from classical literary characters, such as Scheherezade, to the local town characters, real and fictional, such as María Sabida. Ortiz Cofer's readers become aware of a process of initiation and anointment that allows her to pronounce words of incantations and spells that summon a universe of partial truths, controversial memories, conflicting emotions, and ambiguous lessons about life.

Judith Ortiz Cofer was born in 1952 in Hormigueros, a small town on the western coast of Puerto Rico. Her father was in the Navy, based in the Brooklyn Navy Yard, and occasionally had to go on sea tours for up to six months. Her mother never adapted to and never allowed herself to be adopted by the United States. Therefore, everytime the father left for prolonged duty, she would take the children and move back to the island to live with her family. Life there centered around the figure of the grandmother, a woman who held the reins of her household with the power of her stories. Thus began what Ortiz Cofer calls her "gypsy lifestyle," half of the time in Paterson, New Jersey, and the other in a small, rural town in Puerto Rico.

When she was fifteen, her family moved to a rural town in Georgia, where they were probably the first Hispanics in the area. Years later, Ortiz Cofer's father died in a car accident, and her mother moved permanently back to her hometown, having never learned to speak English. Ortiz Cofer, already an adult, carried on with her annual visits to the island to spend the summers with her mother and grandmother.

"Cultural schizofrenia" developed as the family lived two completely different lives: in New Jersey, the father insisted on them acting and looking like Americans, afraid of the prejudicial stereotypes of Puerto Ricans; on the island, she attended the local parochial school and was expected to follow all the traditions of a typical small town. Growing up was a constant struggle against traditions and rituals that threatened to stifle her creative spirit.

Her writing searches for new rituals that will protect, stabilize, and consecrate her identity. She also breaks the traditional paradigms of literary genres, mixing poetry, short stories, creative essays, and fictional autobiography in many of her books. *Terms of Survival* (1987) and *Reaching for the Mainland & Selected New Poems* (1995) are collections of poetry. *The Line of the Sun* (1989), a novel nominated for the Pulitzer Prize, chronicles two generations of a family, especially depicting life in a rural small town in Puerto Rico back in the forties and fifties. *An Island Like You* (1995) is a collection of short stories about male and female teenagers living in New York. Her other three books are mixed genres. *Silent Dancing: A Partial Remembrance of a Puerto Rican Childhood* (1990) is an autobiographical collection of stories, essays, and poems that documents her "gypsy lifestyle" and examines the meaning of conflicting memories. *The Latin Deli* (1993) is a smorgasbord of literary genres and a metaphor of the lives of women in *El Barrio*. *The Year of Our Revolution* (1998) also resorts to poetry, short stories, and "creative non-fiction" to describe the festering rebellion of an adolescent girl during the sixties.

A predominant theme in her work is the tension of living between two cultures. In an interview with Edna Acosta-Belén, Ortiz Cofer declares that she is indeed "a composite of two worlds" (91). But aside from the geographical split of her homes, she recognizes a split of social spheres in both Puerto Rican and American society: the world of men and the world of women (92). During her stays on the island, she notices that the two worlds are very definitely demarcated and that one is not to cross over the boundaries. Gender roles are specifically defined. Cooking, childbearing, child-rearing, housekeeping, and the preservation of morality and local traditions are the realm of women. Working, drinking, sexual entertainment, traveling, and wandering are the men's.

The first part of the *The Line of the Sun* (*LS*) takes place in the small rural town of Salud, which ironically means Health. It chronicles the wild adventures of Guzmán, the uncle of the narrator. The inhabitants of Salud are very serious about the spiritual, emotional, and economic health of their town. Women, and especially the members of the Holy Rosary Society, are the guardians and enforcers of the mores and customs that will ensure a decent life for everyone in the area. There are very specific rules about courtship, appropriate gender behavior, and social responsibilities according to class. Rosa La Cabra (the goat, the pejorative name given to women of doubtful morals) transgresses her role as *espiritista* (Spiritualist) and seduces young Guzmán instead of cleansing him of evil influences. Because of this and the well-known fact that many of the most respectable men in town visit her at night, the women declare war against her until she has been expelled from her childhood house and her hometown. The same women that have sought her potions to restore the love and passion of their husbands, now threaten to expose her to her daughter and ultimately take the child away from her (she is adopted by the president of the society).

Rosario Saturnino is also a victim of this strict morality. She has been condemned to be a spinster and live imprisoned in her own house after her reputation was compromised by Guzmán, who fell down from her balcony awakening everyone in town. The fact that Rosario is still a virgin, since it is obvious that the couple did not have time to consummate their passion, is irrelevant. As far as the town is concerned, she is damaged goods.

There are double standards for the moral expectations of men. Papá Pepe, Guzmán's father, is also an *espiritista*, but well-respected and accepted in town. As opposed to Rosa, nobody accuses him of witchcraft. During the persecution of Rosa, none of the men that have slept with her and sought her favors are accused or even censured. One of the most blatant examples is Don Antonio, the grandfather of the narrator. It is common knowledge that this alcoholic man abuses his family, sold his baby daughter to his American boss to satisfy the needs of a barren wife, and is given to all kinds of vices, from gambling to violence. Yet, at the end, when he commits suicide after spending the night at a seedy bar, everyone, including the local churchgoers, looks the other way and gives him the funeral services and a sacred burial appropriate to a man of his social status.

Women are supposed to attend church on Sundays, covering their heads. Walking to and from church, they are to keep their eyes on the ground so as not to make eye contact with a man and incite sinful desires. They are not to speak or be seen in the company of a man without a proper chaperone.

In her autobiographical text, *Silent Dancing* (*SD*), Ortiz Cofer explains the devotion to the Virgin in her hometown, Hormigueros. Legend has it that the Virgin appeared at the top of a mountain to a poor farmer and saved him from a raging bull. This and other miracles attributed to these apparitions gave origin to the devotion of the Virgen del Pozo (Virgin of the Well, or the Black Virgin, as Ortiz Cofer calls her). A church was built at the top of the mountain with steps that went all the way up to it. Pilgrimages are made to this shrine, and it is not unusual to see some pilgrims climb the steps on their knees. Women, thus, are confined to their "own endless rituals of religion and superstition" (*SD* 40). In the essay "Advanced Biology," in *Latin Deli* (*LD*), the writer explains the significance of religion:

> our Catholic faith determined our family's views on most things, from clothing to the unmentioned subject of sex. Religion was the shield we had developed against the cold foreign city. (120)

Her mother always insisted on the need to "pay your respects to God and all his court with the necessary rituals" (*LD* 120). Consequently, prayers, religious services, and intense devotion to various saints were central to their lives. The Church even prescribes the proper expression of mourning down to the details of clothing and period of time.

It is no wonder, then, that man is "a small-letter god in his home" (*SD* 31). In spite of the "power" that women seem to have in their homes, the ultimate authority, the last word, is that of the husband. Even her father exerts his influence in absentia by constantly sending letters from his various naval posts with detailed instructions for the care and the education of his children. Her mother lives in fear that the children fall and hurt themselves, and she will have to explain a scar or something worse.

As she listens to her grandmother's stories, in *Silent Dancing*, the young Judith realizes that these are indeed lessons on "what it was to be woman, more specifically, a Puerto Rican woman" (*SD* 14). As she looks at the older women around her, she recognizes her maternal and paternal grandmothers, women whose bodies have been ravaged by pregnancies, childbearing, and miscarriages. The maternal grandmother comes up with an ingenious solution. After having her eighth child, she asks her husband to add one more room to the house (additions that were common with the arrival of more children). Once the room is ready with all her specifications in measurements, shelves, furniture, etc., she then informs her husband that *he* can move in. She has to give up "the comfort of Papá's sexual love for something she deemed greater: the right to own and control her body" (*SD* 28).

Toward the end of the autobiographical essays, the adolescent Judith begins to recognize a "subtext of sexual innuendo" in her grandmother's stories and to detect "the sarcasm, and to find hidden clues to their true feelings of frustration in their marriages and in their narrowly circumscribed lives as women in Puerto Rico" (*SD* 142). There is one more lesson to be learned: there are only three choices available to women, and all of them are determined by her body. First, a woman can marry and assume her natural reproductive role. Second, she can become a nun and deny not only the reproductive function but the sexuality of the female body altogether. And last and the least of the options, she can enter *"la vida"³* ("the life" of prostitution) (*SD* 141). The irony of the latter option is that a woman's sexual activity is associated with life, real life; this is painfully recognized by Ortiz Cofer, who also observes how Mamá had become "an automaton programmed for life" and "followed a routine of labor and self-sacrifice into her old age" (*SD* 141). The expansive and spacious *casa* of the beginning, where children can roam freely and play, is now a smothering and suffocating place.

The teenage narrator Isabel / Elenita of *The Year of Our Revolution* is also very aware of the dichotomy between the world of men and women. At home, there is a mother obsessed with religion and always involved in church activities. The father, on the other hand, when he is not working as a janitor in their building, is working at a nightclub as a master of ceremonies. Soon the teenager discovers that the glamorous nightlife of her father is nothing more than introducing striptease acts with lewd jokes.

As the keeper of traditions and morals, the mother establishes the parameters of conduct for her daughter. Conversations at the dinner table are carefully regulated so that the father's work is never discussed, and many other topics remain taboo. In fact, one time Elenita commits the unthinkable offense of mentioning "breasts" as she tries to explain her changing body and the fact that the traditional dresses her mother wants her to wear are too tight. As the girl begins to date, there are more boundaries set up: a Catholic girl cannot go out with Protestants or Jews; and as a Puerto Rican, she is not to date Italian boys. Unfortunately, the teenager discovers her mother's motivations are not only to promote good morals but to protect her from prejudice and rejections. As Nicholasa Mohr depicts in her fiction, becoming a *señorita* brings together a whole set of commandments, the do's and don'ts of female behavior, that can be quite overwhelming and bewildering to a young girl.

In *Reaching for the Mainland* (*RM*, 1995), Judith Ortiz Cofer stretches out her search for a Puerto Rican national and cultural identity that is constantly blurring between tropical colors and shades of winter greys. The first part of the poetry collection, "The Birthplace," includes a number of poems that depict the suffocating customs of her hometown on the island. The section is populated with the quaint characters that strolled the familiar streets and now give title to her poems: "The Woman Who Was Left at the Altar" (5), "Housepainter" (6), "The Man Who Lost His Handwriting" (11), and "The Fruit Vendor," whose ear was cut by a *machete* because of a woman (18). It is not only people who give life to her hometown, but animals such as "The Mule" (10) and the roosters in "Pueblo Waking" (15). "On the Island I Have Seen" provides a picture of everyday life: "Men cutting cane under a sun relentless / . . . / Old men playing dominoes in the plazas / . . . children who pass by on their way to school, / . . . / . . . the starched nun who leads them in silence. / Women in black dresses keeping all the holy days" (9). Underneath the idyllic images of small-town life, there are the "dry fields" "where a man learns the danger or [sic] words, / where even a curse can start a fire."

The oppressive and suffocatingly repetitive ceremonies of daily life are also depicted in "Costumbre" ("Custom"), included in *Terms of*

Survival (*TS*, 1987). The poem summarizes a typical afternoon at the town square: "prostitutes play / dominoes / . . . / with men," while the "wives / who must walk by / on their way / to evening mass / cross themselves / and look away" (*TS* 19). For Juan Bruce-Novoa, "Costumbre" epitomizes the main theme of *Terms of Survival,* denouncing "the central function of religious ritual in maintaining the system of repression that more often than not victimizes women—and that system of repressed desire and macho double standards" (1991, 95). In *The Line of the Sun,* as long as the women go to church and say their prayers, the morality of the town will be strong and "healthy." With the dispensation and blessings secured by the women's prayers, the men can freely pursue their own desires.

The poem "La Fe" ("The Faith") acknowledges the imprint that years of religion have left in the poet, admitting that every time she hears a bell, she has to "fight the urge to genuflect / before marble statues" (*TS* 12). To this day, she has to "pray / to be released from rituals." This, her first published work, depicts Ortiz Cofer's search for survival on her own terms. It will be in the art of storytelling, learned from her grandmother, that she will find the answer to her prayers: rituals of renewal and affirmation.

Cultural anthropologists define rituals as "formal, patterned," "conscious and voluntary, repetitious and stylized" actions or "public performances."[4] Traditionally, rituals are associated with the stability and equilibrium of a society (Evans 1121). However, new studies reveal that these ceremonies or actions can have different objectives. Zuesse categorizes rituals according to purpose. On the one hand, there are the "confirmatory rituals" that "*maintain* distinctions within a divine order" and, on the other, the "transformatory rituals" that "bridge divisions and *effect transformations,* renewing that order" (414, emphasis added). Like many who grow up in a very conservative and strict Catholic environment, with protective parents, Ortiz Cofer could not wait to break out of the rituals of that culture. But as an adult, she admits to Acosta-Belén, that she realizes that "you can both be free of the rituals and use them in a different way. Now they enrich my writing, but I am no longer a prisoner of them" (88). She does recognize sadly that "many Puerto Rican women are still prisoners of their rituals."

Interestingly enough, Ortiz Cofer had to go back to the customs of her childhood on the island to find the tools of her craft. As depicted in *Silent Dancing*, it was a magical kingdom of carefree play and engrossing tales. Whether the women were sitting and doing a chore (such as cleaning the rice), breaking for coffee, or taking the children to play out by the mango tree, the grandmother was always ready with a story. It was a sacred time in which the children knew to keep quiet, and no one was to interrupt or the story would not be finished that day. What the young Judith began to realize was that underneath the entertaining tone of this wealth of stories there were lessons being imparted, warnings given, and formulas for survival being passed on. The grown-up daughters would listen intently, sometimes bowing their heads in silent recognition and acknowledgment that the lesson was for them.

There was also a ritualistic element to these "public" ceremonies. They were always in the afternoon, around four o'clock. Mamá (the grandmother) would sit in a place of honor, either a rocker or on an elevated root of the mango tree, as if on a throne or at an altar. Absolute silence was required; formulaic expressions such as the traditional "colorín, colorado"[5] were used; and the stories were repeated with different names and in varying versions, conveying lessons specific to the circumstances and the audience. Ortiz Cofer calls them "parables," as if they were holy gospels spreading sacred truths (*SD* 18).

Like the grandmother, Ortiz Cofer uses storytelling to dismantle traditional behavioral paradigms and to invoke a "magical" transformation that empowers women to gain control of their bodies, their minds, their sexuality, their own space, and ultimately their lives. On several occasions, Ortiz Cofer explains why storytelling was the natural vehicle for her artistic expression. As she points out to Acosta-Belén, "my literary heritage is non-intellectual in its beginnings" (86). It wasn't until college that she began to "transfer that oral tradition into literature."

Many Latina writers, and especially the Puerto Rican writers discussed in this book, find themselves excluded from literary canons. As she began to read American books, Nicholasa Mohr found that "I, as a Puerto Rican child, never existed in North American letters."[6] The female experience was equally absent in Puerto Rican literature, which up until the seventies was mainly written by men. At the same time, Latina writers confront the prejudices of publishing companies and academia. Departments of modern languages refuse to include their works in the standard curricula because they write in English and/or about experiences in the States and, therefore, do not reflect foreign culture. English departments, on the other hand, argue that these books are the domain of foreign languages and literatures. Similarly, many scholarly journals have policies of publishing only articles dealing with Hispanic literature, i.e., written in Spanish, while others exclude critical work on Latino writers because they are not in the realm of English and/or American literary studies. Chapter 5 examines Luz María Umpierre-Herrera's scathing satire of the prejudices of these intellectual institutions.

Traditionally, the written word is associated with the hegemonic discourse of the government in power, the law, and traditional social institutions. The dichotomy between the written document and the oral text intensifies in colonized territories. In his study of Luis Rafael Sánchez's narrative, Julio Ortega shows how the Puerto Rican novelist uses the popular language of "la oralidad callejera" ("the street orality") to undermine and destabilize everything that pertains to the dominant culture, from traditional literary canons to the most sacred norms of gender roles.[7] Speaking then, not writing, is, according to Ortega, the most "powerful instrument" against the "tyranny" of written codes (15). After all, he argues, "la oralidad representa en América Latina no el lenguaje de la autoridad sino el de la marginalidad" ("orality in Latin America represents not the language of authority but that of marginality" 19). John Beverly seems to agree in his study of *testimonio*, an oral genre, which allows for the "representation" of those who have been excluded from "authorized" texts, mainly "the child, the 'native,' the woman, the insane, the criminal, the proletarian" (93). The *testimonio*, like that of Rigoberta Menchú discussed in his article, becomes a weapon of "resistance" against oppression (Beverly 106).

Marginalized by literary traditions and canons, it is not surprising that Puerto Rican women writers resort to oral traditions, as do many other Hispanic artists in the United States.[8] They actually utilize the antithesis of writing and orality to underline the tension between their marginalized voices and canonical works. For them, writing is a deliberate act of speaking out, of raising their voices to denounce, lament, celebrate, record, and name. They co-opt the formulas of storytelling, folktales and fairy tales, songs and prayers, gossip, phone conversations, and even recipes in order to authorize and inscribe themselves in a sacred tradition of their own. Julio Ortega emphasizes that orality is a viable tool for those who have been disempowered and decentralized too long:

> . . . lo oral pone en duda la jerarquización entre alta cultura y cultura popular [. . .] la palabra hablada busca legitimarse como testimonio frente a la validación de los poderes que hace la escritura . . . las licencias del decir erodan el monoligüismo burgués y su buena conciencia del decoro (24)

> [. . . orality questions the hierarchy of high culture over popular culture . . . the spoken word seeks to legitimize itself as a testimony in opposition to the validation of power granted by writing . . . the licenses of speech corrode bourgeois monolinguism and its good conscience of propriety.]

With the invocation of the spoken word, Latina writers question and subvert traditional gender and cultural roles; they denounce and attack the constricting parameters of proper female behavior; they name and validate themselves; and they initiate themselves as "keepers of the past."[9] Against the prejudices and stereotypes imprinted in written texts, orality emerges as a weapon of liberation. Judith Ortiz Cofer describes her epiphanic moment in the third grade when the teacher hit her on the head with a hardcover spelling book for not understanding the words written on the board. She "understood then that language is the only weapon a child has against the absolute power of adults" and began to build an "arsenal of words" (*SD* 66).

For a shy, confused girl constantly navigating between two cultures and forced at times to be the translator/interpreter for her adult mother, language, words, stories became a source of strength, a refuge, and a weapon. The mother in *The Year of Our Revolution* acknowledges that words were her daughter's domain: "she [the daughter] could use language to her advantage like no one else I knew" (*YOR* 86). Aside from the anecdote of the spelling book, the poem "The Man Who Lost His Handwriting" summarizes best the power of words. It is a poignant homage to Don Andrés, the "town scribe, directing every event / with pen and ink" (*RM* 11). He records the names given to children at their baptism. People would choose a name because of the beauty with which he would write certain letters. But "it was words, they say, that broke Andrés." It was also his job to transcribe the "reams of telegrams" from "two wars / in two decades," informing the mothers in town about their sons' deaths, notices that "stacked on his desk like a tombstone." Little by little, "he lost his alphabet." Years of pronouncing death, of spelling its fatal five letters, sealed the poor man's sentence to roam the streets in silence, searching for things and putting them in his pockets without ever again saying their names.

Puerto Rican women writers refuse to be silenced, like poor Don Andrés, by the oppression of the hegemonic discourse, which tends to isolate and marginalize them until their voices are muted and erased from canonical traditions. In order to avoid this sentence, Sandra María Esteves resorts to *santería* because of its communal spirit. As she invokes an alternative cosmogony of creative powers in her poetry, she is not only "saddled" by the spirits of the protecting saints but also joins a community of "sistas," women poets, jazz singers, and *Salsa* musicians. Like other Nuyorican poets, Esteves also prefers the performance, the spoken word "as an expression of communitas, commonality, communion" (Kanellos 122). Paul Zumthor emphasizes the aspect of oral communication that "bespeaks the totemic repast, the eucharist, cannibalism" (8). Ortiz Cofer wants to participate in that communion. By drinking the sap of the mango tree, she allows her grandmother's stories to flow through her until they become her own:

> as I embroidered my own fable, listening all the while to that inner voice, which, when I was very young, sounded just like Mamá's when she told her stories in the parlor or under the mango tree. And later, as I gained more confidence in my own ability, the voice telling the story became my own. (*SD* 85)

In storytelling, it is important for the teller to anchor herself within a genealogy, a community of oral tradition. In this case, she begins by echoing and repeating the stories heard from her grandmother until she finds her own voice, her own words, her own truth. This process is repeated in "Not for Sale," where the young narrator listens to the stories of Scheherezade, told by an Arabian traveling salesman who sells them a quilt depicting scenes from the *Arabian Nights*. At night, lying on her new quilt, the girl continues to listen to the stories, "since it was in my voice that she spoke to me, placing my dreams among hers, weaving them in" (*LD* 21).

Anchored in a long tradition of storytelling from both the women in her family and fictional characters, Ortiz Cofer begins her own rituals of creation, which she details in her essay, "5:00 A.M.: Writing as Ritual" (*LD* 166–168). Married, with a young child, and teaching on three different campuses, there was no time for herself, much less to do anything creative. She began then to get up at five o'clock in the morning in order to have two hours for herself before the household would awake. One hour was devoted to poetry and the other to a novel, *The Line of the Sun*, which took three-and-a-half years to complete at that pace. Her poignant essay, "Sleeping with One Eye Open," speaks loudly of the sacrifices one must make to be an artist. It also describes her "pantheon of women who sleep with one eye open," watchful of all of the demands of their daily routine that threaten to steal away their time, their energy, their creative soul. She can invoke this "clapboard temple," where she has put her Mamá, María Sabida, and other women who understand "the meaning of *being* an artist" (12).

Her poems are filled with references to the spoken word: prayers, spells, incantations, *las malas lenguas* (wagging tongues), sounds, and voices. As she explains in an interview with Jocelyn Bartkevicius, growing up in her grandmother's house was a sensory experience. Thus, when she speaks of the inspiration of different muses, she does not invoke literary figures, although she acknowledges her indebtedness to Virginia Woolf. For Ortiz Cofer, there is no classical "winged" muse, but "an old lady in Puerto Rico . . . surrounded by the *sounds* of her world" (Bartkevicius 73; emphasis added).

Sounds and words carry with them the cosmic energy of creation and of transformation. Traditionally, the word has been at the center of religious myths of creation. In the Bible, the Word is equated with God (John 1:1). Ortiz Cofer's poem, "They say," similarly proclaims the writer's birth (*SD* 48–49). The repetition of the title phrase is almost an incantation for breathing life into a baby whose blood and soul are literally "leaking" out. As the midwife works to save the child, "the women prayed" while the "Mother's breath" kept threatening to blow out the candles. With every "They say," the relatives affirm the presence of the child in this world, echoing the book of "Genesis," in which every "And then God said" is followed by an emerging portion of the universe.

While people in Ortiz Cofer's hometown go to her grandfather, a spiritualist or medium, to carry messages between the living and the dead, the writer resorts to words and stories to negotiate meaning between two worlds. Many children of Puerto Rican immigrants became literal translators/interpreters for their grown-up parents. Esmeralda Santiago, Nicholasa Mohr, and Ortiz Cofer all narrate embarrassing moments at the welfare office when as young children they had to negotiate with the adult language of "hidden innuendos" and veiled threats about issues they could barely understand. But Ortiz Cofer also recognizes the problematic aspect of translating meaning from one culture to another.[10] For her, translation is a metaphor for what she calls "the habit of movement," the constant pilgrimage from the island to the continent and back, from the apartment decorated in "Early Puerto Rican" to the streets of an American city. In one of her stories, the young adolescent complains that if any of her friends were to come into her apartment, they would suffer "culture shock."

In her interview with Bartkevicius, Ortiz Cofer reaffirms her belief that writing is a way of finding the meaning of all of her bewildering experiences while growing up. It is not a self-indulgent exercise in "self-expression," but of "self-discovery" (67). As she begins rendering the stories heard in her childhood into literature, she uncovers much of the same feminist discourse now current hidden in them. The "simple little stories" of her grandmother were a way of teaching, of giving lessons about survival, about the world, about men, about life. As she records them years later, Ortiz Cofer begins to distill from them the lessons imparted: how to gain control of one's own body, how to survive an abusive man, and how to gain some freedom and independence from a controlling husband. In many ways, the grandmother, a woman with not much formal schooling, was pronouncing a feminist discourse of liberation long before the word had become a movement.

Like her ancestors, Ortiz Cofer admits that her background is not a literary or academic one. She did not learn about the great writers of English, American, and Latin American literature until her college days. Although she began to read all the folk and fairy tales available to her in the children's section of the Paterson Public Library, it was her grandmother's storytelling that introduced her to the power of words, the beauty of language, and the creative energy of metaphors. Instead of trying to conform to literary traditions and genre theory, Judith Ortiz Cofer initiates her own rituals of creation. Inspired by Virginia Woolf, she searches for her own temple of imagination, her own tree laden with fruitful stories in order to consecrate those "moments of being," of truth, that are so important for an artist. Like Scheherezade, like her grandmother, like Eva Luna,[11] like Marisol in *The Line of the Sun*, Ortiz Cofer "would always trade my stories for what I wanted out of life" (283).

The Latin Deli (1993) is an extended metaphor of the power of words and the important role that the storyteller has within the community. At the core of this book is the story "Corazón's Café," chronicling the life of the protagonist, whose name means "heart." This *bodega*, a combination of coffee shop and small grocery store, has established itself after ten years at the heart of the community, where people come for the produce that will bring the island back to them, for a cup of coffee and a few words with others who share the same feelings of exile and loss, where the food for all important occasions, from baptisms, to weddings and funerals, is supplied. With their bags of food, the clients take away nourishment that strengthens their souls. Only in sharing stories, problems, pains, and dreams do they find solace and comfort. There is, for example, Don Cándido, who has a son in a Cuban prison and who comes every day to talk about politics and then leaves "to visit his few surviving old friends, to talk away death for one more day" (*LD* 115).

The poem, "The Latin Deli: Ars Poetica," at the beginning of the book anticipates the story of "Corazón's Café." These "rules of poetry" prescribe the most important ingredients in this temple / deli of refuge. The high priestess sits at the counter as "Patroness of Exiles" with codfish and green plantains "hanging in stalks like votive offerings" (*LD* 3). As she sells "canned memories" to the exiles, she listens to "their dreams and their disillusions." They are "all wanting the comfort / of spoken Spanish." Like the guavas in Santiago's *When I Was Puerto Rican*, reading the labels out loud evokes "the names of lost lovers." As she listens to their grocery lists as if they were poems, "she must divine, conjuring up products / from places that now exist only in their hearts— / closed ports she must trade with" (*LD* 4). As the "Madonna" in charge of the deli, she deals in yearnings and desires that she has to translate into hope and understanding.

Following these rules, the book goes on to a series of poems, stories, and "meditations" describing small ceremonies of transformation. These ultimately make up the ritual of survival that takes place every day at the *Latin Deli*. In "Note for Sale," the traveling Arabian salesman attempts to trade stories of Scheherezade to rescue his son (16–21). The girl has to sit quietly, wearing a ring on her finger and the Arabian quilt wrapped around her. If the story is interrupted, the salesman will start all over again. Soon, the young narrator's parents realize that the Arab wants to buy the girl as a wife for his son, so that he can come to the United States. "The Changeling" describes the game of dressing up as a boy in order to get her father's attention (38). The mother "was not amused / by my transformations" and the child has "to return invisible, / as myself," to eat dinner with the family. The young girl recognizes the need to "tell of life in the mountains," "my tales of battle" in order to come alive and be recognized as an individual. But she is too young, and her creative spirit is soon squelched by the reality of everyday life.

Other pieces speak of the need to "hide my secrets in poems" ("Absolution in the New Year" 40) and of hiding "under my blanket / to read forbidden fictions" ("The Purpose of Nuns" 65). Obviously her new rituals encounter the resistance of traditional conservative religious and cultural institutions. She does admit her admiration for her mother, who finally "has managed to liberate herself from the rituals, the mores, and traditions that 'cramp' her style while retaining her femininity and 'Puertoricanness,'" ("Advanced Biology" 121).

Ortiz Cofer continues to describe how she stepped into the Paterson Public Library, "a Greek temple in the ruins of an American city," and methodically read every book in the children's section (*LD* 130). As she "absorbed" all the fantastic tales that seemed to repeat themselves with some variations from culture to culture, she discovered "the sense of inner freedom, a feeling of power and the ability to fly that is the main reward of the writer" ("The Paterson Public Library" 132).

"The Witch's Husband," a central story in *The Latin Deli* collection, reveals the magical power of storytelling. The author has been summoned to Puerto Rico to convince her grandmother that Grandpa will have to go to a nursing home because of his dementia and that she, in her fragile condition, will need to move in with one of her daughters. As the narrator arrives at the house, she describes a man who "has misplaced his words" (*LD* 42). Of all the symptoms of senility, the lack of words is the one that signals the inability to go on with a normal life at home. Before the narrator has a chance to give her prepared lecture, Mamá asks her if she wants to hear a story as an offering made to invoke the rituals of their childhood. The writer remembers the same offering made whenever she was in the middle of a tantrum. Mamá goes on to tell her about the witch's husband, who found out that his wife went out every night at midnight. He followed her one night only to see her fly away to meet with other witches, in reality his neighbors' wives, and partake in a feast while speaking an incomprehensible language. Upon noticing his presence, the witches flew away. Upon discovering him the next day, the owners of the castle beat the man and left him unconscious and naked in the middle of a public road.

Upon hearing the story, Ortiz Cofer was reminded of the year her grandmother spent in New York without her husband and children, and decided to ask about it. Mamá goes on to explain how she found herself "young and pretty, full of energy and dreams" but married with four young children at that time (*LD* 47). Her husband, realizing that she was sick of heart and spirit, arranged for her sister in New York to come and take care of the kids and the household for a year while his wife went abroad. She worked as a seamstress and "lived" (*LD* 48). When she came back, she promised never to leave him again, and he never asked questions. As she said those words, the grandmother came over to Judith and finished the witch's story: the husband completely forgot what he had seen. Silenced by the beautifully poignant covenant of love of her grandparents, the narrator leaves, ready to defend her grandmother's position of never again abandoning her husband. And the story ends with a wink, a "traditional blessing," and "colorín colorado."

No rhetoric, no arguments would have been as convincing as the "Witch's Husband" story and the truth of her grandparents' commitment. Ortiz Cofer acknowledges that "a simple little story . . . is more powerful in its simplicity than anything that I could lecture her about" (Bartkevicius 64). Aside from the power to transform and change the minds and attitudes of others, these two stories also reveal the powerful need in women for freedom. In the tale, the witch is a devoted wife who always comes back to her husband; and the husband has no reason to complain, except for her nightly forays. But the husband must accept that life goes on with the witch going out every night to a place of her own, where she and other women find their own language, their own particular modes of expression, and find those things that will replenish and fortify their souls. Up until now the family has always believed that the grandmother suffers from heart disease and that she spent a year in New York taking care of her medical problem. The narrator, a grown-up Judith, a writer herself, has failed until now to understand and appreciate the need within her grandmother not just for freedom but "to live." Replenished and fortified by the experiences lived during that year, the grandmother is able to come back and take care of her family, which includes eight children, without losing her spirit or dying of heartache.

Ultimately, the craft of storytelling has empowered the grandmother to conjure up yearnings, dreams, and arguments that have allowed her to claim her body, her space, her life. It has also given her the power to pronounce spells and incantations that carry lessons of survival for all of the women in her family. Judith Ortiz Cofer realizes that she too has inherited this talent, and now she shares "The Medium's Burden," as explained in the last poem of *The Latin Deli*. As a medium, she possesses the secrets, the stories, the dreams of others and it is up to her to negotiate, to translate, to interpret, and ultimately to transform, like her grandmother did, the lives of those around her.

In "The Woman Who Slept with One Eye Open: Notes on Being a Writer," Ortiz Cofer explains how two of her grandmother's stories "have become the germinal point for not only my work as a creative artist but also my development as a free woman" (3). One is about María La Loca ("The Crazy One") and the other one, María Sabida. María La Loca is a woman who, betrayed by her lover, went crazy. Ortiz Cofer's poem, "The Woman Who Was Left at the Altar," chronicles this poor woman's descent into insanity and violence. The poem describes the character, years after being jilted, as a fat old woman who roams the streets of town with live chickens hanging from her waist for sale. With the material of her wedding gown, she makes curtains and doilies for her house. She only wears black, the color of mourning. In her madness, she shows her naked breasts to the church congregation to prove her maternal capabilities, but by now she has lost even the capacity to speak. The knife in her hand betrays her murderous rage as she confronts the dogs that follow the smell of "her skirts of flesh" and "She takes *him* [the fiancée] to the knife time after time" (*SD* 22, emphasis added). In "Casa," the narrative that precedes the poem, the narrator remembers having heard the story many times with the names changed in each new version. Laura, one of Mamá's daughters, seemed to be especially disturbed by the tale as "she knew that the fable was intended for her" (*SD* 20). Barely seventeen and still in high school, she had become engaged to a boy who had then left for New York to work. Although the girl insisted on planning the wedding, Mamá did not believe it would ever happen. The story of María La Loca was about to repeat itself.

For Ortiz Cofer, the lesson of this woman's tragedy is about allowing "love or anything else to defeat you" (Bartkevicius 65). Women, like María La Loca, who have chosen men, marriage, motherhood, and other traditional roles and who only allow themselves those choices, end up completely silenced, defeated, and living life according to the parameters and demands set by others, not by themselves. The passive voice of the title, "was left," reflects the passivity of a woman who stands still waiting for others to direct her actions. To be an artist, to be a writer, to be a "free woman," one has to defy traditional definitions of gender roles and genres and to be constantly on guard, "with one eye open," against everything that threatens to squelch your spirit.

It is in the "crude and violent tale of María Sabida" that the writer finds a model of the discipline and strength necessary for everyday survival. Typical of oral tradition, there are many versions of the María Sabida tale. At the core of the story, there is a young maid, well known for her courage and wisdom, who conquers a thief terrorizing her town. At the end, she agrees to marry the thief but still has to "sleep with one eye open" for the rest of her life. In one version, she and her girlfriends are kidnapped and given "sleep-inducing figs" in order to kill them. María Sabida recognizes the poisonous figs, and only pretends to eat them. She also withstands the pain of hot wax on her skin as the thief makes sure she is asleep. As he turns to call the others, María Sabida jumps and pushes him over the rails, causing him to fall. The thief decides to teach her a lesson, but first convinces her father and her that he wants to marry the girl that has been able to outsmart him. Aware of his deadly intentions, María Sabida makes an adult-size doll filled with honey. As he stabs her, the "blood" splashes onto his face and he realizes how sweet his wife was and how happy he could have been. She comes out of her hiding place, he professes his love, and, *colorín colorado*, they live happily ever after. But she still "slept with an eye open."

Ortiz Cofer includes this tale in *Silent Dancing* (69–85) and in *The Year of Our Revolution* (89–94). For Ortiz Cofer, María Sabida shows "that a woman can have 'macho'" ("Woman" 3). The word, "when divested of gender, . . . means the arrogance to assume that you belong where you choose to stand, that you are inferior to no one, and that you will defend your domain at whatever cost" ("Sleeping" 4). For a woman to become a writer, she has to have "macho," the courage to make a choice, to claim "a room of her own" and the time to devote to her craft.

Upon first hearing the story, Ortiz Cofer acknowledges, one might think it reinforces Catholic notions of the triumph of perseverance and virtue over evil, i.e., a virtuous woman turns a bad man around. But the author recognized long ago the strategies of rebellion subtly taught by her grandmother and to not accept the moral at face value. The more the story is told, the more meanings are revealed, and the more it becomes a metaphor of the "untapped power of creativity" ("Sleeping" 7). She recognizes in the thief "the destroyer of ambition, drive, and talent—the killer of dreams." The thief serves "sleep-inducing figs," the entrapment of daily routines and the veiled seduction of family demands that drain the energy out of women. Many of them will give in and, exhausted from satisfying everyone's needs, they will succumb to sleep. For others, like Ortiz Cofer and the writers discussed in this book, the urgency to write is too strong and, with a macho stance, they make their own choices and sacrifices, they renounce sleep and commit themselves to action and life. They live on the alert, watching out for the "sleep-inducing figs" that constantly threaten a woman's consciousness and creativity.

Within the sacred space of the blank page, Judith Ortiz Cofer performs, again and again, rituals of confirmation and transformation. With the blessing of her *comadres* and anointed with macho, she can proclaim, "I am a writer" ("Sleeping" 4). In the Catholic Church, the sacrament of confirmation allows an adult to reaffirm the faith that was given in baptism as a baby. It also endows the person with the courage of the Holy Spirit to go out and be an active apostle for the Church. Ortiz Cofer confirms her vocation as an artist, and like María Sabida, she too will defend herself courageously against anything that threatens to steal away her time, her talent, her voice.

At the core of most of her work is the problem of memory construction. Both the narrator in *The Line of the Sun* and the biographer in *Silent Dancing* are very much aware of the gaps, incongruencies, and contradictions in the recollections of the events presented. In the novel, Marisol admits that the text we are reading is the result of overheard conversations, letters, and what uncle Guzmán and her own mother have told her. And because she was a young girl, there were things that she was not told. The family's embarrassment and sense of decency obliterated many other incidents. Ultimately, the narrator affirms her own appropriation of Uncle Guzmán's life and adventures and her own reconstruction through her imagination of what his/story was supposed to be. He was her hero, a mythical character that brought life, color, and drama to her world.

The title *Silent Dancing: A Partial Remembrance of a Puerto Rican Childhood* already foreshadows the tension between memory, reconstruction of events, and the power of the imagination in what is supposed to be an autobiographical text. At different times, Ortiz Cofer acknowledges the objections of her mother and other members of the family who do not remember the events the way she does. As a daughter, as a family member, she does need reassurance: "I want my mother to tell me that what I remember is true" (*SD* 163). After all, she considers her mother, "the Keeper of the Past" (*SD* 164). Nevertheless, at the end of the book, when her mother is still insisting on her own version of the events, Ortiz Cofer affirms, "But that is not how *I* remember it" (*SD* 165).

Ortiz Cofer has struggled with her desire to record the stories of her childhood while at the same time not wanting to be a historian or a genealogist. It was Virginia Woolf's ideas about memoir writing that finally "liberated" this Puerto Rican writer. As she explains to Ocasio, "It's your childhood, you reconstruct and re-create it any way that suits you, because memory is mostly fiction" (732). With this understanding of what memory is, it is not surprising that *The Line of the Sun* finishes with the following statement from the narrator: "Right at that point, when he and I tell our best lie, I say, this is the end" (291).

With that purpose in mind, Ortiz Cofer writes what she calls "creative non-fiction," "meditations" about instances in her past. These pieces do not always follow a chronological order, and they may be embellished, hence, the adjective "creative." But as she explains again and again in interviews and lectures, her intention is to elucidate an experience, an emotion, a moment of being. In many instances, a poem emerges as an offering to placate her questions.

If the purpose of "confirmatory rituals" is to define and distinguish, Ortiz Cofer is constantly attempting to negotiate meanings. In *Silent Dancing,* she describes the difficulties when "she [her mother] and I try to define and translate key words for both of us, words such as 'woman' and 'mother'" (152). Storytelling again becomes the ritual through which they can define these terms. The recollection of the conflicts that occurred during the visits to the island is immediately followed by the mother telling the story of "Marina," as they are strolling downtown and spot an old man with a little girl. She had heard the story before about a boy that was raised by his mother as a girl named "Marina." As a shy adolescent, the "boy/girl" befriends Kiki, the mayor's oldest daughter, during the girls' baths at the river. The couple runs away and it is then that everyone finds out about what the disturbed mother had done to her son. "Marino" and Kiki lived happily ever after. Now, apparently a widower, he has returned to town with his granddaughter. The story is about what it takes to make a good husband and provides Ortiz Cofer and her mother with "a new place to begin our search for the meaning of the word *woman*" (*SD* 160).

Like Nicholasa Mohr, who searches for an understanding of the mother-daughter relationship, many of Ortiz Cofer's stories explore paternal and maternal figures and the awkward feelings of an adolescent girl. On several occasions, the writer describes the striking beauty of her petite mother with the jet black hair that gives her a gypsy look. As a young girl trying to fit into a new environment, Ortiz Cofer resented the way her mother stood out wherever they went. "The Way My Mother Walked" (*RM* 28) and "The Other" describe the mixed feelings when "A sloe-eyed dark woman shadows me," forcing her to "make room for her; she crowds me" (*RM* 40). "Meditation of My Hands" becomes an obscure elegy to the strength of her mother's hands that "were a vise / strong and quick" (*RM* 36). She "should have been a pianist, or one / of those Borgia women who strangled / their unfaithful lovers with fingers." What the poem reveals under the dark possibilities of a "vise" or "a strangler" is her admiration for her mother's hands that provided protection ("I would never have been a dropped baby") and the ever-constant comfort of her mother's strength in her life.

Words, in this case poems, also become an outlet for grief over the death of the quiet and melancholic man who was her father. While in the Navy, he was absent a lot. "My Father in the Navy" conveys the exhilaration that his expected arrival provoked:

> His homecomings were the verses
> we composed over the years making up
> the siren's song that kept him coming back

. . . .

like the evening prayer. (*RM* 25)

During the Cuban missile crisis, a young Judith had to accompany her mother to government offices to locate their father, since they had not heard from him in months. The child did not understand about the politics and the events that were taking place out in the world, only about a man that would return home even more taciturn. In "Photographs of My Father," the writer examines pictures of a very young man in his uniform and tries to understand who he was (*RM* 68–69). He died in a car accident a few years after his retirement. In *Terms of Survival*, "El Error" ("The Mistake" 40) and "To My Father" (52) describe with piercing poignancy the crash, the echo of his words, the love letters written to his family that were never delivered.

While the father was on sea duty, the children had to save all their school reports, papers, and exams to show to him on his return. As the title, "Progress Report to a Dead Father," indicates, the poem is a bitter cry for one more report, for "the hoard of words I had stored for you" that were left unsaid (*RM* 53). One of the last poems attached to *Reaching for the Mainland* depicts with painful honesty the awkward experience of meeting her mother's new boyfriend. "Through Climate Changes" takes the reader through the elegant simplicity of its metaphor to the hot humid afternoon when she met "this man who loves my mother" (*RM* 67). In spite of her grief and the picture of her father in the middle of the room, she takes the hand extended to her, a gesture that "is both a greeting / and a plea" (*RM* 66–67). With this simple gesture the daughter acknowledges and affirms the mother's need for her own life.

Judith Ortiz Cofer learned from her grandmother the transformative powers of storytelling. Those tales carried with them the potions, the formulas that could bring change to the lives of those who listened carefully between the lines. Strategies for resistance and liberation were secretly encoded within the repetition of María Sabida's adventures or La Loca's misfortunes. The family sat enthralled as Mamá transported them to different worlds, different lives, making them forget the heat of those summer afternoons, as if they were witnesses to a transfiguration. As an adult, Ortiz Cofer experienced again Mamá's power to conquer enemies with her stories. Once the granddaughter hears the story of "the witch's husband," there will be no more arguments to remove the grandparents from their ancestral home.

Armed with "an arsenal of words," the secret formulas of oral traditions, and strategies for survival, Ortiz Cofer develops her own rituals in order to transform the "cultural schizophrenia" of her childhood into the "habit of movement." Julio Ortega argues that for those within the Commonwealth of Puerto Rico with its colonial status, oral language becomes a source of identity: "Si la patria no otorga la nacionalidad . . . la otorga el habla" ("If the homeland does not grant nationality . . . it is granted by the spoken word" 18). Experiencing the same feelings of ambiguity and ambivalence that Esmeralda Santiago had about her cultural identity, Ortiz Cofer sets out to explore, in the realm of words and metaphors, memories that will make sense of her "gypsy life." The atypical unsteady geographical and spatial mobility of her childhood echoes the cultural, linguistic, and sexual instability that surrounds her. Movement, then, becomes the metaphor of the fluid identity of Puerto Ricans, a fluidity already expressed in the mechanics of liquids by Aurora Levins Morales and Rosario Morales.

Reaching for the Mainland, probably one of Ortiz Cofer's most political works, reaches out in search of a homeland and a cultural heritage. The sections, "The Birthplace," "The Crossing," "The Habit of Movement," hint at the active search, the constant motion of the poems that takes the reader to her hometown on the island, to a school yard in Paterson, to the Maya ruins, and back to New York City.

Juan Bruce-Novoa insists that both *The Line of the Sun* and *Reaching for the Mainland* are projects about cultural identity. The story of Guzmán in the novel is "mostly a product of hearsay, of oral tradition" set between two failed rituals of *santería*, which according to the critic enhances the instability of the text by allowing for "the recontextualizing act of shifting meanings" (1992, 63, 67). According to cultural anthropologists, "transformatory rituals" emerge in response to some disequilibrium, and "aim [for] the restoration of harmony" (Zuesse 416). The rituals reconstructed in *The Line of the Sun* and in "The Habit of Movement" in *Reaching for the Mainland* allow Ortiz Cofer to restore some balance, some equilibrium to an existence constantly lived between two worlds. In order to survive "the nomadic life" as a child, Judith learned not to pack "anything heavier / to carry than a wish" ("The Habit . . ." *RM* 59). She took what she had learned from the books read at the library; she began to carry "the idea of home on our backs;" and she discovered how "our habit of movement kept us safe." If a grown-up Esmeralda Santiago can pack everything she owns in one suitcase, Ortiz Cofer's baggage is as heavy as the stories of her childhood.

Instead of fighting the "quicksand" at her feet, Ortiz Cofer turns the constant shifting into a tool for her craft. According to Bruce-Novoa, "she claims that this in-betweenness is a dynamic state of creativity" (1991, 93). By co-opting the pendular nature of her life, the critic explains how Ortiz Cofer proclaims a "definition of a new Puerto Rican cultural identity [which] demands constant movement, oscillation, which ultimately places identity in the act of movement itself."

Thus, Ortiz Cofer writes texts, like Mamá's stories, constantly shifting in meaning. The instability of her memories in *Silent Dancing* becomes a deliberate strategy to empower herself and her readers with creative mobility so that we can engage, like her, in a dance of constant renewal. It is not surprising that she repeats poems, stories, and creative nonfiction in her various books. They are not fixed pieces in one particular manuscript, but constantly shifting from one text to another, subject to the creative instinct of the writer. Her creativity is not a choice but a primal need at the core of her *being*. After all, "we are all / born equipped with a gland of madness," which forces "those of us who daily waver / between writing a poem and slashing our wrists" ("We Are All Carriers" *RM* 45).

"A Poem" in *Reaching for the Mainland* invokes the ultimate aesthetic experience: ". . . a poem like the 2:30 sun / that shocks you every afternoon" (*RM* 57). Like the other writers studied in this book, Ortiz Cofer recognizes the power that their craft has to transform, to heal, to reinvent, and ultimately to create. If only she could, like a sorcerer, conjure the magic words, "A poem I would write like a fetish; / . . . / one that would change your life a little."

❧ ❧ ❧

Sandra María Esteves, Aurora Levins Morales, Rosario Morales, Nicholasa Mohr, Judith Ortiz Cofer, Esmeralda Santiago, and Luz María Umpierre-Herrera are all carriers of that "gland of madness." They had no choice but to struggle with the "killer" and his "poisonous figs," constantly threatening to silence who they are. They were born with the "medium's burden," with the "witchcraft" of spells and incantations for conjuring new identities, new realities, new experiences. They have danced and kissed the mango tree in rituals where they were anointed as *comadres*, women with macho asserting their creative powers in order to record their own versions of their memories, to own their bodies, and to call themselves "writers." They create poems, novels, short stories, memoirs, and essays that transform the way we look at the process of growing up and becoming a woman, at the relationship with our mothers and our daughters, at the fluidity of our lives, at our notions of nationhood, and our own sexuality. They have written, and their readers now live happily ever after, changed by their words.

¡Y colorín, colorado, este libro se ha acabado!

Notes

1. Juan Flores quotes Mohr in his article "Back Down These Mean Streets: Introducing Nicholasa Mohr and Louis Reyes Rivera," 52.
2. "Comadrazgo" is the bond between two women established through the sacrament of baptism. The mother and godmother of the child become "comadres," agreeing both to take care of the child, regardless of biological maternity. This is a sacred bond that goes beyond blood relationship. Judith Ortiz Cofer feels the same way about the women, real and fictional who have taught her about her craft ("Woman" 4).
3. Puerto Ricans use the euphemism "*la vida*" (the life), since prostitution is considered too ugly a word to mention.
4. See Elizabeth S. Evans's entry, "Ritual," in *Encyclopedia of Cultural Anthropology*, 1120–1123; and Evan M. Zuesse's lengthy discussion of "Ritual," in the *Encyclopedia of Religion*, 405–422.
5. An untranslatable phrase used in Spanish at the end of fairy and folktales to establish the end of the story. Sometimes, it will be followed by another verse that rhymes with it, "este cuento se ha acabado" ("this story has ended").
6. See the Introduction for a more detailed discussion of Mohr's article "Puerto Rican Writers in the U.S., Puerto Rican Writers in Puerto Rico: A

Separation beyond Language (Testimonio)," in *Breaking Boundaries*, 111–116.

7. "Teoría y Práctica del Discurso Popular (Luis Rafael Sánchez y la Nueva Escritura Puertorriqueña)," in *Reapropiaciones*, 9–52.

8. See Nicolás Kanellos' article, "Orality and Hispanic Literature of the United States," 115–123.

9. Albert Lord, in his groundbreaking study of oral tradition, *The Singer of Tales*, emphasizes the singer's "role of conserver of the tradition, the role of the defender of the historic truth" (28).

10. Cicero had already recognized the difficulty of translating from one culture to another while maintaining the same meaning. He compared it to exchanging coins into another currency, one always loses something in the transaction; *De optimo genere oratorum*, trans. H. M. Hubbell (Cambridge: Harvard UP, 1960), 349–73.

11. The main character in two of Isabel Allende's work, who actually survives poverty and saves herself from some difficult situations by telling stories.

Selected Bibliography

Primary Sources

Esteves, Sandra María. *Bluestown Mockingbird Mambo*. Houston: Arte Público, 1990.

_____. "The Feminist Viewpoint in the Poetry of Puerto Rican Women in the United States." Rodríguez de Laguna 171 177.

_____. "Open Letter to Eliana (Testimonio)." *Breaking Boundaries: Latina Writings and Critical Readings*. Ed. Ascunción Horno-Delgado, et al. Amherst: U of Massachusetts P, 1989. 117–121.

_____. *Tropical Rains: A Bilingual Downpour*. Bronx: African Caribbean Poetry Theater, 1984.

_____. *Yerba Buena. Dibujos y Poemas*. Introduction by Louis Reyes Rivera. New York: Greenfield, 1980.

Levins Morales, Aurora. *Medicine Stories: History, Culture and the Politics of Integrity*. Cambridge: South End Press, 1998.

_____. ". . . And Even Fidel Can't Change That!" *This Bridge Called My Back*. Eds. Gloria Anzaldúa and Cherríe Moraga. 53–56.

Levins Morales, Aurora, and Rosario Morales. *Getting Home Alive*. Ithaca: Firebrand Books, 1986.

Mohr, Nicholasa. *All for the Better: A Story of El Barrio*. Stories of America Series. New York: Steck-Vaughn, 1993.

_____. *El Bronx Remembered: A Novella and Stories*. New York: Harper Trophy, 1993.

_____. *Felita*. New York: Penguin, 1999.

_____. *Going Home: Sequel to Felita*. New York: Puffin-Penguin, 1999.

_____. *In My Own Words: Growing Up Inside the Sanctuary of My Imagination*. New York: Julian Messner-Simon & Schuster, 1994.

_____. *In Nueva York*. Houston: Arte Público, 1993.

_____. "Journey Toward a Common Ground: Struggle and Identity of Hispanics in the U.S.A." *The Americas Review* 18.1 (1990): 81–85.

_____. *A Matter of Pride and Other Stories*. Houston: Arte Público, 1997.

_____. *Nilda*. 2nd ed. Houston: Arte Público, 1986.

_____. "Puerto Rican Writers in the U.S., Puerto Rican Writers in Puerto Rico: A Separation beyond Language (Testimonio)." *Breaking Boundaries: Latina Writings and Critical Readings*. Horno-Delgado, et al. 111–116.

_____. "Puerto Ricans in New York: Cultural Evolution and Identity." *Images and Identities*. Ed. Rodríguez de Laguna. 157–160.

_____. *Rituals of Survival: A Woman's Portfolio*. 3rd. ed. Houston: Arte Público, 1990.

Ortiz Cofer, Judith. "And are you a Latina Writer?" *The Americas Review* 24.3–4 (1996): 155–161.

_____. *An Island Like You: Stories of The Barrio*. New York: Orchard Books, 1995.

_____. *The Latin Deli: Prose and Poetry*. New York: W.W. Norton, 1993.

_____. *The Line of the Sun*. Athens: U of Georgia P, 1989.

_____. *Reaching for the Mainland & Selected New Books*. Tempe: Bilingual P/Editorial Bilingüe, 1995.

_____. *Silent Dancing: A Partial Remembrance of a Puerto Rican Childhood*. Houston: Arte Público, 1990.

_____. *Terms of Survival*. Houston: Arte Público, 1987.

_____. "The Woman Who Slept With One Eye Open: Notes on Being a Writer." *Sleeping With One Eye Open: Women Writers and the Art of Survival*. Kallet and Cofer 3–12.

_____. *The Year of Our Revolution*. Houston: Piñata Books-Arte Público, 1998.

Santiago, Esmeralda. *Almost a Woman*. Reading: Merloyd Lawrence-Perseus, 1998.

_____. *America's Dream*. New York: HarperCollins, 1996.

_____. "A Puerto Rican Stew." *New York Times Magazine* 6 June 1994: 6–9.

_____. *When I Was Puerto Rican*. New York: Vintage-Random House,

1993.

Umpierre-Herrera, Luz María. "De la Protesta a la Creación—Una Nueva Visión de la Mujer Puertorriqueña en la Poesía." *Imagine: International Chicano Poetry Journal* 2.1 (Summer 1985): 134–142.

_____. *En el País de las Maravillas (Kempis puertorriqueño)*. Bloomington: Third Woman, 1982.

_____. *For Christine: Poems and One Letter*. Chapel Hill: Professional Press, 1995.

_____. "La ansiedad de la influencia en Sandra María Esteves y Marjorie Agosin," *Revista Chicano-Riqueña* 11.3–4 (1983): 139–147.

_____. *The Margarita Poems*. Bloomington: Third Woman, 1987.

_____. *Nuevas aproximaciones críticas a la literatura puertorriqueña contemporánea*. Rio Piedras: Cultural, 1983.

_____. *Una Puertorriqueña en Penna*. San Juan: Masters, 1979.

_____. *. . . Y Otras Desgracias / And Other Misfortunes. . . .* Bloomington: Third Woman: 1985.

Secondary Sources

Abel, Elizabeth, Marianne Hirsch, and Elizabeth Langland, eds. *The Voyage In: Fictions of Female Development*. Hanover: UP of New England, 1983.

Acosta-Belén, Edna. "A *MELUS* Interview: Judith Ortiz Cofer." *MELUS* 18.3 (Fall 1993): 83–97.

Agra Deedy, Carmen. "Mangoes and Magnolias." *Growing Up Cuban in Decatur, Georgia*. Peachtree Audio Cassette, 1995.

Algarín, Miguel. "Nuyorican Aesthetics." *Images and Identities*. Ed. Rodríguez de Laguna 161–163.

Algarín, Miguel, and Miguel Piñero, eds. *Nuyorican Poetry: An Anthology of Puerto Rican Words and Feelings*. New York: William Morrow, 1975.

Alonso, Manuel A. y Pacheco. *El Jíbaro*. Ed. Luis O. Zayas Micheli. Rio Piedras: Edil, 1992.

Amrine, Frederick. "Rethinking the *Bildungsroman*." *Michigan Germanic Studies* 13.2 (Fall 1987): 119–139.

Alvarez, Julia. *How the García Girls Lost Their Accents*. New York:

Plume-Penguin, 1992.

Andreu Iglesias, César, ed. *Memorias de Bernardo Vega. Contribución a la historia de la comunidad puertorriqueña en Nueva York.* Río Piedras: Huracán, 1994.

Anzaldúa, Gloria. *Borderlands / La Frontera: The New Mestiza.* San Francisco: Aunt Lute Books, 1987.

_____, ed. *Making Face, Making Soul / Haciendo Caras: Creative and Critical Perspectives by Feminists of Color.* San Francisco: Aunt Lute Books, 1990.

_____, and Cherrié Moraga, eds. *This Bridge Called My Back: Writings by Radical Women of Color.* 2nd ed. New York: Kitchen Table, 1983.

Aparicio, Frances. *Listening to Salsa: Gender, Latin Popular Music, and Puerto Rican Cultures.* Hanover: Wesleyan UP, 1998.

_____, and Susana Chávez-Silverman, eds. *Tropicalizations: Transcultural Representations of Latinidad.* Hanover: UP of New England, 1997.

Arcana, Judith. *Our Mother's Daughters.* Berkeley: Shameless Husey P, 1979.

Barnet, Miguel. "La Regla de Ocha: The Religious System of Santería." Olmos and Paravisini-Gerbert, *Sacred* 79–100.

Barradas, Efraín. *Partes de un todo: Ensayos y notas sobre la literatura puertorriqueña en los Estados Unidos.* Puerto Rico: Universidad de Puerto Rico, 1998.

Bartkevicius, Jocelyn. "An Interview with Judith Ortiz Cofer." *Speaking of the Short Story: Interviews with Contemporary Writers.* Eds. Farhat Iftekharuddin et al. Jackson: UP of Mississippi, 1997. 57–74.

Benmayor, Rina. "*Getting Home Alive:* The Politics of Multiple Identities." *The Americas Review* 17. 3–4 (1989): 107–117.

Bergmann, Emilie L., and Paul Julian Smith, eds. *¿Entiendes? Queer Readings, Hispanic Writings.* Durham: Duke UP, 1995. 1–14.

Beverly, John. "The Margin at the Center on *Testimonio* (Testimonial Narrative)." Smith and Watson 91–114.

Booth-Foster, M. Marie. "Voice, Mind, Self: Mother-Daughter Relationships in Amy Tan's *The Joy Luck Club* and *The Kitchen God's Wife.*" Brown-Guillory 208–227.

Braendlin, Bonnie Hoover. "Bildung in Ethnic Women Writers." *Denver Quarterly* 17.4 (Winter 1983): 75–87.

Brown-Guillory, Elizabeth, ed. *Women of Color: Mother-Daughter Relationships in 20th-Century Literature.* Austin: U of Texas P, 1996.

Bruce-Novoa, Juan. "Judith Ortiz Cofer's Rituals of Movement." *The Americas Review* 12.3–4 (1991): 88–99.

———. "Rituals in Judith Ortiz Cofer's *The Line of the Sun.*" *Confluencia* 8.1 (Fall 1992): 61–69.

Buckley, Jerome Hamilton. *Season of Youth: The Bildungsroman from Dickens to Golding.* Cambridge: Harvard UP, 1974.

Burgos, Julia de. *El mar y tú: Otros poemas.* Río Piedras: Huracán, 1986.

———. "Grand River of Loiza." Santiago 46–47.

———. *Obra Poética.* Introducción de José Emilio González. Ed. Consuelo Burgos y Juan Bautista Pagan. San Juan: Instituto de Cultua Puertorriqueña, 1961.

Castro-Klarén, Sara. "La crítica literaria feminista y la escritora en América Latina." *La sartén por el mango: Encuentro de escritoras latinoamericanas.* Eds. Patricia Elena González y Eliana Ortega. Rio Piedras: Ediciones Huracán, 1985. 27–46.

Chávez-Silverman, Susana. "Tropicolada: Inside the U.S. Latino/a Gender B(l)ender." Aparicio and Chávez-Silverman, *Tropicalization* 101–118.

Chodorow, Nancy. *The Reproduction of Mothering: Psychoanalysis and the Sociology of Gender.* Berkeley: U of California P, 1978.

Cienfuegos, Lucky. "Dedicated to María Rodríguez Martínez, February 24, 1975." Algarín and Piñero 156.

Cixous, Hélène, and Catherine Clément. *The Newly Born Woman.* Trans. Betsy Wing. Minneapolis: U of Minnesota P, 1986.

Colón, Jesús. *A Puerto Rican in New York and Other Sketches.* Foreword by Juan Flores. New York: International Publishers, 1991.

Cruz-Malavé, Arnaldo. "Toward an Art of Transvestism: Colonialism and Homosexuality in Puerto Rican Literature." Bergmann and Smith 137–167.

Davidson, Cathy N., and E. M. Broner, eds. *The Lost Tradition: Mothers and Daughters in Literature.* New York: Frederick Ungar, 1980.

Diego, José de. "To be Persecuted." Santiago 7.

Evans, Elizabeth S. "Ritual." *Encyclopedia of Cultural Anthropology.* Eds. David Levinson and Melvin Ember. New York: Henry Holt, 1996.

Fanon, Frantz. *The Wretched of the Earth.* Trans. Constance Farrington. New York: Grove Press, 1963.

Fernández Olmos, Margarite, and Lizabeth Paravisini-Gebert, eds. "Introduction: Religious Syncretism and Carribean Culture." *Sacred Possessions: Vodou, Santería, Obeah, and the Caribbean.* New Brunswick: Rutgers UP, 1997. 1–12.

Ferré, Rosario. "Destiny, Language and Translation, or, Ophelia Adrift in the C & O Canal." *Women's Writing in Latin America: An Anthology.* Eds. Sara Castro-Klaren, Sylvia Molloy, and Beatriz Sarlo. Boulder: Westview Press, 1991. 88–94.

_____. *The House on the Lagoon.* New York: Farrar, Straus, and Giroux, 1995.

_____. *Las dos Venecias.* México: Joaquín Mortiz, 1992.

Flores, Juan. "Back Down These Mean Streets: Introducing Nicholasa Mohr and Louis Reyes Rivera." *Revista Chicano-Riqueña* 8.2 (Primavera 1980): 51–57.

_____. "The Latino Imaginary: Dimensions of Community and Identity." Aparicio and Chávez-Silverman, *Tropicalizations* 183–193.

_____, ed. "'Qué assimilated, brother, *yo soy asimilao'*: The Structuring of Puerto Rican Identity." *Divided Borders: Essays on Puerto Rican Identity.* Houston: Arte Público, 1993.

Freedman, Rita. "Myth America Grows Up." *Beauty Bound.* Lexington: Lexington Books, 1986. 390.

Friday, Nancy. *My Mother, My Self: The Daughter's Search for Identity.* New York: Dell, 1981.

Gautier Benítez, José. "Ausencia." *Antología de la literatura puertorriqueña.* Madrid: Editorial Playor, 1980. 10.

Gil, Rosa María, and Carmen Inoa Vázquez. *La Paradoja de María: Como Pueden Las Latinas Fortalecer Su Autoestima sin Abandonar Sus Tradiciones.* Trans. Mayda Ochoa. New York: G.P. Putnam's Sons, 1996.

Glissant, Edouard. *Caribbean Discourse: Selected Essays.* Trans. J.

Micheal Dash. Charlottesville: UP of Virginia, 1989.

González, José Luis. "La Carta." *Cuentos puertorriqueños de hoy.* Ed. René Marqués. 6th ed. Río Piedras: Cultural, 1977. 87–88.

_____. *Veinte Cuentos y Paisa.* 2nd ed. Río Piedras: Cultural, 1986.

González, María. "Love and Conflict: Mexican American Women Writers as Daughters." Brown-Guillory 153–171.

Grosz, Elizabeth. *Sexual Subversions: Three French Feminists.* Sydney: Allen & Unwin, 1989.

Hardin, James, ed. *Reflection and Action: Essays on the Bildungsroman.* Columbia: U of South Carolina P, 1991.

Hernández Cruz, Víctor. *Tropicalization.* New York: Canon, 1976.

Hirsch, Marianne. *The Mother/Daughter Plot. Narrative, Psychoanalysis, Feminism.* Bloomington: Indiana UP, 1989.

_____. "Spiritual *Bildung*: The Beautiful Soul as Paradigm." Abel 23–48.

Hobsbawm, Eric. *The Age of Empire, 1875–1914.* New York: Vintage Books, 1989.

hooks, bell. *Feminist Theory: From Margin to Center.* Boston: South End P, 1984.

Horno-Delgado, Asunción. "*Señores, don't leibol mi, please!*: ya soy Luz María Umpierre." Trans. Janet N. Gold. Horno-Delgado, et al. *Breaking* 136–145.

_____, et al., eds. *Breaking Boundaries. Latina Writings and Critical Readings.* Amherst: U of Massachusetts P, 1989.

Irigaray, Luce. "And the One Doesn't Stir without the Other." Trans. Helene Vivienne Wenzel. *Signs* 7.1(Autumn 1981): 56–67.

_____. "The Mechanics of Fluids." *This Sex Which is Not One.* Trans. Catherine Porter. Ithaca: Cornell UP, 1985. 106–118.

Kallet, Marilyn, and Judith Ortiz Cofer, eds. *Sleeping With One Eye Open: Women Writers and the Art of Survival.* Athens: U of Georgia P, 1999.

Kaminsky, Amy. *Reading the Body Politics. Feminist Criticism and Latin American Women Writers.* Minneapolis: U of Minneapolis P, 1993.

Kanellos, Nicolás. "Orality and Hispanic Literature of the United States." *Redefining American Literary History.* Eds. A. LaVonne

Brown Ruoff and Jerry W. Ward, Jr. New York: Modern Language Association, 1990. 115–123.

_____. *Thirty Million Strong. Reclaiming the Hispanic Image in American Culture.* Golden: Fulcrum Publishing, 1998.

Kaplan, E. Ann. *Motherhood and Representation: The Mother in Popular Culture and Melodrama.* London & New York: Routledge, 1992.

Karafilis, Maria. "Crossing the Borders of Genre: Revisions of the Bildungsroman in Sandra Cisneros's *The House on Mango Street* and Jamaica Kincaid's *Annie John.*" *The Journal of the Midwest Modern Language Association* 31.2 (Winter 1998): 63–78.

Kelley, Margot. "A Minor Revolution: Chicano/a Composite Novels and the Limits of Genre." *Ethnicity and the American Short Story.* Ed. Julie Brown. New York: Garland, 1997. 63–84.

Kiberd, Declan. *Inventing Ireland.* Cambridge: Harvard UP, 1995.

Kristeva, Julia. *Powers of Horror: An Essay on Abjection.* Trans. Leon S. Roudiez. New York: Columbia UP, 1982.

Laviera, Tato. *La Carreta Made a U-turn.* Houston: Arte Público, 1992.

Lewis, Oscar. *La Vida: A Puerto Rican Family in the Culture of Poverty—San Juan and New York.* New York: Random House, 1965.

Lionett, Françoise. *Autobiographical Voices: Race, Gender, Self-Portraiture.* Ithaca: Cornell UP, 1989.

López Springfield, Consuelo. "*Mestizaje* in the Mother-Daughter Autobiography of Rosario Morales and Aurora Levins Morales." *Autobiography Studies* 8.2 (Fall 1993): 303–315.

Lord, Albert B. *The Singer of Tales.* Cambridge: Harvard UP, 1960.

Lugo-Ortíz, Agnes I. "Community at Its Limits: Orality, Law, Silence, and the Homosexual Body in Luis Rafael Sánchez's '¡Jum!'" Bergmann and Smith 115–136.

Marqués, René. *La Carreta, drama en tres actos.* Río Piedras: Cultural, 1971.

_____. "The Docile Puerto Rican—Literature and Psychological Reality." Trans. Barbara Bockus Aponte. Santiago 155–158.

Martini, Fritz. "Bildungsroman—Term and Theory." Hardin 1–25.

Moane, Geraldine. *Gender and Colonialism: A Psychological Analysis of Oppression and Liberation.* New York: St. Martin's Press, 1999.

Mohanty, Chandra T. "Introduction: Cartographies of Struggle: Third

World Women and the Politics of Feminism." Mohanty, et al., *Third* 1–47.

_____. "Under Western Eyes: Feminist Scholarship and Colonial Discourses." Mohanty, et al., *Third* 51–80.

Mora, Gabriela. "Narradoras hispanoamericanas: Vieja y nueva problemática en renovadas elaboraciones." *Theory and Practice of Feminist Literary Criticism.* Eds. Gabriela Mora and Karen S. Van Hooft. Ypsilanti: Bilingual/Editorial Bilingüe, 1982. 156–174.

Moraga, Cherríe L. *Loving in the War Years.* Expanded ed. Cambridge: South End Press, 2000.

Morales Carrión, Arturo. *Puerto Rico: A Political and Cultural History.* New York: W.W. Norton, 1983.

Negrón de Montilla, Aida. *La americanización de Puerto Rico y el sistema de instrucción pública, 1900–1930.* Río Piedras: Editorial Univeritaria, 1977.

Nice, Vivian E. *Mothers and Daughters: The Distortion of a Relationship.* London: Macmillan, 1992.

Nieves-Squires, Sarah. "Hispanic Women: Making Their Presence on Campus Less Tenuous." Washington, D.C.: Association of American Colleges, 1991.

Oboler, Susana. *Ethnic Labels, Latino Lives: Identity and the Politics of (Re)Presentation in the United States.* Minneapolis: U of Minnesota P, 1995.

Ocasio, Rafael. "The Infinite Variety of the Puerto Rican Reality: An Interview with Judith Ortiz Cofer." *Callaloo* 17.3 (1994): 730–742.

Ortega, Eliana. "Poetic Discourse of the Puerto Rican Women in the U.S.: New Voices of Anacaonian Liberation." Horno-Delgado, et al., *Breaking* 122–135.

Ortega, Julio. *Reapropiaciones (Cultura y Nueva Escritura en Puerto Rico).* Río Piedras: Universidad de Puerto Rico, 1991.

Ortiz-Márquez, Maribel. "From Third World Politics to First World Practices: Contemporary Latina Writers in the United States." *Interventions: Feminist Dialogues on Third World Women's Literature and Film.* Eds. Bishnupriya Ghosh and Brinda Bose. New York: Garland, 1997. 227–244.

Ostalaza Bey, Margarita. *Política Sexual en Puerto Rico.* Río Piedras:

Huracán, 1989.

Osuna, Juan José. *A History of Education in Puerto Rico.* 2nd. ed. Río Piedras: Editorial de la Universidad de Puerto Rico, 1949.

Padilla, Raymond V., and Rudolfo Chávez-Chávez, eds. *The Leaning Tower: Latino Professors in American Universities.* Albany: State University of New York P, 1995.

Paz, Octavio. "Los hijos de la Malinche." *El laberinto de la soledad.* Mexico City: Fondo de Cultura Económica, 1959.

Pedreira, Antonio S. *Insularismo.* Río Pedras: Edil, 1978.

Pérez-Erdélyi, Mireya. "Luz María Umpierre—Poeta Puertorriqueña." *Chasqui* 16.2 (November 1987): 61–68.

Pietri, Pedro. "Puerto Rican Obituary." Santiago 117–126.

Platizky, Roger S. "From Dialectic to Deliverance: Luz María Umpierre's *The Margarita Poems.*" *La Escritora Hispánica.* Actas de la decimotercera conferencia anual de literatura hispánicas en Indiana University of Pennsylvania. Eds. Nora Erro-Orthmann y Juan Cruz Mendizabal. Miamia: Universal, 1987. 261–266.

Rebolledo, Tey Diana, and Eliana S. Rivera, eds. *Infinite Divisions: An Anthology of Chicana Literature.* Tucson: U of Arizona P, 1993.

Redfield, Marc. *Phantom Formations: Aesthetic Ideology and the Bildungsroman.* Ithaca: Cornell UP, 1996.

Reyes, María de la Luz, and John J. Halcón. "Practices of the Academy: Barriers to Access for Chicano Academics." *The Racial Crisis in American Higher Education.* Eds. P. Altbach and K. Lomotey. Albany: State U of New York P, 1991. 167–186.

Rich, Adrienne. *Of Woman Born. Motherhood as Experience and Institution.* 10th ed. New York: W.W. Norton, 1986.

Rodríguez de Laguna, Isela, ed. *Images and Identities: The Puerto Rican in Two World Contexts.* New Brunswick: Transaction Books, 1987.

Rojas, Lourdes. "Latinas at the Crossroads: An Affirmation of Life in Rosario Morales and Aurora Levins Morales' *Getting Home Alive.*" Horno-Delgado, et al., *Breaking* 166–77.

Rosa-Nieves, Cesareo. *Ensayos Escogidos: Apuntaciones de crítica literaria sobre algunos temas puertorriqueños.* Barcelona: Miguiza, 1970.

_____. *La Poesía en Puerto Rico: Historia de los temas poéticos en la literatura puertorriqueña*. San Juan: Editorial Edil, 1969.

Roundberg, Annmari. "Spittle and Splitting." *The Encyclopedia of Religion*. Ed. Mircea Eliade. Vol. 14. New York: Macmillan, 1987. 37–38.

Sammons, Jeffrey L. "The Bildgunsroman for Nonspecialists: An Attempt at a Clarification." Hardin 26–45.

———. "The Mystery of the Missing *Bildungsroman*, or: What happened to Wilhelm Meister's Legacy?" *Genre* 14.2 (Summer 1981): 229–246.

Sánchez, Luis Rafael. *La guagua aérea*. Río Piedras: Cultural, 1994.

Sánchez, Marta E. "La Malinche at the Intersection: Race and Gender in *Down These Mean Streets*." *PMLA* 113.1 (1998): 117–128.

Sandoval, Chéla. "Feminism and Racism: A Report on the 1981 National Women's Studies Association Conference." Anzaldúa 55–71.

Sandoval Sánchez, Alberto. "La identidad especular del allá y del acá: Nuestra propia imagen puertorriqueña en cuestión." *Centro Bulletin* 4.2 (Spring 1992): 28–43.

San Pedro, Teresa. "La esperpéntica realidad del cuento tradicional en el poema 'Cuento sin hadas' de Luz María Umpierre." *The Americas Review* 19.1 (1991): 92–100.

Santiago, Roberto, ed. *Boricuas: Influential Puerto Rican Writings— An Anthology*. New York: One World, 1995. xiii–xxxiii.

Scarano, Francisco A. *Puerto Rico: Cinco siglos de historia*. San Juan: McGraw-Hill, 1993.

Smith, John H. "Sexual Difference, *Bildung*, and the *Bildungsroman*." *Michigan Germanic Studies* 13.2 (Fall 1987): 206–225.

Smith, Sidonie. *A Poetics of Women's Autobiography: Marginality and The Fictions of Self-Representation*. Bloomington: Indiana UP, 1987.

———. *Subjectivity, Identity, and the Body: Women's Autobiographical Practices in the Twentieth Century*. Bloomington: Indiana UP, 1993.

———, and Julie Watson, eds. *De/Colonizing the Subject: The Politics of Gender in Women's Autobiography*. Minneapolis: U of Minnesota P, 1992.

Soto, Pedro Juan. *Spiks*. 6th ed. Rio Piedras: Cultural, 1980.

Suárez Findley, Eileen J. *Imposing Decency: The Politics of Sexuality and Race in Puerto Rico, 1870–1920*. Durham: Duke UP, 1999.

Tan, Amy. *The Bonesetter's Daughter.* New York: G.P. Putnam's Sons, 2001.

_____. *The Joy Luck Club.* New York: G.P. Putnam's Sons, 1989.

_____. *The Kitchen God's Wife.* New York: G.P. Putnam's Sons, 1991.

Thomas, Piri. *Down These Mean Streets.* New York: Vintage Books, 1991.

Torres, Lourdes. "The Construction of Self in U.S. Latina Autobiographies." Mohanty et al., *Third* 271–287.

Valdez, Guadalupe. "Minority and Majority Members in Foreign Languages Departments: Towards the Examination of Established Attitudes and Values." *ADFL Bulletin* 22.2 (Winter 1991): 10–14.

Vázquez, Blanca. "Puerto Ricans in the Media: A Personal Statement." *Centro de Estudios Puertorriqueños Bulletin* 3.1 (1990–91): 4–15.

Vega, Ana Lydia. "Pollito Chicken." *Vírgenes y mártires.* Río Piedras: Editorial Antillana, 1981. 73–79.

Vosburg, Nancy. "Luz María Umpierre-Herrera." *Contemporary Lesbian Writers of the United States: A Bibliographical Critical Sourcebook.* Eds. Sandra Pollack and Denise D. Knight. Westport: Greenwood Press, 1993. 549–555.

Wells, Rebecca. *Divine Secrets of the Ya-Ya Sisterhood.* New York: Harper Perennial, 1996.

Wright, Winthrop R. *Café con Leche: Race, Class, and National Image in Venezuela.* Austin: U of Texas P, 1990.

Yarbro-Bejarano, Yvonne. "The Lesbian Body in Latina Cultural Production." Bergmann and Smith 181–197.

Zeno Gandía, Manuel. *La Charca.* 2nda Ed. Barcelona: Vosgos, 1981.

Zentella, Ana Celia. "The 'Chiquitafication' of U.S. Latinos and Their Language, OR Why We Need Anthro*political* Linguistics." *SALSA* 3 (April 7–9, 1995): 1–18.

Zuesse, Evan M. "Ritual." *Encyclopedia of Religion.* Ed. Mircea Eliade. New York: MacMillan, 1987.

Zumthor, Paul. *Oral Poetry: An Introduction.* Trans. Kathryn Murphy-Judy. *Theory and History of Literature.* Minneapolis: U of Minnesota P, 1990.